P9-CCZ-790

g Health

rmation

ms

Evaluating Health Care Information Systems

Methods and Applications

edited by

**James G. Anderson
Carolyn E. Aydin
Stephen J. Jay**

SAGE Publications
International Educational and Professional Publisher
Thousand Oaks   London   New Delhi

Copyright © 1994 by Sage Publications, Inc.

For information address:

SAGE Publications, Inc.
2455 Teller Road
Thousand Oaks, California 91320

SAGE Publications Ltd.
6 Bonhill Street
London EC2A 4PU
United Kingdom

SAGE Publications India Pvt. Ltd.
M-32 Market
Greater Kailash I
New Delhi 110 048 India

Printed in the United States of America

Library of Congress Cataloging-in-Publication Data

Main entry under title:

Evaluating health care information systems: methods and
    applications / edited by James G. Anderson, Carolyn E. Aydin,
    Stephen J. Jay.
        p.   cm.
    Includes bibliographical references and index.
    ISBN 0-8039-4935-9 (cl)   —ISBN 0-8039-4936-7 (pb)
    1. Information storage and retrieval systems—Medical care—
Evaluation.   2. Information storage and retrieval systems—Medical
care—Cost effectiveness.   3. Health facilities—Administration—
Data processing. I. Anderson, James G., 1936-   . II. Aydin,
Carolyn E.   III. Jay, Stephen J.
R858.E98 1994
362.1'0285—dc20   93-27074

94 95 96 97 10 9 8 7 6 5 4 3 2 1

Sage Production Editor: Astrid Virding

Contents

Preface

Information systems pervade complex organizations. In health care organizations such as hospitals, the U.S. Congressional Office of Technology Assessment has estimated that these computerized systems, when fully implemented, account for 4% to 8% of an institution's total operating budget. As health care costs continue to spiral upward, health care institutions are under increasing pressure from purchasers and payers of services to create a cost-effective system by controlling operating costs while maintaining quality of care and service. Information systems are being marketed for health care organizations to provide management information, control costs, and facilitate total quality management and continuous quality improvement programs. Cost control and quality improvement are the two major premises on which decisions to purchase information systems are based.

There is mounting evidence, however, that the implementation of many information systems has resulted in unforeseen costs, unfulfilled promises, and disillusionment. There is also growing realization that information systems affect the structure and functioning of organizations, the quality of work life of employees within them, and ultimately the cost and quality of the goods and services they provide. Professionals who develop, implement, and evaluate clinical computer systems, however, frequently address only the technical aspects of these systems, whereas the success of implementation and utilization depends on integration of the computer system into a complex organizational setting. Without an evaluation strategy that goes beyond the technical aspects of the system, an institution has no means of knowing how well it is actually functioning within the organization and no firm basis for developing specific interventions to enhance system success. Including these issues in systems evaluations will increase the likelihood of implementing a system that is cost-effective for the organization as a whole.

The purpose of *Evaluating Health Care Information Systems* is to provide computer system developers, administrators, health care policy analysts, chief information officers, investigators, and others with a guide for evaluating the impacts of computerized information systems on (1) the structure and functioning of health care organizations, (2) the quality of work life of individual health care professionals and others working within the organization, and (3) the cost-effective delivery of health care. Evaluating information system impacts requires not only an understanding of computer technology but also an understanding of the social and behavioral processes that affect and are affected by the introduction of this technology into organizational settings. Investigators in the social sciences have developed theoretical foundations and analytical approaches to help understand the impact and use of information systems, but few guidelines exist to help developers, administrators, and evaluators design evaluation strategies and select appropriate methods to study system outcomes.

This book is designed as a practical guide for determining appropriate questions to ask and the most effective methods available to answer those questions. The book begins with the premise that any evaluation must be preceded by a clear statement of study objectives. Next, investigators should recognize their own perspective and assumptions concerning how information systems affect and are affected by the organizational setting in which they are implemented. Only at this point are investigators ready to review and select appropriate methodologies to answer their research questions.

The selection of appropriate methodologies is critical to the successful outcome of any investigation. Given the complex interrelationships between computer systems and their organizational environments, there is no one best method for evaluation. Rather, the selection of methods will be determined by the evaluation objectives. This book advocates a pluralistic approach, providing the reader with detailed information on a number of methods that can be used to evaluate health care information systems. More than one evaluation strategy may be brought to bear on the same problem domain, with each method providing a different, complementary view of the issues under study. The book is designed to assist an investigator in selecting among different methods to build the specific approach that will be most fruitful for investigating a given situation or problem. The chapters also provide a practical overview of established research guidelines for sampling, data collection procedures and instruments, and analytic techniques.

The material presented in this book draws on more than a decade of empirical studies in health care computing conducted by the contributors and others. Individual chapters review specific methods for organizational evaluation such as direct observations, use of archival data, interviewing strategies, survey research, experimental research methods, simulation, social network analysis, and cost-benefit analysis. Part I begins with an overview of theoretical perspectives and evaluation questions, followed by seven chapters covering different methods for evaluating the impacts of information systems using examples specific to health care organizations. Each of these seven chapters provides the reader with a detailed overview of a specific method, followed by annotated references at the end of the chapter for further reading. The example studies in Part II illustrate different evaluation methods and provide the reader with an understanding of the nature and scope of evaluation research and its importance in studying the impact of information systems, including providing information for practical decision making and interventions.

The book also draws from a variety of social science disciplines to integrate the study of information systems with social science theory and methods. We argue that investigators in the social sciences have developed theoretical frameworks and analytical approaches that can help understand how the introduction of computer systems in health care settings affects the quality of the work environment, tasks and skills of health professionals, social interactions among professionals in the organization, and the effective delivery of medical care. We hope to make the developers and users of medical information systems more aware of (1) the extent to which the success of these systems depends on complex social processes, and (2) the contributions the social sciences can make in helping understand these processes.

The study of information systems, however, also requires social scientists themselves to develop new theories, data collection techniques, and analytic methods. This book should provide investigators and students with a starting point for new theoretical and policy-oriented research into the impacts of information systems on health care organizations. We also hope to initiate a dialogue between adherents of different research approaches, helping to clarify the range of methods and their appropriateness, strengths and weaknesses, and the understanding that can be acquired by combining different methods in a single research endeavor.

Finally, there is growing awareness at colleges and universities of the importance of studying and evaluating the use and impact of information systems as evidenced by the growth of curricula and faculty positions in the information sciences; medical, dental, and nursing informatics; and health care administration. Moreover, some schools are developing joint teaching and research programs that draw from diverse disciplines such as medicine, computer science, information systems, the library sciences, organizational behavior, operations management, and the social sciences. This book is meant to provide a useful guide to the research and evaluation of systems for this wide variety of disciplines as well as to system developers, administrators, and practitioners.

We wish to acknowledge Ann West, formerly an editor at Sage Publications, who recognized the importance of our endeavor, and Reed M. Gardner, Professor of Medical Informatics at the University of Utah/ LDS Hospital, who made many useful suggestions regarding the book. Also, we wish to thank Marilyn M. Anderson for her assistance in coordinating and assembling the various contributions.

—*James G. Anderson*
Carolyn E. Aydin
Stephen J. Jay

PART I

Evaluating Health Care
Information Systems:
A Multimethod Approach

Despite the fact that they are technologically sound, more than half of medical information systems fail because of user and staff resistance. Although implementation success depends heavily on the integration of the computer system into a complex organizational setting, few guidelines exist for designing effective evaluation strategies and selecting appropriate methods to examine outcomes of system use.

Predicting organizational changes resulting from information systems requires an understanding of dynamic social and political processes that occur within organizations as well as the characteristics of individuals, work groups, and the information system. Chapter 1 outlines how theories about the impacts of information systems on organizations and the people in them can guide research and evaluation. Models of change based on different assumptions can aid in understanding the implementation of information systems and guide the selection of methodological tools for assessing their organizational impacts. Three general models are discussed. The first views the computer system as an *external force* that brings about predictable change in the behavior of individuals and organizational units. A second perspective views the design of information systems as being *determined by the information needs* of managers and clinicians. It is assumed that the organization has control over the technical aspects of the system and the consequences of its implementation. A third theoretical perspective holds that *complex social interactions* within the organization determine the use and impact of medical computer systems. The chapter concludes with 10 suggested areas for evaluation of health care information systems and an overview of appropriate research methodologies.

Chapters 2 through 8 discuss the major methods that can be used to evaluate an information system. Given the scope and complexity of these projects, there is no "one best approach" to evaluation. The selection of a methodology must be determined by the overall objectives of the evaluation. At the same time, the selection of a methodology for a particular project is critical to the success of the project. In order to select an appropriate methodology, the investigator needs to be aware of the various methods that are available as well as their advantages and limitations. Each chapter provides an overview of a specific approach to evaluation. Examples provide the reader with a resource for understanding the nature and scope of the specific approach. Extensive references at the end of each chapter provide useful sources for the reader to learn more about each method.

Chapter 2 focuses on the design of evaluation studies. An effective evaluation plan begins with a focused research question or hypothesis, followed by the selection of a study design. Study designs discussed and illustrated include: cohort studies, time series studies, cross-sectional studies, experimental and quasi-experimental studies, and post-intervention studies. The next step in the planning process is to determine how to measure important concepts and how many subjects will be needed. The discussion includes factors that determine sample size and an examination of the reliability and validity of the data collection instruments chosen for use.

Chapter 3 provides an overview of qualitative research methods. These methods attempt to understand the process by which organizational change occurs after the introduction of an information system from the point of view of the participants and their social and institutional context. Five major advantages of qualitative methods are cited, namely, (1) understanding how users perceive and evaluate the system; (2) understanding the influence of the social and cultural context on system use; (3) investigating causal processes; (4) providing information that can be used to improve a system under development; and (5) providing information to decision makers. These issues are illustrated by a study of a clinical laboratory system.

Chapter 4 provides a guide to survey methods that can be used to evaluate the impacts of computer systems on the functioning of health care organizations and the work life of individuals within them. Survey research involves gathering information from a sample of a population using standardized instruments. The author points out that, where possible, standard measures with established validity and reliability should be used. The chapter describes a number of survey instruments drawn from the literature on information systems, organizations and organizational behavior, and work attitudes and values. These instruments have been developed and used in health care organizations and other organizational settings and have documented reliabilities and validities. Many of the instruments are included in the chapter appendix or references are provided to enable the reader to obtain a copy of the instrument.

Chapter 5 outlines how experimental research methods can be used to evaluate health care information systems. These methods are characterized by the following: (1) the study is conducted in a laboratory or field setting; (2) whenever possible, subjects are randomly assigned to treatment and control groups; (3) one or more independent or experimental variables are manipulated by the investigator; (4) other independent variables that might affect the outcome are controlled as far as possible; and (5) one or more outcome measures or dependent variables are measured. Three different types of experimental research are discussed and illustrated: laboratory experiments, field or quasi-experiments, and computer simulation experiments. These research strategies are compared in terms of the amount of control the investigator has over subjects and the research setting and the generalizability of the findings to the real organizational environment.

Chapter 6 describes social network approaches to evaluating health care information systems. First, the authors discuss how the introduction of an information system affects and is affected by characteristics of the organization's structure and by relationships such as interdependence, interaction, and integration. Second, network concepts and analytical methods are reviewed. Third, examples of this approach are provided from two sets of studies of medical information systems.

Chapter 7 provides a critique of cost-benefit analyses of health care information systems. The authors also discuss barriers to cost-benefit analyses of these systems, namely: (1) physicians, nurses, and administrators who adopt the system do not bear the cost consequences of their decision; (2) the cost of evaluation is thought to be too high; and (3) once adopted, it is unlikely that the system will be discarded even if many of its benefits are not realized. Finally, guidelines for cost-benefit analysis are provided.

Chapter 8 outlines a methodology that can be used to test clinical information systems prior to adoption using simulated cases. Clinical

Information Processing Scenarios (CLIPS) are simulated cases that occur within the practice setting that generally require deviations from standard procedures. These cases can be used to evaluate a system's range of operation, ease of use, and ability to support specific groups of users.

1

Overview

Theoretical Perspectives and Methodologies for the Evaluation of Health Care Information Systems

James G. Anderson
Carolyn E. Aydin

The Need for Evaluation

Health care organizations—long-time users of computers—are considering many new computer-based products in the hope of increasing efficiency, reducing costs, and improving patient care (Anderson & Jay, 1987, 1990; Freudenheim, 1990). These products include a growing number of medical computer applications in which health care providers interact directly with the computer. These applications are referred to generally as *medical or clinical information systems.* Medical information systems involve computer-stored databases containing patient information to support medical order entry, results reporting, decision support systems, clinical reminders, and other health care applications (Anderson, 1992a, 1992b). In some health care organizations, a comprehensive system coordinates patient care activities by linking computer terminals in patient care areas to all departments through a central or integrated information system. Other organizations use smaller separate systems that link patient care areas to only one department such as the laboratory, radiology, or the pharmacy. These systems provide communication networks between departments as well as storage and retrieval of medical information. Other computerized databases or expert systems may serve a single department or group of practitioners.

A recent survey of 620 hospitals indicated that "hospitals use less than one-quarter of the abilities built into their computer systems" (Gardner, 1990). Moreover, these systems often fail because developers frequently emphasize the technological and economic aspects of the systems and neglect social and political considerations such as the organizational environment, social interactions, political issues, and hidden costs such as interruptions of established organizational routines (King & Kraemer, 1980; Kling, 1980; Kling & Scacchi, 1982; Kumar & Bjorn-Andersen, 1990; Lyytinen, 1987; Mouritsen & Bjorn-Andersen, 1991). Dowling (1980) found in a survey of 40 randomly selected hospitals that 45% of the information systems failed because of user resistance and staff interference despite the fact that they were technologically sound. Lyytinen (1988) and Lyytinen and Hirschheim (1987) also report a 50% failure rate for information systems. The authors suggest that failure may be due to technical problems; problems with the format and content of the data; user problems related to skills, competence, and motivations; and organizational problems. At present there are few published studies about the reasons for failure and their relative importance.

At the same time, the current emphasis on cost-effectiveness in health care is creating new pressures on organizations to justify expenditures through detailed evaluations of the impacts of new information systems. Although implementation success depends heavily on the integration of the computer system into a complex organizational setting, professionals who develop, implement, and evaluate health care computer systems have few guidelines for designing effective evaluation strategies and selecting appropriate methods to examine the outcomes of system use in health care organizations. To ensure that newly adopted systems accomplish their intended purpose, vendors and purchasers alike need to develop detailed plans prior to system implementation for ongoing implementation and post-installation evaluation to examine the use and long-term impacts of these systems.

Evaluating the impact of computer-based medical information systems requires not only an understanding of computer technology but also an understanding of the social and behavioral processes that affect and are affected by the introduction of the technology into the practice setting. As technological developments result in the widespread use of computers in health care, the social and behavioral sciences can provide an important perspective to guide the establishment of research agendas and the conduct of policy-relevant investigations. According to the conceptual framework developed by Ives, Hamilton, and Davis (1980) and Kraemer and Dutton (1991), for example, research and evaluation of information systems may involve any or all of the following categories: (1) the external environment of the organization; (2) the internal environment of the organization; (3) the information system users; (4) the systems development environment and staff; (5) the management and operational environment of the system; (6) the nature of the system including the information processed; (7) patterns of utilization; (8) organizational impacts; (9) and social impacts. These impacts may be direct or indirect, intended or unintended. The following sections outline how different theories about the impacts of information systems influence research and evaluation by suggesting different research questions and demanding different methodological tools for assessing their impacts on organizations and the people in them.

Assumptions About Change

Theories about change embody conceptions of the nature and direction of causal influences. Information systems research may be based on a number of different theories or models of change with different or competing assumptions. These models of change influence which research questions will and will not be asked and guide the selection of research methodologies (Babbie, 1983; Kuhn, 1962).

Three common "storylines" with contrasting assumptions characterize the consequences associated with computer systems: optimist, pessimist, and pluralist (Hirschheim, 1985; Kling, 1980). The optimist position predicts increased productivity, improved skill requirements, more interdependent jobs, and enhanced communication (i.e., workers share information with workers in other departments by means of common access to a system). The pessimist position, in contrast, predicts that information technology will rob workers of their expertise and decrease their interactions through job routinization and fragmentation (i.e., workers only access information remotely through computer terminals) and generate conflicts about control over information and other resources (Braverman, 1974; Hirschheim, 1985; Kling, 1980). The present book adopts the third or pluralist position that, although computer systems can have both isolating and integrating capabilities, actual impacts depend on what the organization and its members do with the technology and how the implementation is managed.

According to this position, the introduction of computer systems in health care organizations may be accompanied by changes on several different levels. These include changes for: (1) individuals and their jobs, (2) departments as a whole and how the department's work is performed, (3) the structure and functioning of the entire organization, and (4) the quality of both the service patients receive and the medical care that is delivered. Some of these changes may be immediate and evident in the performance of the daily work of health care. Other changes may occur slowly and be more difficult to detect. The changes that occur, however, are not simply caused by the computer system. Rather, these changes are viewed as a result of complex interactions between the capabilities of the system itself, administrative decisions on how to use the system in a particular organization, and actions of individual employees as they adapt to the system in their everyday work (Aydin & Rice, 1992; Kling, 1980; Markus, 1983, 1984).

The pluralist perspective also maintains that research about the effects of computers on managerial decision making, authority, and control; the work environment, productivity, and job enhancement; the frequency, nature, and quality of interpersonal relationships among organizational members; and relations between organizations and their environment can enhance our insights into the complex effects of introducing computers into organizational settings (Attewell & Rule, 1984; Kraemer & Danziger, 1990). To date, however, research findings suggest that these effects are complicated, diverse, and contingent on the specific organizational context. In some instances the availability of the new technology even generates new organizational needs to which it is applied (King & Kraemer, 1980). Understanding the changes that may occur, however, can help analysts predict impacts of individual systems, including both desired and unanticipated effects on the organization in which they are being implemented.

Evaluation Research and Models of Change

Evaluation research differs from scientific inquiry. Although both use the same logic of inquiry and research procedures, scientific studies focus primarily on meeting specific research standards. Although scientific rigor is important in evaluation studies as well, evaluation research must also recognize the interests of organizational stakeholders and be conducted in a way that is most useful to decision makers. Although evaluation studies may strive to meet the criteria for scientific rigor, the primary purpose of evaluation research is to provide information to organization stakeholders and decision makers (Rossi & Freeman, 1985).

Although evaluation studies may not specify an explicit paradigm or theoretical framework, underlying and often unconscious assumptions about models of change may influence both the questions selected for study and the accompanying research strategies (Kaplan, 1991). Different assumptions will lead researchers to ask different questions and focus on different outcomes to the computer implementation process. Thus it is important that evaluation researchers also recognize the influence of their own and the organization stakeholders' underlying assumtions about change in selecting specific questions for investigation.

The following sections detail three different models of change prevalent in information systems research, including: (1) the computer system as an external force, (2) system design determined by user information needs, and (3) complex social interactions as determinants of system use. Examples are also included to illustrate the different theoretical perspectives. Many of these examples, as well as those cited in subsequent chapters, both meet the rigorous requirements of scientific investigation and provide evaluation information to stakeholders in the organization under study as well.

The Computer System as an External Force

Theories about how information systems affect organizations imply quite different conceptions of what causes change to occur (Kaplan, 1991; Kling, 1980; Markus, 1983; Markus & Robey, 1988; Pfeffer, 1982; Slack, 1984). The simplest approach views the computer system as an exogenous or external force that brings about change in the behavior of individuals and organizational units. Information systems are developed and implemented to support management goals. Participants who are expected to use the new technology are viewed as passive, resistant, or dysfunctional if they fail to use the system. Evaluation in this instance usually focuses on technical performance (e.g., cost, speed, accuracy). Studies are frequently undertaken in the laboratory using controlled clinical trials and there may be little or no investigation of how systems fit into the daily work of the organization into which they will be introduced (Benbasat, 1989a; Forsythe & Buchanan, 1992).

In general, studies based on this theoretical perspective treat organizational and technological characteristics as invariant rather than as changing over time. They also fail to include characteristics of the organizational environment and social interaction that may have important effects on outcomes (Lyytinen, 1987). A variant of this theoretical approach, however, does include the examination of the impact of the computer on specific characteristics of the organization. Leifer and McDonough (1985), for example, found that departments that used a computer system were more centralized, less complex, and less uncertain about their environment to begin with than departments that didn't use the system, even when task routineness was controlled.

System Design Determined by User Information Needs

A second theoretical perspective views the design of information systems as determined by the information needs of managers and clinicians (Kaplan, 1991; Markus & Robey, 1988). In this view, the information system is considered to be endogenous to the organization with organization members having control over the technical aspects of the system and the consequence of its implementation. According to this theory, change occurs in a rational fashion as needs are identified and problems solved. Much of the literature from this perspective is optimistic about the amount of influence that designers and implementers have over system capabilities and characteristics (Bjorn-Andersen, Eason, & Robey, 1986; Olson, 1982).

Complex Social Interactions as Determinants of System Use

A third theoretical perspective holds that complex social interactions within the organization determine the use and impact of medical computer systems (Anderson & Jay, 1987; Kaplan, 1991; Kling & Scacchi, 1982; Markus & Robey, 1988; Rogers, 1983). This theoretical perspective is more complex than the two perspectives outlined above. According to this view, the way technology is ultimately implemented and utilized in a particular organizational setting depends on conflicting objectives, preferences, and work demands. From this viewpoint, predicting organizational change resulting from information systems requires an understanding of the dynamic social and political processes that occur within organizations as well as the characteristics of individuals and the information system. The prediction of outcomes requires knowledge of the processes that occur during system planning, implementation, and use rather than simply the levels of independent variables hypothesized to predict change (Kimberly & Evanisko, 1981; Markus & Robey, 1988; Mohr, 1982).

Barley (1986), for example, focused on social interactions in his study of the introduction of computerized tomography scanners in two community hospitals. Results showed that the new technology challenged traditional role relations and patterns of interaction among radiologists and radiological technologists in both settings. Only one of the departments, however, became more decentralized as a result. Moreover, professionals who adopt an innovation may adapt it to their own specific needs and organizational contexts, in a sense "reinventing" the innovation (Anderson & Jay, 1985; Johnson & Rice, 1984; Kaplan, 1991; Rogers, 1983).

In another example, Lundsgaarde, Fischer, and Steele (1981) studied the reactions of physicians, nurses, and ancillary personnel to the implementation of the Problem Oriented Medical Information System (PROMIS). Physicians resisted using the system because of fears that it would disrupt traditional staff relations. Nurses and other staff readily accepted the system, however, because it allowed them to utilize their professional expertise more fully. Aydin (1989) also addressed social interactions in her study of the effects of a computerized medical information system on the pharmacy and nursing departments in two hospitals. The results indicated changes in tasks and greater interdependence between the two departments.

Awareness of these different models of change can help system evaluators recognize their own implicit assumptions and consider additional areas of study and the research strategies that accompany them. The next section outlines 10 general research questions suggested by these and other theoretical perspectives. The questions are followed by a discussion of the research methodologies appropriate to each of the different perspectives.

Evaluation Questions and Research Methods

In evaluating the impacts of a new computer system, an essential step is to determine what questions to ask. This section suggests a number of potential questions for evaluation studies. The selection of appropriate questions will be determined by both implicit assumptions about change and the explicit purpose of the evaluation for the organization itself.

The suggested questions cover a variety of theoretical frameworks, including those detailed above. Research on the relationship between acceptance of a computer system and individual variables such as personality style or resistance to change, for example, treats the computer as an exogenous force and adds a psychological framework in which the investigator assumes that individual differences will influence actions in the workplace (e.g., Counte, Kjerulff, Salloway, & Campbell, 1984). In contrast, investigators who look for differences between professions or departments in acceptance of medical systems focus on social interactions and the political nature of information systems, making the assumption that professional or departmental issues will be important in determining individual reactions to new computer systems (e.g., Aydin & Rice, 1991, 1992). The use of network methods (see Chapter 6) in investigating computer impacts, however, implies a diffusion model in which acceptance of the innovation is transmitted through channels of communication, over time, among members of a social system.

The 10 questions detailed below, although not exhaustive, provide a beginning framework for addressing system impacts. Additional questions and approaches are suggested in later chapters in this book. Recognizing the purpose of a specific system evaluation will also help determine the focus of the investigation. If, for example, the organization is committed to maintaining the system, evaluators will most likely focus on issues such as how to encourage more individuals to use the system, ensure adequate training, enhance satisfaction with improved system support, encourage the formation of user groups, and so on. If, however, discontinuing the system is an option, the focus may be on determining how well the system is functioning, the level of system use, and its cost-effectiveness. The evaluator who is knowledgeable about different models of change may also be able to suggest additional questions that may provide important information for the decisions to be made for the organization.

The suggested areas for evaluation are organized around the following 10 questions. These questions and the detailed issues they encompass are meant to encourage system evaluators to go beyond obvious questions of user attitudes and system acceptance and attempt to address some of the more difficult issues that will, in the long run, prove important in the implementation of successful, cost-effective systems. Table 1.1 links each question with the models of change detailed above and includes suggested evaluation methods. The final section in this chapter provides an overview of the evaluation methods that are described in detail in subsequent chapters of the book.

Evaluation Questions

1. Does the system work technically as designed?

The first step is usually to determine whether the system actually works. For an order entry system, for example, does the computer actually transmit the needed information about physician orders between nursing stations and the appropriate ancillary department? Does a physician expert system provide the physician with the necessary information to

TABLE 1.1 Evaluation Questions, Models of Change, and Suggested Research Methods

Evaluation Question	Models of Change	Suggested Methods	Further Description
1. Does the system work as designed?	External force	Qualitative (interviews, observation, documents)	Chapter 3
	User needs	Survey	Chapter 4
	Interactions	Laboratory/quasi-experiment	Chapters 2 & 5
		Cost-benefit analysis	Chapter 7
		Clinical information processing scenarios	Chapter 8
2. Is the system used as anticipated?	External force	Qualitative (interviews, observation, documents)	Chapter 3
	User needs	Survey	Chapter 4
	Interactions	Quasi-experiment	Chapters 2 & 5
		Cohort/time series study	Chapter 2
		Post-intervention study	Chapter 2
3. Does the system produce the desired results?	External force	Qualitative (interviews, observation, documents)	Chapter 3
	User needs	Survey	Chapter 4
	Interactions	Laboratory/quasi-experiment/simulation	Chapters 2 & 5
		Cohort/time series study	Chapter 2
		Post-intervention study	Chapter 2
		Cost-benefit analysis	Chapter 7
4. Does the system work better than the procedures it replaced?	External force	Qualitative (interviews, observation, documents)	Chapter 3
	User needs	Survey	Chapter 4
		Quasi-experiment	Chapters 2 & 5
		Simulation	Chapter 5
		Cohort/time series study	Chapter 2
		Cost-benefit analysis	Chapter 7

TABLE 1.1 Continued

Evaluation Question	Models of Change	Suggested Methods	Further Description
5. Is the system cost-effective?	External force	Cost-benefit analysis	Chapter 7
	User needs		
6. How well have individuals been trained to use the system?	External force	Qualitative (interviews, observation, documents)	Chapter 3
	User needs	Survey	Chapter 4
		Cohort/time series study	Chapter 2
7. What are the anticipated long-term impacts on how departments interact?	Interactions	Qualitative (interviews, observation)	Chapter 3
		Survey	Chapter 4
		Quasi-experiment	Chapters 2 & 5
		Cohort/time series study	Chapter 2
		Network analysis	Chapter 6
8. What are the long-term effects on the delivery of medical care?	User needs	Qualitative (interviews, observation, documents)	Chapter 3
	Interactions	Survey	Chapter 4
		Quasi-experiment	Chapters 2 & 5
		Cost-benefit	Chapter 7
9. Will the system have an impact on control in the organization?	Interactions	Qualitative (interviews, documents)	Chapter 3
		Survey	Chapter 4
		Network analysis	Chapter 6
		Cost-benefit analysis	Chapter 7
10. To what extent do impacts depend on practice setting?	Interactions	Qualitative (interviews, observation, documents)	Chapter 3
		Survey	Chapter 4
		Quasi-experiment	Chapters 2 & 5

arrive at a diagnosis and make treatment decisions? Do the appropriate professionals actually use the system?

A system that seems to work perfectly in tests or simulations may encounter a number of difficulties when actually implemented in a hospital or medical practice. For the purposes of the present volume, we will assume that the technical aspects of the system are operating correctly and focus on evaluating system impacts that stem from determining who actually uses the system, how they use it, and the impacts of its use on individuals, groups, and the delivery of medical care.

2. *Is the system being used as anticipated?*

Who uses the system, how much, and for what purposes? If system use is optional, is the system used by enough individuals to warrant continuation? Who doesn't use the system, and why? What factors influence individual decisions to use the system (e.g., personality styles, professional issues, age, departmental norms for how work should be done, communication networks)? What is its impact on individual jobs (e.g., work overload, job satisfaction, new skills development, new job classifications)?

Even systems that work are often not used as anticipated. Thus it is important to determine whether the system (1) meets the needs of projected users, (2) is convenient and easy to use, and (3) fits the work patterns of the professionals for whom it is intended. These issues are particularly important for computer systems designed for health care professionals. In other industries such as banking, insurance, or travel, for example, workers may be required to use a computer system continuously in order to perform their work. Health care systems, however, are frequently an adjunct to enhance or speed medical work performed on and for patients. Using the computer may require changes in daily work patterns that health care professionals may be unwilling or unable to make if the system is inconvenient or difficult to use (Griffin, 1991). Other systems may potentially meet user needs but be too confusing or complicated to encourage use, particularly if individuals only need to use the system on a sporadic basis. For example, a physician with admitting privileges at several different hospitals may be unwilling or unable to learn and remember different computer protocols for each hospital. Furthermore, even when computer use is required, errors are likely when the system is not tailored to the needs of the user. All of these are issues for consideration when evaluating system impacts.

3. Does the system produce the desired results?

Desired by whom? Administrators? Physicians? Other professionals or departments? What competing interests are involved? Decisions to adopt centralized systems are often made by hospital administrators with varying amounts of consultation with the departments and individuals who will use the system. Ideally, however, system implementation will be preceded by agreement on expected system outcomes for the organization as a whole. Individual departments may actually agree to the adoption of a system that does not meet their own specific needs but provides benefits for the institution. Sometimes these agreements involve other negotiated benefits for the department in question.

Aydin (1989), for example, found that the pharmacy department in a major medical center agreed to use what it considered to be a "nursing" order entry system. In return for agreeing to the system, the pharmacy negotiated a return to the expanded consultant role that they had been forced to give up under previous budget cuts. In contrast, however, the PROMIS system was discontinued despite its use by radiologists, pharmacists, and nurses because it lacked acceptance by the medical staff, the primary decision-making power in the organization (Kaplan, 1991; Lundsgaarde, Fischer, & Steele, 1981).

4. Does the system work better than the procedures it replaced?

Computer system implementation requires expenditures for hardware, software, and user training, as well as possible increases in staff for data entry tasks, especially where more information is being gathered and stored than in the past. Thus system evaluators must address system benefits as well as operating efficiency. Has computerization resulted in cost savings in staff time spent in data collection and analysis? If not, is the additional data and analysis made possible by computerization worth the time and money spent (e.g., to meet regulatory requirements, control other costs, increase patient or physician satisfaction, or deliver better health care to patients)?

5. Is the system cost-effective?

For whom? Individual practitioners? Departments? Patients? The organization as a whole? Medical information systems have the potential to reduce costs by improving information flows between departments as well as by providing information that may not have been readily available before the implementation of the system. However, costs may

squeezing the balloon

need multiple perspective

increase for employee training and higher salaries when new computer skills are added to job descriptions. Increased personnel expenses in nursing for clerks to enter orders in the computer, for example, may be balanced by cost savings in the pharmacy where the order entry system automatically bills patients for pharmacy charges. However, direct order entry by physicians may save clerical costs. Order entry may also result in the "capture" of charges that were frequently "lost" with manual systems. Chapter 7 addresses issues in determining the cost-effectiveness of medical information systems.

6. How well have individuals been trained to use the system?

How many errors occur? Are data entry errors widespread, or limited to a few users? Do individuals communicate with colleagues about new ways to use the computer system? Is system support readily available when problems arise? Are improvements needed in the training provided, "user-friendliness" of the system, time available for users to practice and become familiar with the system, communication with users, and support in solving system problems?

7. What are the anticipated long-term impacts on the ways departments linked by computer interact with each other?

Is communication and coordination between departments more or less efficient using the computer system? If departments worked well together before the computer system, has computer implementation created any new problems? Has the computer system resolved ongoing problems such as slow transmission of orders, and the like? Are lab results reported faster with the computer system? Does one department feel they are bearing more than their share of the new job responsibilities related to the computer system (e.g., nurses or clerical staff doing order entry for pharmacy or radiology)? Is another department concerned with errors in order entry (e.g., errors in radiology orders made by clerical staff on nursing units)? Do these issues affect system effectiveness?

8. What are the anticipated long-term effects on the delivery of medical care?

Will lab/radiology results reporting be faster? If so, will the increases in efficiency be evident in decreased lengths of stay? Will computer-based monitoring of physician orders eliminate duplicate and/or unnecessary tests? If so, what will be the impact on the cost or quality of care? On physician satisfaction? If an order entry system, for example, requires nurses, clerks, or physicians to enter the reason for requesting a specific radiology test along with the order, will radiologists be able to document that having this information enables them to better meet physicians' diagnostic needs?

9. Will system implementation have an impact on control in the organization?

Will the new system enable administrators to monitor or control physician practice behavior and decrease departmental independence in professional decision making? If so, what is the impact on physician attitudes, cost of medical care, and so on? Is there a shift in the balance of power between clinical personnel and managers, between departments, between the institution and attending physicians (Kaplan, 1992)? Is there an impact on the competitive position of the institution? Who determines what information is to be included in new systems and how it is to be collected and used (Kaplan, 1992)?

10. To what extent do medical information systems have impacts that depend on the practice setting in which they are implemented?

Under what circumstances and in what organizational settings do certain effects occur? How common are these effects? What are the impacts of organization, size, culture, values, and the like on system outcomes? What evaluation questions are appropriate in different settings?

The following section provides a brief overview of some of the research methods appropriate to these evaluation questions and the models of change they represent (see Table 1.1).

Research Methods

Numerous research methods are available to support investigation of the research questions and the underlying models of change described above. This section provides a brief overview of some of these methods with examples of their contributions to research on information systems in health care organizations. The discussion includes qualitative methods, survey research, experimental research methods, mathematical and computer simulation models, research strategies that combine quantitative and qualitative methodologies, and network analysis. Each of these methods is described in detail in subsequent chapters of this book.

Qualitative Research. Described in detail in Chapter 3, qualitative research is conducted in natural settings and is characterized by the use of data in the form of words rather than numbers, primarily from observations, interviews, and documents. These methods attempt to understand change from the point of view of the participants and their social and institutional context. Qualitative methods are particularly useful in determining *how* and *why* specific outcomes occur (Yin, 1984). In instances where the investigator is attempting to build a theory of how a medical information system affects the organization and its members, for example, these methods provide important insights into the reasons for change. Although particularly useful when the major purpose of the investigator is theory building (Van Maanen, Dabbs, & Faulkner, 1982), qualitative methods are equally important in theory testing. Case studies, which may combine quantitative and qualitative methods, are used both for theory construction (Benbasat, Goldstein, & Mead, 1987; George & McKeown, 1985; Yin, 1984), and for testing theories or hypotheses about causes and effects (Markus, 1989; Mohr, 1985). In theory testing, specific theoretical propositions need to be developed in advance to guide data collection and hypothesis testing (Yin, 1989).

Qualitative methods are also particularly useful in collecting and analyzing data pertinent to the design of medical information systems. Fafchamps (1991), for example, describes an ethnographic work flow analysis of physician behavior in the clinics of two health care institutions. Information about physician needs, practice behavior, and the clinical setting was collected by (1) asking physicians to describe what they were doing and conducting a guided tour of the clinics; (2) structured observations of meetings and interpersonal interactions; (3) focused interviews; and (4) analyzing formal and informal notes and reports. These data were analyzed and used to help design a physician workstation.

Survey Research Methodologies. Survey research methodologies are also widely used to study the impact of information systems (see Chapter 4). In survey research, responses to predefined questions or items are collected from a sample of individuals, departments, or organizations to produce quantitative descriptions of population characteristics or of relationships between variables. Zmud and Boynton (1991) provide summary data and statistical analysis on 119 scales that have been used to study information systems.

In considering attitudes toward computers, for example, a comparative survey of physicians, pharmacists, lawyers, and CPAs by Zoltan-Ford and Chapanis (1982) found that physicians and lawyers expressed dissatisfaction with what they perceived to be the depersonalizing nature of computers and with the complexity of computer languages. Surveys by Teach and Shortliffe (1981) and Singer, Sacks, Lucente, and Chalmers (1983) concluded that physicians generally accept applications that enhance their patient management capabilities but tend to oppose applications that automate clinical activities traditionally performed by physicians themselves. Anderson, Jay, Schweer, and Anderson's (1986b) survey of medical students, residents, and practicing physicians found that, although physicians recognize the potential of computers to improve patient care, they express concerns about the possibility of increased control over their practices, threats to privacy, and legal and technical problems.

Surveys can also be used to collect descriptive data needed to establish policies or to solve problems. Survey data may indicate the existence of problems, as well as their seriousness and pervasiveness. In this instance the methodology is problem-driven (Attewell & Rule, 1984; Kraemer & Dutton, 1991). Kaiser and King (1982), for example, used survey research in their study of the emerging role of information analysts. Kraemer and Dutton (1991) provide a useful propositional inventory based on a meta-analysis of the findings from a large number of surveys. In general, studies based on surveys fail to examine the relationships between information systems and their external environments, the dynamics of how change takes place, and societal impacts of the information system.

Cohort/Time Series Studies. These studies can be used to follow individuals or performance measures over a period of time in order to evaluate the impact of implementing a computer system (see Chapter 2). For example, Counte et al. (1984) surveyed a sample of hospital clerical workers prior to, 6 months after, and 12 months after the implementation of an admission discharge and transfer component of a medical information system (MIS). The study found that workers' orientation toward change, need for order and structure, as well as their initial attitude toward the MIS, predicted their adaptation to the new system.

A second study used a time series design to evaluate a computerized physician reminder system (Rind et al., 1991). Physicians' responses to laboratory test results were measured for 3 months prior to and during a 6-month period after implementation of the reminder system. The findings indicated that physicians adjusted or discontinued medications an average of 21.1 hours sooner in response to the reminders.

Experimental Research Methods. Experimental research methods can also be used to study the effects of information systems on individuals, work groups, and the organizations in which they function (Benbasat, 1989b; DeSanctis, 1989). To date, most experimental research has been conducted in the laboratory. This research methodology is characterized by: (1) random assignment of subject to treatment and control conditions; (2) manipulation of one or more independent variables; (3) measurement of their effects on the dependent variables; and (4) control over other independent and intervening variables that affect the dependent variable (Fromkin & Streufert, 1976).

A major advantage of laboratory experiments is that they permit the investigator to test hypotheses derived from theories or other empirical studies under controlled conditions (see Chapter 5). Although laboratory experiments have a high degree of internal validity, however, they lack external validity since it is difficult to generalize the results to the actual organizational settings in which the information system will be implemented (Campbell & Stanley, 1963).

An alternative strategy is to employ quasi-experimental designs or field experiments (Cook & Campbell, 1979). These methodologies permit the investigator to test hypotheses about the impacts of an information system in a natural organizational setting, making the results more generalizable than those derived from laboratory experiments (see Chapters 2 and 5). Although true experimental designs incorporate random assignment of subjects and experimental control of independent variables, field experiments involve compromises when the investigator must work with intact groups or lacks control over many extraneous and potentially confounding variables. Nevertheless, there are many settings in which quasi-experimental design allows the investigator to collect data and make inferences about the impact of information systems. Zmud, Olson, and Hauser (1989), for example, found 10 quasi-experimental studies of information systems. Anderson, Jay, Perry, and Anderson (1990) also used a quasi-experimental design to test a network intervention strategy to increase physician use of a hospital information system (see Chapter 13).

Mathematical and Computer Simulation Models. Mathematical and computer simulation models can also be used to study medical information systems (see Chapter 5). This approach provides researchers with a relatively inexpensive means of studying operational effectiveness and predicting the effects of changing the operational environment without actually interfering with the ongoing work of the organization. In one study, Anderson, Jay, Schweer, and Anderson (1986a) developed

decision models -
regression models -
other models

a mathematical model to characterize the process by which physicians change their use of a medical information system. A structural equation model was constructed using data collected from members of a hospital medical staff. The model indicated that consultation with other physicians on the hospital service led to greater exposure to and a more favorable attitude toward potential computer applications. Physicians who were more knowledgeable about computers were more likely to tailor the system to their individual practices. All of these factors resulted in increased use of the system by physicians. The results of the study led to a number of policy recommendations regarding strategies for introducing computer technology to physicians.

In a second study, a computer simulation model of the order entry process for a hospital information system was developed and used to perform computer simulation experiments to estimate the effects of two methods of order entry on several outcome measures (Anderson et al., 1988a, 1988b). The results indicated that the development and use of personal order sets for order entry could result in a significant reduction in manpower, salaries, fringe benefits, and errors for the hospital.

Combining Methods. Studies that attempt to examine complex social interactions as determinants of system use generally require a combination of qualitative and quantitative methods. Qualitative data, for example, can be used to gain critical insights into motivations and interactions within the organization. Detailed observations in the actual organizational setting can also be used to interpret the findings and explain how and why information systems bring about changes. Subsequently, qualitative data, surveys, and experimental methods can all be used for empirical testing of hypotheses. This combination of qualitative and quantitative methods produces insights that neither method alone can provide. Furthermore, the findings are considered to be more robust and generalizable (Kaplan & Duchon, 1988).

In one example, both qualitative and quantitative methods were used to study the impact of a clinical laboratory computer system (Kaplan, 1987; Kaplan & Duchon, 1988, 1989). Quantitative results showed differences between technicians in their reactions to the computer system. Shedding further light on these differences, qualitative data indicated that laboratory employees differed in their orientation to the nature of their work. One group of technicians focused on workload increases; the other emphasized improved results reporting and service. The users' response to the computer system depended on their perception of the extent to which the system supported or interfered with the performance of their jobs as they defined them.

Network Analysis. Another approach to the study of social interactions, frequently termed *social network analysis* or *structural analysis*, focuses on interactions that occur between individuals and/or departments as a medical information system is adopted and its use diffuses throughout the organization. The network or structural approach hypothesizes that individuals' responses to the information system are affected and constrained by their positions and roles in the social system of which they are a part. Individual adoption and use is seen as dependent on group interaction (Anderson, Jay, Schweer, Anderson, & Kassing, 1987; Kaplan, 1991; Rice & Aydin, 1991; Rogers 1983, 1987). This perspective differs fundamentally from those that assume that individuals and organizational units are somewhat independent of one another in the ways in which they respond to and use an information system. Instead, this approach attempts to identify the communication structure or the underlying social structure, generally unknown to organizational participants, by collecting and analyzing relational data. Network analysis methods are based on graph theory, clustering methods, and multidimensional scaling and are described in detail in Chapter 6.

Anderson and Jay (1985), for example, used network analysis in their study of the time-of-adoption of a computer-based hospital information system. Medical doctors adopted the innovation (i.e., began entering their orders) in clusters, with all of the doctors in a clique adopting at about the same time. "Network location was found to have a significant effect on the adoption and utilization of the HIS (the computer-based-innovation) independently of background and practice characteristics of physicians" (Anderson & Jay, 1985). In other words, the network variable added additional unexplained variance in innovativeness to that explained by such individual characteristics of the doctors as age and medical specialty. Furthermore, utilization patterns were similar among physicians belonging to each group.

Conclusion

Each of the methods described above is explained in detail, with sample evaluation instruments where appropriate, in Chapters 2 through 8. The chapters also include examples of studies that make different theoretical assumptions, address different evaluation questions, and employ different research methodologies. Each study also has important practical policy implications for the organization under study.

Additional Readings

The Social Impact of Computers

Anderson and Jay (1987) and Anderson (1992a, 1992b) review evaluation studies of the use and impact of health care information systems. Dunlop and Kling (1991) provide an important collection of readings outlining the different positions in the debates about social issues surrounding computerization.

Evaluation and Models of Change

Kling (1980), Kling and Scacchi (1982), Lyytinen (1987), and Markus and Robey (1988) provide detailed theoretical research frameworks for information systems and research dealing with information systems problems.

Rice's (1992) chapter is a detailed review of the different paradigms and theoretical frameworks adopted by information system researchers.

Research Methods

The three volumes from the Harvard Business School Research Colloquium on research methodologies that can be used to study information systems cover qualitative research methods (Cash & Lawrence, 1989), experimental research methods (Benbasat, 1989a), and survey research methods (Kraemer, 1991). Jenkins (1985) also provides a useful overview of methods used in MIS research.

Nissen, Klein, and Hirschheim's (1991) edited volume provides comprehensive documentation of current research methods and approaches in information systems today.

Rossi and Freeman (1985) is an excellent textbook on evaluation research. Patton (1990) provides an excellent introduction to qualitative approaches to evaluation. Yin (1984) is an excellent monograph on case study research. Fromkin and Streufert (1976) provide a good discussion of laboratory experiments, and Cook and Campbell (1979) contains an overview of quasi-experimental research designs.

Scott (1991) provides a good readable introduction to network analysis.

References

Anderson, J. G. (1992a). Medical information systems. In A. Kent & J. G. Williams (Eds.), *Encyclopedia of microcomputers* (vol. 9., pp. 39-65). New York: Marcel Dekker.

Anderson, J. G. (1992b). Computerized medical record systems in ambulatory care. *Journal of Ambulatory Care Management, 15*, 1-8.

Anderson, J. G., & Jay, S. J. (1985). Computers and clinical judgment: The role of physician networks. *Social Science and Medicine, 10*, 969-979.

Anderson, J. G., & Jay, S. J. (Eds.). (1987). *Use and impact of computers in clinical medicine*. New York: Springer-Verlag.

Anderson, J. G., & Jay, S. J. (1990). Computers and the future practice of medicine: Issues and options. *Cahiers de Sociologie et de Demographie Médicales, 30*, 295-312.

Anderson, J. G., Jay, S. J., Perry, J., & Anderson, M. M. (1990). Diffusion of computer applications among physicians: A quasi-experimental study. *Clinical Sociology Review, 8*, 116-127.

Anderson, J. G., Jay, S. J., Schweer, H. M., & Anderson, M. M. (1986a). Physician utilization of computers in medical practice: Policy implications based on a structural model. *Social Science and Medicine, 23*, 259-267.

Anderson, J. G., Jay, S. J., Schweer, H. M., & Anderson, M. M. (1986b). Why doctors don't use computers: Some empirical findings. *Journal of the Royal Society of Medicine, 79*, 142-144.

Anderson, J. G., Jay, S. J., Schweer, H. M., Anderson, M. M., & Kassing, D. (1987). Physician communication networks and the adoption and utilization of computer applications in medicine. In J. G. Anderson & S. J. Jay (Eds.), *Use and impact of computers in clinical medicine* (pp. 185-198). New York: Springer-Verlag.

Anderson, J. G., Jay, S. J., Cathcart, L., Clevenger, S. J., Kassing, D. R., Perry, J., & Anderson, M. M. (1988a). A computer simulation of physician use of a hospital information system. In W. E. Hammond (Ed.), *Proceedings AAMSI Congress 1988* (pp. 114-118). Washington, DC: American Association for Medical Systems and Informatics.

Anderson, J. G., Jay, S. J., Clevenger, S. J., Kassing, D. R., Perry, J., & Anderson, M. M. (1988b). Physician utilization of a hospital information system: A computer simulation model. In *Proceedings 12th Annual Symposium on Computer Applications in Medical Care* (pp. 858-861). Los Angeles, CA: IEEE Computer Society Press.

Attewell, P., & Rule, J. B. (1984). Computing and organizations: What we know and what we don't know. *Communications of the ACM, 27*, 1184-1192.

Attewell, P., & Rule, J. B. (1991). Survey and other methodologies applied to IT impact research: Experiences from a comparative study of business computing. In K. L. Kraemer (Ed.), *The information systems research challenge: Survey research methods* (vol. 3, pp. 299-315). Boston, MA: Harvard Business School.

Aydin, C. E. (1989). Occupational adaptation to computerized medical information systems. *Journal of Health and Social Behavior, 30*, 163-179.

Aydin, C. E., & Rice, R. E. (1991). Social worlds, individual differences, and implementation: Predicting attitudes toward a medical information system. *Information & Management, 20*, 119-136.

Aydin, C. E., & Rice, R. E. (1992). Bringing social worlds together: Computers as catalysts for new interactions in health care organizations. *Journal of Health and Social Behavior, 33*, 168-185.

Babbie, A. (1983). *The practice of social research* (3rd ed.). Belmont, CA: Wadsworth.

Barley, S. R. (1986). Technology as an occasion for structuring: Evidence from observations of CT scanners and the social order of radiology departments. *Administrative Science Quarterly, 31*, 78-108.

Benbasat, I. (1989a). Laboratory experiments in information systems studies with a focus on individuals: A critical appraisal. In I. Benbasat (Ed.), *The information systems research challenge: Experimental research methods* (vol. 2, pp. 33-47). Boston, MA: Harvard Business School.

Benbasat, I. (Ed.). (1989b). *The information systems research challenge: Experimental research methods.* Harvard Business School Research Colloquium, Vol. 2. Boston, MA: Harvard Business School.

Benbasat, I., Goldstein, D. I., and Mead, M. (1987). The case research strategy in studies of information systems. *MIS Quarterly, 11*, 369-386.

Bjorn-Andersen, N., Eason, K., & Robey, D. (1986). *Managing computer impact: An international study of management and organization.* Norwood, NJ: Ablex.

Braverman, H. (1974). *Labor and monopoly capital—The degradation of work in the twentieth century.* New York: Monthly Review Press.

Campbell, D., & Stanley, J. (1963). *Experimental and quasi-experimental designs for research.* Chicago: Rand McNally.

Cash, J. I., & Lawrence, P. R. (Eds.). (1989). *The information systems research challenge: Qualitative research methods.* Harvard Business School Research Colloquium, Vol. 1. Boston, MA: Harvard Business School.

Cook, T. D., & Campbell, D. T. (1979). *Quasi-experimentation: Design and analysis issues for field settings.* Boston: Houghton Mifflin.

Counte, M. A., Kjerulff, K. H., Salloway, J. C., & Campbell, B. (1984). Implementing computerization in hospitals: A case study of the behavioral and attitudinal impacts of a medical information system. *Journal of Organizational Behavior Management, 6*, 109-122.

DeSanctis, G. (1989). Small group research in information systems: Theory and methods. In I. Benbasat (Ed.), *The information systems research challenge: Experimental research methods* (vol. 2, pp. 53-82). Boston, MA: Harvard Business School.

Dowling, A. F. (1980). Do hospital staff interfere with computer system implementation? *Health Care Management Review, 5*, 23-32.

Dunlop, C., & Kling, R. (1991). *Computerization and controversy: Value conflicts and social choices.* Boston: Academic Press.

Fafchamps. D. (1991). Ethnographic workflow analysis: Specification for design. In J. H. Bullinger (Ed.), *Proceedings of the 4th International Conference on Human-Computer Interaction.* Amsterdam: Elsevier.

Forsythe, D. E., & Buchanan, B. G. (1992). Broadening our approach to evaluating medical information systems. In *Proceedings 15th Annual Symposium on Computer Applications in Medical Care* (pp. 8-12). New York: McGraw-Hill.

Freudenheim, M. (1990). Hospitals increase use of computers. *New York Times*, September 11, 1990, p. C2.

Fromkin, H. L., & Streufert, S. (1976). *Laboratory experimentation, industrial and organizational psychology* (pp. 415-465). Chicago: Rand McNally.

Gardner, E. (1990). Information systems: Computers' full capabilities often go untapped. *Modern Healthcare*, May 28, 38-40.

George, A., & McKeown, T. (1985). Case studies and theories of organizational decision making. In R. F. Coulam & R. A. Smith (Eds.), *Advances in information processing in organizations* (vol. 6, pp. 21-58). Greenwich, CT: JAI Press.

Griffin, B. (1991). Effects of work redesign on employee perceptions, attitudes, and behaviors: A long-term investigation. *Academy of Management Journal, 34*, 425-435.

Hirschheim, R. (1985). *Office automation—A social and organizational perspective.* New York: John Wiley.

Ives, B., Hamilton, S. , & Davis, G. B. (1980). A framework for research in computer-based management information systems. *Management Science, 26*, 910-934.

Jenkins, A. M. (1985). Research methodologies and MIS research. In E. Mumford, R. Hirschheim, G. Fitzgerald, & T. Wood-Harper (Eds.), *Research methods in information systems* (pp. 103-117). Amsterdam: Elsevier.

Johnson, B. M., & Rice, R. E. (1984). Reinvention in the innovation process: The case of word processing. In R. E. Rice & Associates (Eds.), *The new media* (pp. 157-183). Beverly Hills, CA: Sage.

Kaiser, K. M., & King, W. R. (1982). The manager-analyst interface in systems development. *MIS Quarterly, 6*, 49-59.

Kaplan, B. (1987). Initial impact of a clinical laboratory computer system: Themes common to expectations and actualities. *Journal of Medical Systems, 11*, 137-147.

Kaplan, B. (1991). Models of change and information systems research. In H. E. Nissen, H. K. Klein, & R. Hirschheim (Eds.), *Information systems research: Contemporary approaches and emergent traditions* (pp. 593-611). Amsterdam: North Holland Press.

Kaplan, B. (1992). National Health Service reforms: Opportunities for medical informatics research. In K. C. Lun et al. (Eds.), *Medinfo 92: Proceedings of the 7th World Congress on Medical Informatics* (pp. 116-1171). Amsterdam: Elsevier.

Kaplan, B., & Duchon, D. (1988). Combining qualitative and quantitative methods in information systems research: A case study. *MIS Quarterly, 12*, 571-586.

Kaplan, B., & Duchon, D. (1989). A job orientation model of impact on work seven months post implementation. In B. Barber, D. Cao, D. Qin, & G. Wagner (Eds.), *MEDINFO 89* (pp. 1051-1055). Amsterdam: North Holland.

Kimberly, J. R., & Evanisko, M. J. (1981). Organizational innovation: The influence of individual, organizational, and contextual factors on hospital adoption of technological and administrative innovations. *Academy of Management Journal, 24*, 689-713.

King, J. L., & Kraemer, K. (1980). *Cost as a social impact of telecommunications and other information technologies.* Irvine, CA: Public Policy Research Organization.

Kling, R. (1980). Social analyses of computing: Theoretical perspectives in recent empirical research. *Computing Surveys, 12*, 61-110.

Kling, R., & Scacchi, W. (1982). The web of computing: Computer technology as social organization. In M. C. Yovits (Ed.), *Advances in computers* (Vol. 21, pp. 2-90). New York: Academic Press.

Kraemer, K. L. (Ed.). (1991). *The information systems research challenge: Survey research methods.* Harvard Business School Research Colloquium, Vol. 3, Boston, MA: Harvard Business School.

Kraemer, K. L., & Danziger, J. N. (1990). The impacts of computer technology on the worklife of information workers. *Social Science Computer Review, 8*, 592-613.

Kraemer, K. L., & Dutton, W. H. (1991). Survey research in the study of management information systems. In K. L. Kraemer (Ed.), *The information systems research challenge: Survey research methods* (vol. 3, pp. 3-57). Boston, MA: Harvard Business School.

Kuhn, T. S. (1962). *The structure of scientific revolutions.* Chicago: University of Chicago Press.

Kumar, K., & Bjorn-Andersen, N. (1990). A cross-cultural comparison of information systems designer values. *Communications of the ACM, 33*, 528-538.

Leifer, R., & McDonough, III, E. F. (1985). Computerization as a predominant technology effecting work unit structure. *Proceedings 6th Annual Conference on Information Systems* (pp. 238-248). New York: Association for Computing Machinery.

Lundsgaarde, H. P., Fischer, P. J., & Steele, D. J. (1981). *Human problems in computerized medicine.* University of Kansas Publications in Anthropology, No. 13. Lawrence: University of Kansas.

Lyytinen, K. (1987). Different perspectives on information systems: Problems and solutions. *ACM Computing Surveys, 19,* 5-46.

Lyytinen, K. (1988). Expectation failure concept and systems analysts' views of information systems failure: Results of an exploratory study. *Information & Management, 14,* 45-56.

Lyytinen, K., & Hirschheim, R. (1987). Information systems failure—A survey and classification of empirical literature. *Oxford Surveys in Information Technology, 4,* 257-309.

Markus, M. L. (1983). Power, politics, and MIS implementation. *Communications of the ACM, 26,* 430-444.

Markus, M. L. (1984). *Systems in organizations: Bugs and features.* Boston, MA: Pitman.

Markus, M. L. (1989). Case selection in a disconfirmatory case study. In J. I. Cash & P. R. Lawrence (Eds.), *The information systems research challenge: Qualitative research methods* (vol. 1, pp. 20-26). Boston, MA: Harvard Business School.

Markus, M. L., & Robey, D. (1988). Information technology and organizational change: Causal structure in theory and research. *Management Science, 34,* 583-598.

Mohr, L. B. (1982). *Explaining organizational behavior.* San Francisco: Jossey-Bass.

Mohr, L. B. (1985). The reliability of the case study as a source of information. In R. F. Coulam & R. A. Smith (Eds.), *Advances in information processing in organizations* (vol. 6, pp. 65-93). Greenwich, CT: JAI Press.

Mouritsen, J., & Bjorn-Andersen, N. (1991). Understanding third wave information systems. In C. Dunlop & R. Kling (Eds.), *Computerization and controversy: Value conflicts and social choices* (pp. 308-320). San Diego, CA: Academic Press.

Nissen, H. E., Klein, H. K., & Hirschheim, R. (Eds.). (1991). *Information systems research: Contemporary approaches and emergent traditions.* Amsterdam: North Holland.

Olson, M. H. (1982). New information technology and organizational culture. *MIS Quarterly, 6,* 71-92.

Patton, M. Q. (1990). *Qualitative research and evaluation methods* (2nd ed.). Newbury Park, CA: Sage.

Pfeffer, J. (1982). *Organizations and organization theory.* Marshfield, MA: Pitman.

Rice, R. E. (1992). Contexts of research on organizational computer-mediated communication: A recursive review. In H. Lea (Ed.), *Contexts of computer-mediated communication.* London, UK: Harvester-Wheatsheaf.

Rice, R. E., & Aydin, C. (1991). Attitudes toward new organizational technology: Network proximity as a mechanism for social information processing. *Administrative Science Quarterly, 36,* 219-244.

Rind, D. M., Safran, C., Phillips, R. S., Slack, W. V., Calkins, D. R., Delbanco, T. L., & Bleich, H. L. (1991). The effect of computer-based reminders on the management of hospitalized patients. In P. Clayton (Ed.), *Proceedings of the 15th Annual Symposium on Computer Applications in Medical Care* (pp. 28-32). Los Angeles, CA: IEEE Computer Society.

Rogers, E. M. (1983). *Diffusion of innovation* (3rd ed.). New York: The Free Press.

Rogers, E. M. (1987). Progress, problems and prospects for network research: Investigating relationships in the age of electronic communication technologies. *Social Networks, 9,* 285-310.

Rossi, P. H., & Freeman, H. E. (1985). *Evaluation: A systematic approach.* Newbury Park, CA: Sage.

Scott, J. (1991). *Social network analysis: A handbook.* Newbury Park, CA: Sage.

Singer, J., Sacks, H. S., Lucente, F., & Chalmers, T. C. (1983). Physician attitudes toward applications of computer database systems. *Journal of the American Medical Association, 249,* 1610-1614.

Slack, J. D. (1984). *Communication technologies and society: Conceptions of causality and the politics of technological intervention.* Norwood, NJ: Ablex.

Teach, R. L., & Shortliffe, E. H. (1981). An analysis of physician attitudes regarding computer-based clinical consultation systems. *Computers and Biomedical Research, 14,* 542-558.

Van Maanen, J., Dabbs, J. M., & Faulkner, R. R. (1982). *Varieties of qualitative research.* Newbury Park, CA: Sage.

Yin, R. K. (1984). *Case study research.* Beverly Hills, CA: Sage.

Yin, R. K. (1989). Research design issues in using the case study method to study management information systems. In J. I. Cash & P. R. Lawrence (Eds.), *The information systems research challenge: Qualitative research methods* (vol. 1, pp. 1-6). Boston, MA: Harvard Business School.

Zmud, R. W., & Boynton, A. C. (1991). Survey measures and instruments in MIS: Inventory and appraisal. In K. L. Kraemer (Ed.), *The information systems research challenge: Survey research methods* (vol. 3, pp. 149-180). Boston, MA: Harvard Business School.

Zmud, R. W., Olson, M. H., & Hauser, R. (1989). Field experimentation in MIS research. In I. Benbasat (Ed.), *The information systems research challenge: Experimental research methods* (vol. 2, pp. 97-111). Boston, MA: Harvard Business School.

Zoltan-Ford, E., & Chapanis, A. (1982). What do professional persons think about computers? *Behaviour and Information Technology, 1,* 55-68.

2

Research Methods to Measure Impacts of Medical Computer Systems

Kristen H. Kjerulff

Introduction

There is a growing awareness of the importance of evaluating new and existing medical computer systems and measuring the impacts of these systems. In an era of cost-consciousness in health care it is important to know if the money that is spent on computer technology is making the health care system function more effectively and efficiently. If computer systems are not being used to the extent intended they may never be able to achieve their objectives. An effective plan for the evaluation of a medical computer system must take into account the extent to which the targeted players use the system and incorporate it effectively into professional practice. A computer system that is technically sound but is not used effectively will not achieve its intended benefits.

Because there is usually very little if any money set aside to evaluate new computer systems, evaluation efforts must often be fairly small-scale, inexpensive, easy to do, and fast. Within these constraints, researchers should strive to develop evaluation studies that will allow valid inferences (internal validity) and be meaningful to others (external validity). An effective evaluation plan begins with a focused research question or hypothesis.

Research Questions and Hypotheses

Although evaluation is, in essence, making a judgment about the value of something, simply asking if a computer system is good or bad is not focused enough to allow for the design of an informative study. A good research question or hypothesis is specific and focused on the factors to be measured. A useful research question might ask, "What percentage of physicians use the personal order sets at least three times a week?" or "What percentage of nurses do care planning on the computer system at the beginning of each shift?" The choice of a research question or hypothesis depends on what one needs to know. If the purpose of the evaluation is to decide whether to keep the current system or upgrade to a new system, the focus of the study may be on what the system is currently used for and what tasks cannot currently be performed with the computer system. In that case there will be multiple research questions such as, "What tasks do unit clerks currently perform on the computer system?" and "What tasks would the unit clerks like to be able to perform on the computer system?"

Hospitals and other health care systems are complex and interesting organizations. The introduction of computerization also provides for an opportunity to conduct basic studies of social, psychological, and organizational processes. These studies may not be purely evaluative in nature but may provide valuable insight into factors of relevance to the success or failure of computer systems. Example research questions that may fall into this category of basic research are "To what extent do physician referral networks affect use of the hospital computer system?" and "To what extent is technology anxiety related to nursing use of the hospital computer system?"

If possible, it is often helpful to begin with a hypothesis rather than a research question. A good research hypothesis is specific as to subjects, variables, and the relationship under investigation. The hypothesis serves as the guide for the choice of the statistical test. An example hypothesis is "Nurses scoring above the median on the Technology Anxiety Inventory will use the hospital computer system less often over the course of a 1-month period than nurses scoring below the median on the Technology Anxiety Inventory."

Evaluation Study Designs

There are a variety of study designs that a researcher may consider when deciding how best to answer the research question or hypothesis.

The choice of study design will depend on financial constraints, how quickly questions must be answered, and the extent to which the researcher is free to experimentally manipulate specific interventions. Following are descriptions of six study designs and example studies for each design. The study designs discussed are as follows: cohort, time series, cross-sectional, experimental, quasi-experimental, and post-intervention.

Cohort Studies

Cohort studies follow individuals over a specific period of time. Because cohort studies occur over time they allow for the description of the natural history of a particular phenomenon, such as the implementation of a computer system, and they allow for the measurement of the temporal sequence of events. Cohort studies are particularly useful for descriptive purposes and for examining the association between predictor and outcome variables of interest. Prospective cohort studies involve sampling of subjects and assessment of predictor variables before an event or intervention occurs and the assessment of outcomes of interest after the event has occurred.

A prospective cohort design applied to the study of the impacts of a medical information system (MIS) was conducted by Counte, Kjerulff, Salloway, and Campbell (1984). In this study, a random sample of hospital clerical workers was drawn and individuals were interviewed shortly prior to the implementation of the Admission Discharge and Transfer (ADT) component of a MIS. Two attitude-toward-computer scales were administered, one to measure attitudes toward computers in general, and a second to measure attitudes toward the specific medical information system that the clerical workers had been trained to use but had not yet begun to use. These attitude scales were described in more detail in Kjerulff and Counte (1988). In addition, participants were administered personality scales to assess two traits that were considered potentially relevant to adaptation to computerization (Jackson, 1967). The first scale was called "Orientation toward Change," which measured the degree to which an individual seeks, enjoys, and accepts change in his or her life. The second scale was called "Cognitive Structure" and measured the degree to which a person seeks order and structure and avoids ambiguity in his or her life. Job perceptions were also measured, including job satisfaction via the Job Description Index (Smith, Kendall, & Hulin, 1969), and role ambiguity and conflict via the Job Perceptions Inventory (House & Rizzo, 1972). Work role activities were also measured by asking participants to indicate the approximate amount of time they had spent the previous working day performing nine activities, including talking on the telephone, filling out forms, talking with patients or their families, extraneous paper work, data processing, traveling around the hospital, and attending meetings.

The primary outcomes of interest in this study were adaptation to the system, satisfaction with the system, and changes in work functioning measured at 6 and 12 months after implementation of the computer system. Adaptation was measured via self-ratings of use of the system, perceived changes as a function of the new computer system, and ratings of adaptation to the system made by the subject's supervisors (Kjerulff, Counte, Salloway, & Campbell, 1983). Satisfaction was measured by response to open-ended questions concerning problems experienced with the MIS, ways the MIS had made their jobs better, and ways the MIS had made their jobs worse (Kjerulff, Counte, & Salloway, 1988). The results of the study indicated that both of the personality scales as well as the attitudes toward the MIS were predictive of adaptation to the computer system (Counte, Kjerulff, Salloway, & Campbell, 1987). Specifically, individuals who reported the greatest difficulty adapting to the MIS had a more negative orientation toward change in general and were lower on cognitive structure. Individuals who were more positive about the changes created by the new MIS had a more positive attitude toward the system even before it was implemented. Attitude toward the MIS was correlated with satisfaction with the system both at 6 months and at 1 year post-implementation (Kjerulff, Counte, & Salloway, 1988). Work role activities changed over time, reflecting increased utilization of and reliance on the computer system, and satisfaction with the system increased over time.

Prospective cohort studies allow investigators to examine potential cause-and-effect relationships. The study described above provides evidence to support the hypothesis that attitudes toward computers and basic personality traits, exhibited prior to implementation, play a role in the process of adaptation to computerization. These types of studies are, however, expensive and time-consuming to conduct. In addition, prospective studies require investigators to measure many potential predictors in hopes that at least some will play a role in the outcomes of interest. There also exists the potential for unmeasured confounding variables to be causing the apparent relationship between the predictors and outcomes of interest. If investigators measure potentially confounding variables (such as subject educational level and prior computer experience) along with predictor variables and examine the impact of these factors, then potential confounders can often be ruled out.

Another potential problem with cohort studies is that subjects may leave the study over time for some reason that is related to the predictor of outcome variables. In a study of the implementation of a pharmacy computer system, Kjerulff, Counte, and Salloway (1986) noted an unusual increase in employee turnover during the first 6 months after implementation of the system. Questionnaire data collected prior to the implementation of the system indicated that those who left the hospital were less positive toward computers than those who stayed, and they also differed on a variety of personality and job perception measures.

Time Series Studies

Sometimes a researcher may not be interested in following specific individuals over time but may need to measure some particular factor over time, such as adverse drug events, patient mortality, lost medical records, or medication errors. Factors such as these can be measured repeatedly in a particular setting utilizing a time series design.

A time series design applied to the study of a computerized physician reminder system was conducted by Rind et al. (1991). The reminder system was designed to provide computerized prompts to physicians when lab tests indicated that patients were developing worsening renal function during treatment with nephrotoxic or renally excreted drugs, as evidenced by rising creatinine levels. Physician response to lab results indicating rising creatine levels was measured during a 3-month period prior to implementation and during a 6-month period after implementation of the reminder system. During the 6-month period after the reminder system was implemented, physicians adjusted or discontinued medications an average of 21.1 hours sooner than prior to the reminder system. This time series study suggests that computerized reminders can have an impact on physician behavior. Research is continuing to examine the impacts of this reminder system on patient outcomes.

Cross-Sectional Studies

In a cross-sectional study all data is collected at one point in time. Cross-sectional studies are often done to compare several groups of individuals on some factor of interest, and they are relatively inexpensive and fast to conduct. In addition, researchers conducting such studies don't have to worry about subject attrition. The major weakness of cross-sectional studies is that it is difficult to establish causal relationships because there is no information on temporal sequencing of events. For that reason, cross-sectional studies are often conducted for descriptive purposes and not for purposes of examining causal relationships.

Anderson, Jay, Schweer, and Anderson (1986) conducted a cross-sectional study to examine physician attitudes toward computer applications in medicine and to compare the attitudes of medical students, residents, and practicing physicians. The authors found that all three groups recognized the potential of computers to reduce costs and improve the quality of health care, but medical students and residents were more positive toward these applications than practicing physicians. Practicing physicians were also more concerned with the potential for computers to increase governmental and hospital control of their practices, threaten privacy, and result in legal and ethical problems. Attitudes toward computers among the residents and physicians were related to use of the hospital information system.

Experimental Studies

Experimental studies are essentially cohort studies in which the experimenter randomly assigns individuals to one of two groups and then applies some type of intervention to one group. True experimental studies are rare in the field of research on health care computing because researchers rarely have the luxury of randomly assigning people to use or not use a new computer system or of implementing the system for some and not for others. Most medical computer systems are developed and implemented to fill a specific and practical need, and researchers must work around an implementation schedule that is dependent on a variety of nonresearch-related factors, such as hospital finances and staffing needs.

Experimental studies are nonetheless very useful for examining causal relationships. If individuals are randomly assigned to groups, most potentially confounding variables should occur in equal proportions in each group, thus allowing researchers to control for the influence of confounding variables.

After individuals are randomly assigned to groups, baseline measurements are usually made concerning a variety of potential predictor and confounding variables, such as age, prior computer experience, education, role in the organization, and so on. In addition, it is sometimes feasible to measure the outcome of interest prior to the intervention and examine outcome changes as a function of the intervention. For example, a researcher could measure medication errors prior to and after implementation of a pharmacy information system.

There are very few true experimental studies conducted in the field of computers and health care because of the difficulties involved with randomly assigning some individuals to use the computer and others not. The closest example found of an experimental design was a study of a computerized nurse care planning system (CNCP) conducted by Keller, McDermott, and Alt-White (1991). In this study, nursing units were matched and randomly assigned to be intervention or control units. There were two intervention and two control units. Data was collected in all four units 2 months prior to implementation on the intervention units, and 3 months after implementation. Chart review was conducted to measure nursing care planning, health teaching, and discharge planning. Patients who were on the units during the data collection phases were interviewed by telephone shortly after discharge concerning their satisfaction with nursing care, readiness for self-care, and perceived nurse involvement. In addition, the nurses working on the units were surveyed concerning their job satisfaction, intent to stay, perceived competency, and use of care planning. Keller et al. found that 3 months after implementation there were no significant differences between the treatment and control units on any of the factors under investigation, with the exception of nursing care planning. Contrary to expectation, results indicated that the quality of the care planning decreased on the treatment units. On the basis of a simultaneous qualitative assessment, Keller et al. found that there were many problems with the system that had not been resolved by the post-implementation data collection stage.

Clearly, in a study of this type subjects are aware that they are in the treatment or control group. In that case there is always the potential for subjects to change their behavior in such a way that the hypotheses are supported or refuted. Experimental studies also have the potential problem of differential attrition over time between the control and experimental groups. Nurses who dislike computers could choose to transfer from the units scheduled to be computerized during implementation. If this occurred and was not taken into account, only the nurses who were positive toward computers would be left during the post-implementation data collection phase and positive changes in behavior could be a function of this attrition bias. In addition, studies involving intact groups, such as nursing units, cannot be considered truly experimental, even when random assignment to treatment and control conditions are involved, because the intact groups may differ in unmeasured ways that could contribute to differences found in the study variables of interest. Nonetheless, studies involving experimental designs have the potential for providing strong evidence of the impact of computerization when potential confounding variables can be taken into account.

Quasi-Experimental Studies

Because researchers in health care computing rarely have the luxury of randomly assigning individuals to treatment and control groups, quasi-experimental designs are often the most feasible method for examining a particular intervention or new system. Quasi-experimental studies are similar to experimental studies in that there is usually a treatment group and a control or comparison group. However, treatment groups or individuals are usually chosen because they are willing guinea pigs for a particular intervention. Comparison groups or individuals are then chosen that match as closely as possible the treatment groups or individuals. Because treatment groups may be chosen for their enthusiasm or willingness to try a new computer system, there is an obvious bias built into this strategy. A computer system can be wildly successful on a unit of enthusiastic users and a dismal failure on units of individuals who are not willing to learn to use the system or to overlook its idiosyncracies. In reality though, hospital units and departments are often quite autonomous and simply would not be willing to be assigned to use a new computer system, even in the interest of good science. In that case the best choice is a quasi-experimental design, matching control units as closely as possible to willing treatment units.

An interesting quasi-experimental design study was conducted by Anderson, Jay, Perry, and Anderson (1989) to examine the effectiveness of a strategy to increase usage of an existing hospital information system. Four hospital services were selected to receive the intervention. These services were as follows: cardiovascular disease, general surgery, obstetrics and gynecology, and orthopedic surgery. Ten other hospital services were chosen as the control groups. Particularly influential physicians were identified on each of the experimental services on the basis of referral patterns and committee membership. Individual meetings occurred with each of the influential physicians to provide them with information about their use of the computer system and to explain the potential benefits of using the system. The results of the study indicated that use of the computer system increased on the experimental services and did not change on the control services.

There are several strengths and weaknesses of a study of this type. Because the study groups were not randomly assigned to treatment and control they could differ to begin with on the parameters of interest. In the study described, the treatment units were higher initially and throughout the study on use of the system. This difference can be controlled for by simply looking at change in use as a function of the intervention, which Anderson and colleagues did do. However, had this intervention been randomly assigned to units, it may not have worked as well on units with lower initial usage levels or less willing levels of participation. A major strength of this study is that use of the computer system was measured unobtrusively via system logs. Frequently, participants in control groups are clearly aware that they are being studied and may change their behavior for that reason. In that case, changes occur in both the experimental and treatment groups and it may be difficult to see a treatment effect. If the outcome of interest can be measured unobtrusively this solves the problem of participant awareness quite nicely.

Post-Intervention Studies

Post-intervention studies are similar to cross-sectional studies in that data is collected at one point in time, but their primary purpose is not to compare across several groups as with cross-sectional studies but to describe the nature of a particular phenomenon. In the field of health care computing the phenomenon of interest in a post-intervention study is usually how things are going after a system has been implemented. The strength of this type of study is that a specific factor of interest can be studied in-depth. After a system has been implemented there may be some aspect of the system or the organization that is creating difficulties or appears to be particularly interesting, which would not have been evident prior to implementation. The weakness of this type of study is that no data is available from before the intervention and it is difficult to make inferences about changes as a function of the intervention or to examine cause-and-effect relationships. However, it is often just as useful to measure how people perceive that things have changed as it is to measure how things have actually changed as a function of a new computer system.

A post-intervention study to examine the effects of a computerized order entry system was conducted by Aydin and Ischar (1989). In this study, nurses who had worked at the hospital for at least 8 years responded to a questionnaire concerning communication between the nursing and pharmacy departments and perceived changes since the system had been implemented 7 years earlier. On average, these nurses did not perceive that spoken communication between nursing and pharmacy had decreased since the system had been implemented. In addition, the nurses felt that they knew the pharmacy personnel better than they had prior to implementation of the system. Because the relationship between the two departments had always been good, most of the nurses indicated either that things were just as good as ever since implementation of the system or that the working relationship had improved. Only 7% noted negative changes in the relationship between nursing and pharmacy as a function of the medication order entry system. This study provided a description of how nurses perceived a medication order entry system 7 years after implementation. Although Aydin and Ischar note the weakness of a design that asks people to remember how things were 7 years previously, this study provides valuable insight into how the nurses perceived the medication order entry system at the time of the study, regardless of whether perceived changes were accurate.

Frequently the opportunity, funding, or time to study a computer system of interest may not occur until after the system has been implemented. In that case a post-intervention design may be the only design that is feasible. This is a design that lends itself well to description rather than to the examination of change or a cause-and-effect relationship.

Study Subjects

As part of the process of planning a study, an investigator must usually decide in advance how many subjects will be needed. A variety of factors enter into this decision-making process. Sometimes there are only a small and finite number of subjects available to study a particular phenomenon. Sometimes an investigator will only have the time and or money to interview 100 people, for example, or the resources to mail 200 questionnaires once. No matter how large or small the study is in scope, it is very important that the investigator estimate the probability that there will be enough people to adequately test the hypothesis under investigation. Besides the practical factors of subject availability, resources, and time there are a variety of other factors that normally enter into sample size determination. These factors will be illustrated in terms of a hypothetical study of an expert system.

Let us say that an expert system was developed to help obstetricians decide whether or not to perform cesarean sections at any point in time for women experiencing prolonged labor. Data would be entered into this expert system concerning the time in labor, stage of labor, age of the woman, number of previous births, size and status of the baby, size and status of the mother, and so on. The expert system would recommend a variety of treatments, including cesarean section under specific conditions. The investigators wish to test the hypothesis that use of the expert system at Good Faith Hospital will cause the cesarean section rate to change for women in prolonged labor. In that case, the research hypothesis is two-tailed because the investigator wishes to explore the possibility that the cesarean section rate may increase or decrease. The null hypothesis is that there will be no change in the cesarean section rate. When testing this hypothesis, the investigators could reject a null hypothesis that is actually true (Type I error), or they could fail to reject a null hypothesis that is actually false (Type II error). If the sample size is not adequate, the investigators may not be able to reject a false null hypothesis and would therefore make a Type II error. In order to determine the sample size needed to conduct this study the investigators must decide how much of a change in the cesarean section rate would be clinically meaningful, and how much risk they would be willing to take of making Type I and Type II errors. Let us say that the investigators know from previous studies that the usual cesarean section rate for women in prolonged labor is .30, and they wish to be able to reject the null hypothesis if the cesarean section rate decreases or increases by 30%. The investigators decide that they are willing to take a 5% risk of making a Type I error and a 10% chance of making a Type II error. In that case, sample size tables (Lipsey, 1990) indicate that the investigators will need to measure the cesarean section rate for 390 women in prolonged labor prior to implementation of the expert system and for another 390 women in prolonged labor after implementation of the expert system.

At this point the investigators may decide that they do not have the resources to conduct the study on 780 women in prolonged labor, but that they could do a study of 500 women. A look at the sample size tables (Lipsey, 1990) indicates that with a total sample size of 500 (250 in each group), the researchers are taking a 24% chance of making a Type II error. If the investigators are willing to take this level of risk that they will fail to reject a false null hypothesis, then they should proceed with the study.

As the reader may have noticed, there are several pieces of information that enter into the sample size estimation procedure that are guesses. The investigator does not know for sure what the cesarean section rate will be prior to implementation of the expert system or how great a change the expert system will create in the cesarean section rate in the women experiencing prolonged labor. If these guesses are not fairly close to the obtained results the study may need more or fewer subjects than estimated. Despite the fact that sample size estimation prior to the beginning of a study is at best a ballpark estimate, it is important that investigators follow the appropriate procedures and obtain a sample size estimate. In that way investigators will be able to make an educated decision as to whether or not they have the resources to adequately test the hypothesis of interest.

Measurement Procedures: Reliability and Validity

An integral part of any study is the measurement or observation of something of interest. How a researcher decides to measure a particular concept is an important decision. There are many ways to measure attitudes toward computers, or satisfaction with a computer system, for example. The results of a study measuring these concepts will depend, in part, on how these concepts are measured. One researcher may choose to measure satisfaction with a new computer system by interviewing hospital administrators. Another researcher may choose to measure the same concept by interviewing the hospital staff. These two approaches may yield totally different results. It may appear that Hospital X likes a particular computer system while Hospital Y does not simply because satisfaction was measured differently at these two hospitals. It is, therefore, very important that researchers clearly define how they plan to measure a particular concept and make certain that they are well aware of the ramifications of choosing one approach versus another to measure that concept.

Research in the health field uses a wide range of procedures to collect data of interest. Sometimes the variable of interest may be as simple as mortality. However, even a variable as simple as mortality may not be as clear-cut as one would think. In large data sets, for example, patients have been coded as dead who were clearly not dead, and vice versa. Patients have also been coded as being 1 or 2 years old, who were by all other evidence well over age 65. It is generally wise to develop procedures to double-check even the simplest of parameters in order to reduce the error in the data to be analyzed. Even a small amount of error can obscure what would otherwise be significant and meaningful study results.

When working with scaled data collection instruments such as attitude and satisfaction questionnaires there are standard procedures for helping investigators judge the quality of the instruments and the appropriateness for a particular study.

A scaled data collection instrument is one in which answers to two or more items are added together to make a total score. This total score is presumed to represent a particular concept, such as attitudes toward computers. In a good scaled data collection instrument all of the items are measuring the same concept and a total score reflects the degree to which the respondent is high or low (or positive or negative) on the concept of interest. If the items are each measuring something different a total score is meaningless. It is important, therefore, that investigators examine the extent to which the items are measuring the same concept when choosing or developing a particular instrument. This characteristic is called *internal consistency reliability* and is usually measured via a statistical procedure called Cronbach's alpha, which is available in SAS, SPSS, and a variety of PC based statistical packages (Cronbach, 1951). Cronbach's alpha can range from 0.0 to 1.0. A Cronbach's Alpha below .60 is not considered acceptable, while a Cronbach's alpha of .80 or above is quite respectable.

In addition to internal consistency reliability researchers may also choose to measure the test-retest reliability of a data collection instrument. If the instrument is designed to measure a concept that should be fairly stable, such as mechanical ability, when the instrument is given more than once to the same person the results should be the same or similar each time it is given. The instrument should not indicate that a person is high on that trait one day and low the next. To measure test-retest reliability a particular instrument is usually administered twice to the same group of people, at least 6 weeks apart. The correlation between scores at these two points in time should be at least .80 in order for the instrument to be considered "test-retest" reliable.

A data collection instrument or procedure may be quite reliable but may not be measuring what the investigator thinks it is measuring. In that case it is not a valid instrument. It's important when judging the quality of a questionnaire or other data collection procedure that the validity also be explored. *Validity* is generally measured in terms of the relationship between an instrument of interest and other variables that it should logically be related to. Technology anxiety should logically be related to avoidance of technologies or difficulty using these technologies, for example.

Kjerulff and Counte (1984, 1988) present an examination of the reliability and validity of two instruments developed to measure attitudes toward computers. One instrument was developed to measure attitudes toward computers in general (ACG), and the second was designed to measure attitudes toward a particular medical information system (ATMIS) that was scheduled to be implemented in a large Midwestern hospital. Both instruments involved the summation of items and were therefore appropriate for the assessment of internal consistency reliability via Cronbach's alphas. The ACG questionnaire obtained an alpha of .85 and the ATMIS questionnaire obtained an alpha of .89. Validity was measured in terms of the extent to which these instruments were related to adaptation to the computer system, satisfaction with the system, satisfaction with training, job satisfaction, perceived competence at working with the MIS, and turnover during implementation of the computer system. Both instruments were related logically to the variables of interest, both in terms of their ability to predict these factors over time and in terms of their ability to relate concurrently to these factors.

Conclusion

This chapter provides a review of basic research methodology essential for the conduct of good research in the field of medical information systems evaluation. It's important to begin with a specific and feasible research question or hypothesis, to understand the strengths and weaknesses of various study designs, to choose an adequate sample size given a variety of constraints, and to examine the reliability and validity of the data collection instruments chosen for use.

Additional Reading

Counte, Kjerulff, and Salloway (1988) provide a historical overview of medical information systems and diffusion patterns, discuss individual and social impacts, adaptation to automation, and issues to consider when planning for the implementation of a medical information system.

Shelly (1984) provides an introduction to research methodology with sections on research hypotheses and questions, experimental and descriptive designs, sampling and measurement issues, as well as basic statistical procedures.

Kjerulff, Pillar, Mills, and Lanigan (1992) provide an example of a cross-sectional study of technology anxiety (a fear of working with medical equipment) and factors related to individual differences in technology anxiety.

References

Anderson, J. G., Jay, S. J., Perry, J., & Anderson, M. M. (1989). Diffusion of computer applications among physicians. In R. Salamon, D. Protti, & J. Moehr (Eds.), *Proceedings: International symposium of medical informatics and education* (pp. 339-342). British Columbia, Canada: University of Victoria.

Anderson, J. G., Jay, S. J., Schweer, H. M., & Anderson, M. M. (1986). Why doctors don't use computers: Some empirical findings. *Journal of the Royal Society of Medicine, 79*, 142-144.

Aydin, C., & Ischar, R. (1989). The effects of computerized order entry on communication between pharmacy and nursing. In L. C. Kingsland, III (Ed.), *Proceedings of the 13th Annual Symposium on Computer Applications in Medical Care* (pp. 796-801). Washington, DC: IEEE Computer Society Press.

Counte, M. A., Kjerulff, K. H., & Salloway, J. C. (1988). Implementing medical information systems. In. J. Rabin & M. Steinhaur (Eds.), *Handbook on human services administration* (pp. 555-593). New York: Marcel Dekker.

Counte, M. A., Kjerulff, K. H., Salloway, J. C., & Campbell, B. C. (1984). Implementing computerization in hospitals: A case study of the behavioral and attitudinal impacts of a medical information system. *Journal of Organizational Behavior Management, 6*, 109-122.

Counte, M. A., Kjerulff, K. H., Salloway, J. C., & Campbell, B. C. (1987). Adapting to the implementation of a medical information system: A comparison of short- versus long-term findings. *Journal of Medical Systems, 11*, 11-20.

Cronbach, L. J. (1951). Coefficient alpha and the internal structure of tests. *Psychometrika, 16*, 297-334.

House, R., & Rizzo, J. (1972). Role conflict and ambiguity as critical variables in a model of organizational behavior. *Organizational Behavior and Human Performance, 7*, 467-505.

Jackson, D. (1967). *Personality research form manual.* Goshen, NY: Research Psychologists Press.

Keller, L. S., McDermott, S., & Alt-White, A. (1991). Effects of computerized nurse care planning on selected health care effectiveness measures. In P. Clayton (Ed.), *Proceedings of the 15th Annual Symposium on Computer Applications in Medical Care* (pp. 38-42). New York: McGraw-Hill

Kjerulff, K. H., & Counte, M. A. (1984). Measuring attitudes toward computers: Two approaches. In G. S. Cohen (Ed.), *Proceedings of the 8th Annual Symposium on Computer Applications in Medical Care* (pp. 529-535). Los Angeles, CA: IEEE Computer Society Press.

Kjerulff, K. H., & Counte, M. A. (1988). Attitudes and adaptation: Employees respond to computerization. *Journal of Health and Human Resources Administration, 11*, 110-138.

Kjerulff, K. H., Counte, M. A., & Salloway, J. C. (1986). Attitudes toward computers and employee turnover during implementation of a pharmacy information system. In. R. Salaman, B. Blum, & M. Jorgensen (Eds.), *Medinfo 86: Proceedings of the 5th Conference on Medical Informatics* (pp. 1046-1051). Amsterdam: Elsevier.

Kjerulff, K. H., Counte, M. A., & Salloway, J. C. (1988). Hospital employee's satisfaction with a medical information system. *Journal of Health and Human Resources Administration, 11*, 141-158.

Kjerulff, K. H., Counte, M. A., Salloway, J. C., & Campbell, B. C. (1983). Measuring adaptation to medical technology. *Hospital and Health Services Administration, 28*, 30-40.

Kjerulff, K. H., Pillar, B., Mills, M. E., & Lanigan, J. (1992). Technology anxiety as a potential mediating factor in response to medical technology. *Journal of Medical Systems, 16*, 7-13.

Lipsey, M. W. (1990). *Design sensitivity: Statistical power for experimental research.* Newbury Park: CA. Sage.

Rind, D. M., Safran, C., Phillips, R. S., Slack, W. V., Calkins, D. R., Delbanco, T. L., & Bleich, H. L. (1991). The effect of computer-based reminders on the management of hospitalized patients. In P. Clayton (Ed.), *Proceedings of the 15th Annual Symposium on Computer Applications in Medical Care* (pp. 28-32). Los Angeles, CA: IEEE Computer Society Press.

Shelly, S. I. (1984). *Research methods in nursing and health.* Boston, MA: Little, Brown.

Smith, P., Kendall, L., & Hulin, C. (1969). *The measurement of satisfaction in work and retirement.* Chicago: Rand McNally.

3

Qualitative Research Methods for Evaluating Computer Information Systems

Bonnie Kaplan
Joseph A. Maxwell

Introduction

Computer information systems can significantly improve patient care, hospital management and administration, research, and health and medical education. However, many systems do not achieve these goals. Dowling (1980) estimates that 45% of computer-based medical information systems fail because of user resistance, even though these systems are sound technologically. Thus, the stakes in developing, implementing, and evaluating such systems are high.

Different evaluation objectives require different methodological approaches. Medical computer information systems may be assessed in terms of cost/benefit criteria, timeliness, completeness, error rate, retrievability, usage rates, and user satisfaction (Blum, 1986; Krobock, 1984; Simborg & Whiting O'Keefe, 1982). Quantitative methods are excellent for studying these kinds of evaluation questions, in which selected features of the information technology, the organization, the user, and the information needs generally are treated as independent, objective, and discrete entities and as unchanging over the course of the study (Kling & Scacchi, 1982).

When a researcher or evaluator wishes to study issues that are not easily partitioned into discrete entities, or to examine dynamics of a process rather than its static characteristics, qualitative methods are more

useful than solely quantitative ones. The strengths of qualitative research methods lie in their helpfulness for understanding the meaning
and context of the phenomena studied and the particular events and
processes that make up these phenomena over time, in real-life, natural
settings. When evaluating computer information systems, these contextual issues include social, cultural, organizational, and political concerns surrounding an information technology; the processes of information systems development, installation, and use (or lack of use); and how
all these are conceptualized by the participants in the setting studied
(Bakos, 1987; Kaplan & Duchon, 1988; Kling, 1980; Kling & Scacchi,
1982; Lyytinen, 1987).

Qualitative methods for studying computer systems development and
use have been discussed by Shneiderman and Carroll (1988) and by
Forsythe and Buchanan (1991). In medicine and health care, qualitative
methods have been used in evaluations and studies of clinical laboratory
information systems (Kaplan, 1986, 1987a; Kaplan & Duchon, 1988,
1989); systems intended for use throughout a hospital by a variety of clinical staff (Fischer, Stratmann, Lundsgaarde, & Steele, 1980; Lundsgaarde,
Fischer, & Steele, 1981); special functions of such systems, such as pharmacy orders (Aydin, 1989; Aydin & Ischar, 1989); visualization systems
in neurology (Nyce & Graves, 1990); imaging systems that store photo-
graphic, video, and radiologic images as part of the patient record (Kaplan
& Lundsgaarde, n.d.); and systems for patient education (Forsythe,
1992). Studies of computer information systems using qualitative
methods have been conducted in numerous business settings as well
(Mumford, Hirschheim, Fitzgerald, & Wood-Harper, 1985; Nissen, Klein,
& Hirschheim, 1991; Walsham, 1993).

Qualitative research methods have undergone significant development in recent years (Hammersley & Atkinson, 1983; Miles & Huberman,
1984; Patton, 1990) and are being increasingly used in evaluation
research (Campbell, 1988; Cook, 1985; Pitman & Maxwell, 1992; Rossi
& Berk, 1991). There also is a growing literature on combining qualitative and quantitative methods (Cook & Reichardt, 1979; Jick, 1983;
Kaplan & Duchon, 1988; Kidder & Fine, 1987; Maxwell, Bashook, &
Sandlow, 1986). The purpose of this chapter is to explain what qualitative approaches can contribute to medical computer systems evaluations. We begin by describing the nature and goals of qualitative
research and evaluation and illustrate these with an example of the use
of qualitative methods in computer information systems evaluation. We
then discuss some key considerations in qualitative evaluation research
and present the most important methods used in this approach.

The Nature of Qualitative Research

Qualitative research refers to a variety of approaches that differ significantly among themselves but that share some defining characteristics and purposes. These approaches are known by a variety of terms: qualitative research, field research, naturalistic research, interpretive research, ethnographic research, postpositivistic research, phenomenological research, hermeneutic research, humanistic research, and some kinds of case studies (Wolcott, 1990, p. 10). Despite some differences in meaning among these terms, we use *qualitative research* to refer to all of these.

Qualitative research consists of systematic and detailed study of individuals in natural settings, instead of in settings contrived by the researcher. Qualitative methods employ data in the form of words: transcripts of open-ended interviews, written observational descriptions of activities and conversations, and documents and other artifacts of people's actions. Such data are analyzed in ways that retain their inherent textual nature. This is because the goals of qualitative research involve understanding a phenomenon from the points of view of the participants and in its particular social and institutional context. These goals largely are lost when textual data are quantified.

As a result of these goals, qualitative research primarily is inductive in its procedures; qualitative researchers assume that they do not know enough about the perspectives and situations of participants in the setting studied to be able to formulate meaningful hypotheses in advance and instead develop and test hypotheses during the process of data collection and analysis. For the same reasons, qualitative evaluations tend to be in-depth case studies of particular systems. When systems are compared, usually comparative case studies are done instead of surveys of larger populations. Aydin (1989), for example, compared changes in pharmacy and nursing in two hospitals, one using a commercial medical information system that included drug ordering, and the other using a pharmacy system developed in-house.

Attributes of Qualitative Research

There are five main reasons for using qualitative methods in evaluating computer information systems:

1. Understanding how systems' users perceive and evaluate a system and what that system means to them. Users' perspectives generally are not known in advance. It is difficult to ascertain or understand these through purely quantitative approaches. By allowing researchers to investigate users' perspectives, qualitative methods can contribute to the explanation of users' behavior with respect to the system and thus to the system's successes and failures.

2. *Understanding the influence of social and organizational context on systems use.* Computer information systems do not exist in a vacuum; their implementation, use, and success or failure occur in a social and organizational context that shapes what happens when that system is introduced. In important respects, a system is not the same system when it is introduced into different settings (Rogers, 1983). As is true for users' perspectives, the researcher usually does not know in advance what all the contextual influences are. Qualitative methods are useful for discovering and understanding what is happening and also for developing testable hypotheses and theories.

3. *Investigating causal processes.* Although experimental interventions can demonstrate *that* causal relationships exist, they are less useful in showing *how* causal processes work (Cook, 1985). Qualitative methods often allow the researcher to get inside the black box of experimental and survey designs and to discover the actual processes involved (Britan, 1978). Qualitative research is particularly good for developing explanations of the actual events and processes that lead to specific outcomes (Miles & Huberman, 1984, p. 132). In this way, qualitative methods can yield theories and explanations of how and why processes and outcomes occur (Markus & Robey, 1988).

4. *Providing formative evaluation—evaluation aimed at improving a program under development, rather than assessing an existing one.* Although quantitative and experimental designs often are valuable in assessing outcomes, they are less helpful in giving those responsible for systems design and implementation timely feedback on their actions. Using qualitative methods can help in identifying potential problems as they are forming, thereby providing opportunities to improve the system as it develops (Lundsgaarde, Gardner, & Menlove, 1989).

5. *Increasing the utilization of evaluation results.* Administrators, policy-makers, systems designers, and practitioners often find purely quantitative studies of little use because these studies do not seem related to their own understanding of the situation and the problems they are

encountering. Qualitative methods, by providing evaluation findings that connect more directly with these individuals' perspectives, can increase the credibility and usefulness of evaluations for such decision makers (Patton, 1990).

An Example: Evaluating a Clinical Laboratory Computer Information System

These attributes of qualitative research are illustrated by a study of a clinical laboratory computer information system used by different laboratories within one department of an academic medical center (Kaplan, 1986, 1987a; Kaplan & Duchon, 1988, 1989). This system was evaluated by combining both quantitative and qualitative methods. A survey questionnaire was designed to assess the impact of the computer system on work in the laboratories. Qualitative data gathered from interviews, observations, and open-ended questionnaire questions were used to determine what changes were attributed to the computer system. Statistical analysis of the survey data initially revealed no differences among laboratory technologists' responses. Qualitative data analysis of their answers to open-ended questions indicated that laboratory technologists within each laboratory differed in their reactions to the system, as did laboratories as a whole. Some focused on work increases, whereas others emphasized improved laboratory results reporting and service.

Although the quantitative survey data provided no apparent reason for these differences, the qualitative data did, leading to further investigation. This investigation revealed that different technologists had different views of their jobs, and these different views affected their attitudes toward the computer system. For some technologists, the system enhanced their jobs, whereas for others it interfered with their jobs, even though they ostensibly had "the same jobs" and were using "the same system." Neither the researchers nor the laboratory personnel expected this finding, though the finding rang true. Further analysis of the quantitative data supported this explanation for the differences among laboratories and among technologists. In the original quantitative analysis, few differences were discernible among technologists or among laboratories from the quantitative data because standard quantitative measures of job characteristics assumed a uniformity of job situations and perceptions. However, this uniformity did not exist, as revealed in qualitative data that identified technologists' own views of their jobs and of the system.

This example illustrates several features of qualitative research. First, it was not possible to design, in advance, a quantitative study that would have tested the right hypotheses, because appropriate hypotheses could not be known in advance. A qualitative approach enabled the researchers to see how individuals construed the information technology, their jobs, and the interaction between the laboratory computer information system and their jobs. Thus the researchers were able to generate productive hypotheses and theory.

Second, the qualitative data enabled the researchers to make sense of their quantitative findings. The qualitative data helped to explain why the quantitative results were as they were. This is one example of the point made above—that qualitative research often can uncover the causal processes that explain quantitative results.

Third, the qualitative data were able to serve these purposes because they helped the researchers understand the system from the points of view of those involved with it. These points of view are crucial to studying issues such as computer systems acceptance or rejection, or the changes that occur when a new system is introduced.

Fourth, qualitative data enabled the researchers to understand the contexts in which the system was developed, installed, and used, and thus to understand differences among laboratories. Such contextual factors as systems designers' philosophies (Hirschheim & Klein, 1989; Kaplan, 1982, 1983, 1987b), changes in status of clinical personnel (Fischer et al., 1980; Lundsgaarde, Fischer, & Steele, 1981), changes in communication patterns among occupational groups (Aydin, 1989), and the professional values of physicians (Kaplan, 1982) all can affect what happens with a computer information system.

Last, the results had face validity. They were believable to the laboratory director in the hospital where the study was done, to laboratory personnel in other hospitals, and even outside of hospitals where workers showed characteristics similar to the laboratory technologists. Because the results were credible and the description of the laboratory technologists recognizable, they were useful for others. This is the primary means by which qualitative studies can be generalized: not by statistical inference to some defined population, but through the development of a theory that has applicability beyond the setting studied (Yin, 1984, p. 21).

In the remainder of this chapter, we discuss some important considerations in designing and conducting evaluations that use qualitative methods.

Getting Started

The most important initial question for an evaluator is whether qualitative methods are appropriate for conducting the study. For this, it is important to consider what qualitative methods can add to an evaluation: what kinds of questions they are capable of answering, and what value they have.

Research Questions and Evaluation Goals

Qualitative methods typically are used to understand the perception of an information system by its users and the context within which the system is implemented or developed. They usually focus on issues of process rather than correlation of variables and tend to be used for understanding a particular case rather than for comparison or for generalization to a specified population.

Thus the questions posed in a qualitative study are initially framed as "What," "How," and "Why" queries rather than as whether a particular hypothesis is true or false. The fundamental question is "What is going on here?" This question is progressively narrowed, focused, and made more detailed as the evaluation proceeds. Qualitative studies may begin with specific concerns or even suppositions about what is going on, but the major strength of qualitative methods is avoiding tunnel vision, seeing the unexpected, disconfirming one's assumptions, and discovering new ways of making sense of what is going on. Qualitative evaluators typically begin with questions such as these:

- What is happening here?
- Why is it happening?
- How has it come to happen in this particular way?
- What do the people involved think is happening?
- How are these people responding to what is happening?
- Why are these people responding that way?

To answer these questions, qualitative evaluators attempt to understand the way others construe, conceptualize, and make sense of what is happening in a particular situation. In doing this, they must become familiar with the everyday behaviors, habits, and attitudes of the people involved as these people go about their daily business. It also is important for evaluators to become familiar with the language or specialized jargon used by people involved with the system. Knowledge of behaviors, habits, attitudes, and language provides a way of identifying key concepts and values. This knowledge enables the evaluator not only to better understand what is going on but also to present findings in terms meaningful to the participants. Policymakers, department administrators, systems designers, and others will be able to recognize the situations being reported and, therefore, know better how to address them. In addition, individuals outside the organization where the evaluation is conducted will have sufficient context to develop a good understanding of it.

Further, qualitative methods can be used throughout the entire systems development and implementation process. They treat a computer information system as a process, rather than as an object or event. By doing this, the evaluator can play an active role in the project (Lundsgaarde, Gardner, & Menlove, 1989), offering evaluations as the project progresses (formative evaluations) instead of having to wait until the project is completed (summative evaluations). In this way, evaluators can serve as a bridge between the interests of systems developers and systems users (Lundsgaarde & Moreshead, 1991).

Recognizing diversity of perceptions also is important: "various individuals . . . may perceive it [an innovation] in light of many possible sets of values" (Rogers, 1983, p. 99). For example, in Lundsgaarde, Fischer, and Steele's (1981; Fischer et al., 1980) evaluation of PROMIS, individuals who thought their professional status was enhanced by the system were more positive than those who felt their status was lowered. Other values also can play a role; Hirschheim and Klein (1989) illustrate this for systems developers, and Kaplan (1982, 1983, 1987b) discusses the effect of values on systems development and use. A major strength of qualitative approaches is their sensitivity to this diversity and to unique events and outcomes.

Role of Theory

Many, though not all, qualitative researchers attempt to avoid prior commitment to theoretical constructs or to hypotheses formulated before gathering any data (cf. Yin, 1984, p. 25). Two different approaches may be taken, or combined. In the first, the evaluator works within an explicit theoretical framework. In the second, the evaluator tries not to be constrained by prior theory and instead sees the development of relevant theory, hypotheses, and categories as a purpose of the project. These approaches may be combined because, in each approach, qualitative researchers develop categories and hypotheses from the data. The difference between the two approaches is not whether the evaluator has some prior theoretical bent—that is unavoidable—but whether the evaluator deliberately works within it or tries to work outside it.

Regardless of which approach is used, an evaluator has a prior theoretical orientation that affects research and evaluation questions—as well as the methods chosen for investigating those questions. Theory is useful for guiding a study. Familiarity with the subject of study or with a wide range of theories and situations, for example, can help the researcher make sense of occurrences in the particular study being conducted. It can help the evaluator to not overlook important issues and help provide a set of constructs to be investigated. Theory also will guide a researcher's interpretation and focus. For example, Kaplan (1991) describes how three different theoretical perspectives would lead to different interpretations of Lundsgaarde, Fischer, and Steele's findings in their evaluation of PROMIS.

Gaining Entry

An evaluation begins with the process of the researcher gaining access to the setting and being granted permission to conduct the evaluation. How this is done shapes the researcher's relationship with the participants in the study and, consequently, affects the nature of the entire study. Some of these effects bear on validity issues, as discussed below. In addition to practical and scientific issues, negotiating a research or evaluation study raises ethical ones (Guba & Lincoln, 1989; Patton, 1990; Pitman & Maxwell, 1992). To help address some of the ethical concerns, we believe that, to the extent possible, all participants in the setting being evaluated should be brought into the negotiation process, and that simply imposing a study on unwilling subjects is a violation of research ethics.

Qualitative Research Design

Qualitative research design involves considerable flexibility (Miles & Huberman, 1984), for two reasons. First, the processes being studied change over time. As they change, the study itself also may need changing. Second, qualitative inquiry necessarily is inductive and iterative. The evaluator goes through repeated cycles of data collection and analysis to generate hypotheses inductively from the data. These hypotheses need to be tested by further data collection and analysis. The researcher starts with a broad research question, such as "What effects will those information systems engendered by the National Health

Service reforms in the United Kingdom have on relative power and status among clinical and administrative staff in a teaching hospital?" (Kaplan, 1992). The researcher narrows the study by continually posing increasingly specific questions and attempting to answer them through data already collected and through new data collected for that purpose. These questions cannot all be anticipated in advance. As the evaluator starts to see patterns, or discovers behavior that seems difficult to understand, new questions arise. The process is one of generating hypotheses and explanations from the data, testing them, and modifying them accordingly. New hypotheses may require new data and, consequently, potential changes in the research design.

Data Collection

The most important principle of qualitative data collection is that everything is potential data. The evaluator does not rigidly restrict the scope of data collection in advance nor use formal rules to decide that some data are inadmissible or irrelevant. However, this approach creates two potential problems: validity and data overload.

The qualitative approach to validity is to use all relevant data but to use them critically. Data are collected as rigorously and systematically as possible, but no unexpected or serendipitous information is ruled out of consideration. These unexpected data might provide important evidence for understanding the system being investigated. However, all inferences drawn from the data are critically assessed for potential validity threats, in ways discussed below.

The problem of data overload is in some ways more intractable. The evaluator must continually make decisions about what data are relevant and may change these decisions over the course of the project. The evaluator must work to focus the data collection process but not to focus so narrowly as to miss or ignore data that would contribute important insights or evidence.

Sources of Data

Qualitative evaluation almost always involves the researcher's direct engagement in the setting studied, what often is called *fieldwork*. Thus the researcher is the instrument for collecting and analyzing data; the researcher's impressions, observations, and confusions all become data, and they are vital to the successful conduct of the evaluation.

Qualitative evaluators use three main sources for data: (1) observation, (2) open-ended interviews and survey questions, and (3) documents and texts. Qualitative studies generally collect data by using several of these methods to give a wider range of coverage (Bonoma, 1985). Qualitative data are recorded in detailed, often verbatim, form as field notes or interview transcripts. Such detail is essential for the types of analysis that are used in qualitative research. We discuss each of these data sources in turn, drawing again on Kaplan and Duchon's (1988, 1989) study and several other studies for examples.

Observation

Observation in qualitative studies (often referred to as *participant observation*) produces detailed descriptive accounts of what was going on (including verbal interaction). Such observation often is crucial to the assessment of a system. For example, Kaplan and Duchon went to the laboratories to observe what technologists actually did, rather than simply depend on verbal reports or job descriptions; Forsythe (Forsythe, Buchanan, Osheroff, & Miller, 1992; Osheroff et al., 1991), in her study of physicians' information needs, attended hospital rounds and recorded each request for information.

Observation also can be conducted when evaluating the potential uses of a proposed computer information system. Kaplan, for example, observed how the flow sheets in the patient record were used in an intensive care unit when it was suggested that flow sheets be replaced by a computer terminal that would display laboratory data in graphic form. She observed that only the pharmacist consulted the flow sheets. When a physician came to see the patient, or a new nurse came on duty, he or she assessed the patient's condition by talking to the nurse who had been caring for that patient, rather than by consulting the patient's record. These observations raised a number of issues that would need addressing if a computer display of flow sheet information were to be implemented successfully.

Open-Ended Interviews and Survey Questions

Open-ended interviewing requires a skillful and systematic approach to questioning participants that can range from informal and conversational interviews to those with a specific agenda. There are two distinctive features of open-ended interviewing. First, the goal is to elicit the respondent's views and experiences in his or her own terms, rather than to collect data that are simply a choice among preestablished response categories. Second, the interviewer is not bound to a rigid interview format or set of questions but should elaborate on what is being asked if a question is not understood, follow up on unanticipated and potentially valuable information with additional questions, and probe for further explanation.

For example, Kaplan and Duchon interviewed laboratory directors and chief supervisory personnel to determine what they expected the potential effects of the computer system would be on patient care, laboratory operations, and hospital operations. They asked such questions as "What effects do you expect the computer system to have?" so as not to constrain what the interviewees would answer. They also asked "What do you think this study should focus on?" so as to explore issues they had not anticipated.

A close analogue to open-ended interviewing, for large groups of respondents, is using open-ended survey questions. Kaplan and Duchon included in their survey such open-ended questions as "What important changes do you think the computer system has caused?" The final question on the survey was a request for any additional comments. Such questions are important to include in interviews and questionnaires to ensure that unanticipated issues are explored.

Documents and Texts

Documents and texts also can be valuable sources of qualitative data. For example, Nyce and Graves (1990) analyzed published texts, case memoirs, and novels written by physicians in their study of the implications of knowledge construction in developing visualization systems in neurology. In Kaplan's studies of the acceptance and diffusion of medical information systems (1982, 1983, 1987b, 1988), she did close readings of original source documents: published research papers; popularizations in medical magazines, newsletters, and books; conference reports; memoirs of individuals who developed the systems; and books commissioned by federal agencies.

Data Analysis

The basic goal of qualitative data analysis is understanding: the search for coherence and order. The purpose of data analysis is to develop an understanding or interpretation that answers the basic question of "What is going on here?" This is done through an iterative process that starts by developing an initial understanding of the setting and perspectives of the people being studied. That understanding then is tested and modified through cycles of additional data collection and analysis until an adequately coherent interpretation is reached (Bredo & Feinberg, 1982, p. 124; Glaser & Strauss, 1967; Van Maanen, 1983).

Thus, in qualitative research, data analysis is an ongoing activity that should start as soon as the first interview or observation is done—in some cases, even before—and continue through the entire course of the research. As with data collection, data analysis methods usually cannot be precisely specified in advance. As noted previously, qualitative data collection and analysis have an inductive, cyclic character. As Agar describes it:

> You learn something ("collect some data"), then you try to make sense out of it ("analysis"), then you go back and see if the interpretation makes sense in light of new experience ("collect more data"), then you refine your interpretation ("more analysis"), and so on. The process is dialectic, not linear. (1980, p. 9)

All forms of qualitative data analysis presuppose the existence of detailed texts, such as observational field notes, interview transcripts, or documents. A necessary first step in data analysis, prior to all of the subsequent techniques, consists of reading the data. This reading is done to gain familiarity with what is going on and what people are saying or doing and to develop initial ideas about the meaning of these statements and events and their relationships to other statements and events. Even at later stages in data analysis, it often is valuable to go back and reread the original data in order to see if the developing hypotheses make sense. All of the analysis techniques described below depend on this prior reading; they require the ongoing judgment and interpretation of the researcher.

Qualitative methods produce large amounts of data that are not readily amenable to mechanical manipulation, analysis, or data reduction. There are four basic techniques of qualitative data analysis: (1) coding, (2) analytic memos, (3) displays, and (4) contextual and narrative analysis. They are used, separately and in combination, to help identify themes; develop categories; and explore similarities and differences in the data and relationships among them. None of these methods is an algorithm that can be applied mechanically to the data to produce "results." However, computer software now is available to facilitate the process of qualitative data analysis (Fielding & Lee, 1991; Tesch, 1990). Such programs perform some of the mechanical tasks of sorting and aggregating previously coded data but cannot replace the evaluator's task of making sense of the data.

We briefly discuss each of the four techniques:

1. Coding. Coding, in qualitative research, involves segmenting the data into units (Hammersley & Atkinson, 1983, p. 167) and rearranging them into categories that facilitate insight, comparison, and the development of theory (Strauss & Corbin, 1990). Although some coding categories may be drawn from existing theory or prior knowledge of the setting and system, others are developed inductively by the evaluator during the analysis, and still others are taken from the conceptual structure of the people studied. The key feature of most qualitative coding is that it is grounded in the data (Glaser & Strauss, 1967), that is, it is developed in interaction with, and is tailored to the understanding of, the particular data being analyzed.

2. Analytic Memos. An analytic memo is anything that a researcher writes in relationship to the research, other than direct field notes or transcription. It can range from a brief marginal comment on a transcript, or a theoretical idea incorporated into field notes, to a full-fledged analytic essay. All of these are ways of getting ideas down on paper and of using writing as a way to facilitate reflection and analytic insight. Memos are a way to convert the researcher's perceptions and thoughts into a visible form that allows reflection and further manipulation (Miles & Huberman, 1984; Strauss & Corbin, 1990). Writing is an important analysis technique and should begin early in the study, perhaps even before starting the study (Wolcott, 1990).

3. Displays. Displays, such as matrices, flowcharts, and concept maps, are similar to memos in that they make ideas, data, and analysis visible and permanent. They also serve two other key functions: data reduction, and the presentation of data or analysis in a form that allows it to be grasped as a whole. These analytic tools have been given their most detailed elaboration by Miles and Huberman (1984) but are employed less self-consciously by many other researchers. Such displays can be primarily conceptual, as a way of developing theory, or they can be primarily data-oriented. Data-oriented displays can be used as an elaboration of coding, in which the coding categories are presented in a single display in conjunction with a reduced subset of the data in each category.

4. Contextual and Narrative Analysis. Contextual and narrative analysis has developed mainly as an alternative to coding (e.g., Mishler,

1986). Instead of segmenting the data into discrete elements and resorting them into categories, these approaches to analysis seek to understand the relationships between elements in a particular text, situation, or sequence of events (Kaplan & Dorsey, 1991; Maxwell & Miller, n.d.). Methods such as discourse analysis (Gee, Michaels, & O'Connor, 1992), narrative analysis (Mishler, 1986), profiles (Seidman, 1991), and ethnographic microanalysis (Erickson, 1992) identify the relationships among the different elements and their meanings for the persons involved.

Validity

Validity in qualitative research addresses the necessarily "subjective" nature of data collection and analysis. Because the researcher is the instrument for collecting and analyzing data, the study is subjective in the sense of being different for different researchers. Different researchers may approach the same research question by collecting different data or by interpreting the same data differently.

Qualitative researchers acknowledge their role as research instruments by making it an explicit part of data collection, analysis, and reporting. As in collecting and analyzing any data, what the evaluator brings to the task—his or her biases, interests, perceptions, observations, knowledge, and critical faculties—all play a role in the study.

Qualitative researchers include in their studies specific ways to understand and control the effects of their background and role. They recognize that the relationships they develop with those studied have a major effect on the data that can be gathered and the interpretations that can be developed (Hammersley & Atkinson, 1983; Pitman & Maxwell, 1992). The researcher's rapport with systems users or developers significantly influences what people will reveal in interviews and the extent to which they alter their behavior in response to an observer's presence. Similarly, researchers recognize that their personal experiences and theoretical bents influence their choice of evaluation questions, data, and interpretation. Qualitative researchers consider it their responsibility to carefully articulate previous beliefs and constantly question every observation and every interpretation so as to help avoid being blinded or misdirected by what they bring to the study (Eckert, 1989, p. 27). They also report their backgrounds to study participants and the audience for the evaluation, including the research community, so that others may consider the potential influence on study results.

The product of any qualitative analysis is an interpretation, rather than a purely "objective" account. It often is valuable for several researchers to analyze the same data and compare results, but discrepancies between different researchers' interpretations do not automatically invalidate the results. Because of the flexibility and individual judgment inherent in qualitative methods, reliability generally is weaker than in quantitative designs, but validity often is stronger; qualitative researchers' close attention to meaning, context, and process make them less likely to ask the wrong questions or overlook or exclude important data (Kirk & Miller, 1986). Thus, the loss of reliability is counterbalanced by the greater validity that results from the researcher's flexibility, insight, and ability to use his or her tacit knowledge.

To further ensure validity, qualitative researchers typically assess specific validity threats during data collection and analysis by testing these threats against existing data or against data collected specifically for this purpose (Eisenhart & Howe, 1992; Kirk & Miller, 1986; Maxwell, 1992; Miles & Huberman, 1984). Particular strategies include: (1) collecting rich data, (2) paying attention to puzzles, (3) triangulation, and (4) feedback. We discuss each of these in turn.

1. Rich data. Rich data are detailed and comprehensive. They are holistic in that the researcher tries to capture what is going on in the entire situation under study. Collecting rich data makes it difficult for the researcher to see only what supports his or her prejudices and expectations (Becker, 1970, p. 53).

2. Puzzles. One underlying assumption of qualitative methods is that things make sense (Bredo & Feinberg, 1982, p. 124)—at least the people involved in the setting understand the situation in ways the research must discover or determine. If the evaluator has not understood how sense is to be made of a situation, the evaluator has not yet achieved an adequate interpretation, perhaps because not enough data have been collected or because the problem is being approached from the wrong perspective or theoretical framework. In particular, the evaluator must pay careful attention to surprises, puzzles, and confusions (Agar, 1986, p. 20) and see them as ways of developing a valid interpretation. The evaluator also identifies and analyzes discrepant data (puzzles) and negative cases, and sometimes even forces breakdowns in interpretation (Agar, 1986, pp. 25-27, 49), in attempting to disconfirm research hypotheses or interpretations.

3. Triangulation. Qualitative researchers typically collect data from a range of individuals and settings. Multiple sources and methods increase the robustness of results. Using more than one source of data and more than one method of data collection allows findings to be strengthened by cross-validating them. This process generally is known as *triangulation* (Jick, 1983).

When data of different kinds and sources converge and are found congruent, the results have greater credibility than when they are based on only one method or source (Benbasat, Goldstein, & Mead, 1987; Bonoma, 1985; Jick, 1983; Yin, 1984). However, when the data seem to diverge, in line with the assumption that things make sense and the importance of focusing on puzzles or discrepancies, an explanation must be sought to account for all of them (Trend, 1979).

4. Feedback. Another way of validating an interpretation is by systematically gathering feedback about one's conclusions from participants in the setting studied (Guba & Lincoln, 1989) and from others familiar with the setting. The researcher checks that the interpretation makes sense to those who know the setting especially well.

We illustrate how issues of reliability and validity can be addressed by drawing on Kaplan and Duchon's study.

In the clinical laboratory information system evaluation, Kaplan had a systems designer's working knowledge of computer hardware and software and of terminology in clinical settings, in particular, with order entry and results reporting systems for a clinical laboratory. She was aware that this background influenced her study. As the primary field researcher, she could listen to, and participate in, discussions among laboratory staff and have a better understanding of them. In designing the study, Kaplan, an information systems specialist, sought colleagues with backgrounds different from hers. Duchon, a specialist in organizational behavior, was unfamiliar with clinical laboratories and with information systems. Each of these two researchers had to be convinced of the other's interpretations. Further, the study's sponsors and participants were aware of the researchers' backgrounds, which also were reported in publications so that others would be able to consider for themselves what effects the researchers' backgrounds might have.

Kaplan and Duchon collected data from multiple sources using several different methods. This provided them with rich data that led to puzzles and discrepancies that required resolving. Resolving these resulted in significant insights. For example, Kaplan and Duchon explored the puzzle presented by interviewees repeatedly saying the computer system would not change laboratory technologists' jobs but that it would change what technologists did. Kaplan and Duchon developed hypotheses and tentative theories to explain how the interviewees might not see a contradiction in their statements.

They also cross-validated their results by comparing their data. Qualitative and quantitative data at first seemed not to agree. The quantitative data initially indicated no differences among laboratories in their response to the computer system, yet differences were evident in the qualitative data. Disparities also occurred in only the qualitative data because technologists in the same laboratory disagreed over whether the computer system was a benefit. Rather than assuming that some technologists simply were wrong, or that either the qualitative or quantitative data was in error, an explanation was needed to allow for all these responses.

Resolving these puzzles and reconciling all the data contributed to a much richer final interpretation that resulted in a theory of how views of one's job and views of a computer system are related. Study results were made available to laboratory managers for comment and presented to laboratory directors for discussion, thus creating opportunities for feedback so as to check the researchers' interpretations. Further feedback was obtained by presenting the theory to staff from the laboratories studied as well as to knowledgeable individuals from other, related settings.

Conclusion

We have presented an overview of qualitative research and how it can be used for evaluating computer information systems. This chapter has covered techniques for data collection and analysis and discussed how and why such methods may be used.

We believe that qualitative methods are useful because they provide means of answering questions that cannot be answered solely by other methods. The strengths of qualitative methods relate primarily to the understanding of a system's specific context of development and use, the ways developers and users perceive the system, and the processes by which the system is accepted, rejected, or adapted to a particular setting. We believe that these are crucial issues for the development, implementation, and evaluation of computer information systems. Consequently, qualitative methods can make an important contribution to research and evaluation of computer information systems.

Additional Reading

Qualitative Methods

Patton (1990) is an excellent introduction to qualitative research methods. It also is one of the best works on qualitative approaches to evaluation. More advanced discussion of theory and methods of qualitative research can be found in Hammersley and Atkinson (1983) and in LeCompte, Millroy, and Preissle (1992).

Specific techniques for qualitative data analysis are presented in Miles and Huberman (1984) and in Strauss and Corbin (1990). A useful guide to both data analysis and writing of qualitative research is Wolcott (1990).

Rogers's (1983) work on the adoption of innovations is relevant to the introduction of computer information systems. This volume and the second edition (Rogers & Shoemaker, 1971) each include an extensive compilation and analysis of literature in the field.

Information Systems Research Theory and Methodological Frameworks

Useful discussions of theoretical perspectives in information systems research can be found in several papers. Kling (1980), Kling and Scacchi (1982), Lyytinen (1987), and Markus and Robey (1988) present theoretical frameworks that are relevant to studies of the social aspects of computing. The paradigms of information systems development Hirschheim and Klein (1989) discuss also are applicable to research approaches and, in fact, were derived from such a framework. Kaplan (1991) illustrates the influences of theoretical stance using a medical information system as an example.

Evaluation Studies of Computing Systems

Krobock (1984) gives a framework for past evaluation studies of medical information systems.

Lundsgaarde, Fischer, and Steele (1981) conducted an exemplary evaluation of a medical information system that combines both qualitative and quantitative methods. The study's primary results are summarized in Fischer et al. (1980).

Kaplan and Duchon (1988) give a detailed account of how a medical system evaluation actually progressed, including issues pertaining to combining qualitative and quantitative methods. Kaplan (1986, 1987a) reports qualitative methods and findings of the study, and Kaplan and Duchon (1989) include quantitative results.

Forsythe and Buchanan (1991) explain the advantages of using qualitative methods for evaluating medical expert systems. Reports of their studies are in Forsythe et al. (1992) and Osheroff et al. (1991). Forsythe (1992) discusses their use in designing patient education systems.

Turkle (1984) and Zuboff (1988), though not concerned with applications of computers in medicine, superbly illustrate the kind of observations and analysis possible by using qualitative methods.

References

Agar, M. H. (1980). *The professional stranger: An informal introduction to ethnography.* New York: Academic Press.

Agar, M. H. (1986). *Speaking of ethnography.* Beverly Hills, CA: Sage.

Aydin, C. (1989). Occupational adaptation to computerized medical information systems. *Journal of Health and Social Behavior, 30,* 163-179.

Aydin, C., & Ischar, R. (1989). The effects of computerized order entry on communication between pharmacy and nursing. In L. C. Kingsland, III (Ed.), *Proceedings of the 13th Annual Symposium on Computer Applications in Medical Care* (pp. 796-801). Washington, DC: IEEE Computer Society Press.

Bakos, J. Y. (1987). Dependent variables for the study of firm and industry-level impacts of information technology. In J. I. DeGross & C. H. Kriebel (Eds.), *Proceedings of the 8th International Conference on Information Systems* (pp. 10-23). New York: Association for Computing Machinery.

Becker, H. S. (1970). Field work evidence. In H. Becker, *Sociological work: Method and substance.* New Brunswick, NJ: Transaction Books.

Benbasat, I., Goldstein, D. K., & Mead, M. (1987). The case research strategy in studies of information systems. *MIS Quarterly, 11,* 369-386.

Blum, B. I. (1986). *Clinical information systems.* New York: Springer.

Bonoma, T. V. (1985). Case research in marketing: Opportunities, problems, and a process. *Journal of Marketing Research, 22,* 199-208.

Bredo, E., & Feinberg, W. (1982). Part two: The interpretive approach to social and educational research. In E. Bredo & W. Feinberg (Eds.), *Knowledge and values in social and educational research* (pp. 115-128). Philadelphia, PA: Temple University Press.

Britan, G. M. (1978). Experimental and contextual models of program evaluation. *Evaluation and Program Planning, 1,* 229-234.

Campbell, D. T. (1988). *Methodology and epistemology for social science: Selected papers.* Chicago: University of Chicago Press.

Cook, T. D. (1985). Postpositivist critical multiplism. In R. L. Shotland & M. M. Marks (Eds.), *Social science and social policy* (pp. 21-62). Beverly Hills, CA: Sage.

Cook, T. D., & Reichardt, C. S. (1979). *Qualitative and quantitative methods in evaluation research.* Beverly Hills: Sage.

Dowling, A. F., Jr. (1980). Do hospital staff interfere with computer system implementation? *Health Care Management Review, 5,* 23-32. Reprinted in J. G. Anderson & S. J. Jay (Eds.). (1987), *Use and impact of computers in clinical medicine* (pp. 302-317). New York: Springer Verlag.

Eckert, P. (1989). *Jocks and burnouts: Social categories and identity in the high school.* New York: Teachers College Press.

Eisenhart, M. A., & Howe, K. R. (1992). Validity in educational research. In M. D. LeCompte, W. L. Millroy, & J. Preissle (Eds.), *The handbook of qualitative research in education* (pp. 643-680). San Diego: Academic Press.

Erickson, F. (1992). Ethnographic microanalysis of interaction. In M. D. LeCompte, W. L. Millroy, & J. Preissle (Eds.), *The handbook of qualitative research in education* (pp. 201-225). San Diego: Academic Press.

Fielding, N. G., & Lee, R. M. (1991). *Using computers in qualitative research*. Newbury Park, CA: Sage.

Fischer, P. J., Stratmann, W. C., Lundsgaarde, H. P., & Steele, D. J. (1980). User reaction to PROMIS: Issues related to acceptability of medical innovations. In J. T. O'Neill (Ed.), *Proceedings of the 4th Annual Symposium on Computer Applications in Medical Care* (pp. 1722-1730). Silver Spring, MD: IEEE Computer Society Press. Reprinted in J. G. Anderson & S. J. Jay (Eds.). (1987), *Use and impact of computers in clinical medicine* (pp. 284-301). New York: Springer Verlag.

Forsythe, D. E. (1992). Using ethnography to build a working system: Rethinking basic design assumptions. In M. E. Frisse (Ed.), *Proceedings of the 16th Annual Symposium on Computer Applications in Medical Care* (pp. 505-509). New York: McGraw-Hill.

Forsythe, D., & Buchanan, B. G. (1991). Broadening our approach to evaluating medical expert systems. In P. D. Clayton (Ed.), *Proceedings of the 15th Annual Symposium on Computer Applications in Medical Care* (pp. 8-12). New York: McGraw-Hill.

Forsythe, D. E., Buchanan, B. G., Osheroff, J. A., & Miller, R. A. (1992). Expanding the concept of medical information: An observational study of physicians' information needs. *Computers and Biomedical Research, 25*, 181-200.

Gee, J. P., Michaels, S., & O'Connor, M. C. (1992). Discourse analysis. In M. D. LeCompte, W. L. Millroy, & J. Preissle (Eds.), *The handbook of qualitative research in education* (pp. 227-291). San Diego: Academic Press.

Glaser, B. G., & Strauss, A. L. (1967). *The discovery of grounded theory: Strategies for qualitative research*. New York: Aldine.

Guba, E. G., & Lincoln, Y. S. (1989). *Fourth generation evaluation*. Newbury Park, CA: Sage.

Hammersley, M., & Atkinson, P. (1983). *Ethnography: Principles in practice*. London: Tavistock.

Hirschheim, R., & Klein, H. K. (1989). Four paradigms of information systems development. *Communications of the ACM, 32*, 1199-1216.

Jick, T. D. (1983). Mixing qualitative and quantitative methods: Triangulation in action. In J. Van Maanen (Ed.), *Qualitative methodology* (pp. 135-148). Beverly Hills, CA: Sage.

Kaplan, B. (1982). The influence of medical values and practices on medical computer applications. In *MEDCOMP '82: The first IEEE Computer Society International Conference on Medical Computer Science/Computational Medicine* (pp. 83-88). Silver Spring, MD: IEEE Computer Society Press. Reprinted in J. G. Anderson & S. J. Jay (Eds.). (1987), *Use and impact of computers in clinical medicine* (pp. 39-50). New York: Springer Verlag.

Kaplan, B (1983). The computer as Rorschach: Implications for management and user acceptance. In R. E. Dayhoff (Ed.), *Proceedings of the 7th Annual Symposium on Computer Applications in Medical Care* (pp. 664-667). Silver Spring, MD: IEEE Computer Society Press.

Kaplan, B. (1986). Impact of a clinical laboratory computer system: Users' perceptions. In R. Salamon, B. I. Blum, & M. J. Jørgensen (Eds.), *Medinfo 86: Fifth World Congress on Medical Informatics* (pp. 1057-1061). Amsterdam: North Holland.

Kaplan, B. (1987a). Initial impact of a clinical laboratory computer system: Themes common to expectations and actualities. *Journal of Medical Systems, 11*, 137-147.

Kaplan, B. (1987b). The medical computing 'lag': Perceptions of barriers to the application of computers to medicine. *International Journal of Technology Assessment in Health Care, 3*, 123-136.

Kaplan, B. (1988). Development and acceptance of medical information systems: An historical overview. *Journal of Health and Human Resources Administration, 11*, 9-29.

Kaplan, B. (1991). Models of change and information systems research. In H. -E. Nissen, H. K. Klein, & R. Hirschheim (Eds.), *Information systems research: Contemporary approaches and emergent traditions* (pp. 593-611). Amsterdam: North Holland Press.

Kaplan, B. (1992). National Health Service reforms: Opportunities for medical informatics research. In K. C. Lun et al. (Eds.), *Medinfo 92: Seventh World Congress on Medical Informatics* (pp. 1166-1171). Amsterdam: Elsevier.

Kaplan, B., & Dorsey, P. (1991). *Requirements analysis interviewing: Alternative perspectives.* Technical Report 91-020. Washington, D.C. : The American University, Department of Computer Science and Information Systems.

Kaplan, B., & Duchon, D. (1988). Combining qualitative and quantitative methods in information systems research: A case study. *MIS Quarterly, 12*, 571-586.

Kaplan, B., & Duchon, D. (1989). A job orientation model of impact on work seven months post-implementation. In B. Barber, D. Cao, D. Qin, & G. Wagner (Eds.), *Medinfo 89: Sixth World Congress on Medical Informatics* (pp. 1051-1055). Amsterdam: North Holland.

Kaplan, B., & Lundsgaarde, H. (n.d.). *Using qualitative methods to discover and identify strategic benefits of a clincial imaging information system.* Unpublished manuscript.

Kidder, L. H., & Fine, M. (1987). Qualitative and quantitative methods: When stories converge. In M. M. Mark & R. L. Shotland (Eds.), *Multiple methods in program evaluation* (pp. 57-75). San Francisco: Jossey-Bass.

Kirk, J., & Miller, M. L. (1986). *Reliability and validity in qualitative research.* Beverly Hills, CA: Sage.

Kling, R. (1980). Social analyses of computing: Theoretical perspectives in recent empirical research. *Computing Surveys, 12*, 61-110.

Kling, R., & Scacchi, W. (1982). The web of computing: Computer technology as social organization. In M. C. Yovits (Ed.), *Advances in computers* (Vol. 21, pp. 2-90). New York: Academic Press.

Krobock, J. R. (1984). Hospital information systems evaluation methodologies. *Journal of Medical Systems, 8*, 419-429.

LeCompte, M. D., Millroy, W. L., & Preissle, J. (Eds.). (1992). *The handbook of qualitative research in education.* San Diego: Academic Press.

Lundsgaarde, H. P., Fischer, P. J., & Steele, D. J. (1981). *Human problems in computerized medicine.* University of Kansas Publications in Anthropology, No. 13. Lawrence: University of Kansas.

Lundsgaarde, H. P., Gardner, R. M., & Menlove, R. L. (1989). Using attitudinal questionnaires to achieve benefits optimization. In L. C. Kingsland, III (Ed.), *Proceedings of the 13th Annual Symposium on Computer Applications in Medical Care* (pp. 703-708). Silver Spring, MD: IEEE Computer Society Press.

Lundsgaarde, H. P., & Moreshead, G. E. (1991). Evaluation of a computerized clinical information system (Micromedex). In P. D. Clayton (Ed.), *Proceedings of the 15th Annual Symposium on Computer Applications in Medical Care* (pp. 18-22). New York: McGraw-Hill.

Lyytinen, K. (1987). Different perspectives on information systems: Problems and solutions. *ACM Computing Surveys, 19,* 5-46.

Markus, M. L., & Robey, D. (1988). Information technology and organizational change: Causal structure in theory and research. *Management Science, 34,* 583-598.

Maxwell, J. (1992). Understanding and validity in qualitative research. *Harvard Educational Review, 62,* 279-300.

Maxwell, J. A., Bashook, P. G., & Sandlow, L. J. (1986). Combining ethnographic and experimental methods in educational research: A case study. In D. M. Fetterman & M. A. Pitman (Eds.), *Educational evaluation: Ethnography in theory, practice, and politics* (pp. 121-143). Beverly Hills, CA: Sage.

Maxwell, J., & Miller, B. (n.d.). *Two aspects of thought and two components of qualitative data analysis.* Unpublished manuscript.

Miles, M. B., & Huberman, A. M. (1984). *Qualitative data analysis: A sourcebook of new methods.* Beverly Hills: Sage.

Mishler, E. (1986). *Research interviewing: Context and narrative.* Cambridge, MA: Harvard University Press.

Mumford, E., Hirschheim, R., Fitzgerald, G., & Wood-Harper, T. (Eds.). (1985). *Research methods in information systems.* Amsterdam: North Holland.

Nissen, H.-E., Klein, H. K., & Hirschheim, R. (Eds.) (1991). *Information systems research: Contemporary approaches and emergent traditions.* Amsterdam: North Holland.

Nyce, J. M., & Graves, W. III. (1990). The construction of neurology: Implications for hypermedia system development. *Artificial Intelligence in Medicine, 2,* 315-322.

Osheroff, J. A., Forsythe, D. E., Buchanan, B. G., Bankowitz, R. A., Blumenfeld, B. H., & Miller, R. (1991). Physicians' information needs: Analysis of clinical questions posed during patient care activity. *Annals of Internal Medicine, 14,* 576-581.

Patton, M. Q. (1990). *Qualitative research and evaluation methods* (2nd ed.). Newbury Park, CA: Sage.

Pitman, M. A., & Maxwell, J. A. (1992). Qualitative approaches to evaluation. In M. D. LeCompte, W. L. Millroy, & J. Preissle (Eds.), *The handbook of qualitative research in education* (pp. 729-770). San Diego: Academic Press.

Rogers, E. M. (1983). *Diffusion of innovations* (3rd ed.). New York: The Free Press.

Rogers, E. M., & Shoemaker, F. F. (1971). *Communication of innovation: A cross-cultural approach.* New York: The Free Press.

Rossi, P. H., & Berk, R. A. (1991). A guide to evaluation research theory and practice. In A. Fisher, M. Pavlova, & V. Covello (Eds.), *Evaluation and effective risk communications workshop proceedings* (pp. 201-254). Interagency Task Force on Environmental Cancer and Heart and Lung Disease, Committee on Public Education and Communication, Document EPA/600/9-90/054.

Seidman, I. E. (1991). *Interviewing as qualitative research: A guide for researchers in education and the social sciences.* New York: Teachers College Press.

Shneiderman, B., & Carroll, J. M. (1988). Ecological studies of professional programmers: An overview. *Communications of the ACM, 31,* 1256-1258.

Simborg, D. W., & Whiting O'Keefe, Q. E. (1982). Evaluation methodology for ambulatory care information systems. *Medical Care 20,* 255-265.

Strauss, A., & Corbin, J. (1990). *Basics of qualitative research: Grounded theory procedures and techniques.* Newbury Park, CA: Sage.

Tesch, R. (1990). *Qualitative research: Analysis types and software tools.* New York: Falmer Press.

Trend, M. G. (1979). On the reconciliation of qualitative and quantitative analyses: A case study. In T. D. Cook & C. S. Reichardt (Eds.), *Qualitative and quantitative methods in evaluation research* (pp. 68-86). Beverly Hills, CA: Sage.

Turkle, S. (1984). *The second self: Computers and the human spirit.* New York: Simon & Schuster.

Van Maanen, J. (1983). Epilogue: Qualitative methods reclaimed. In J. Van Maanen (Ed.), *Qualitative methodology* (pp. 247-268). Beverly Hills, CA: Sage.

Walsham, G. (1993). *Interpreting information systems in organizations.* Chichester, UK: Wiley.

Wolcott, H. (1990). *Writing up qualitative research.* Newbury Park, CA: Sage.

Yin, R. K. (1984). *Case study research: Design and methods.* Beverly Hills, CA: Sage.

Zuboff, S. (1988). *In the age of the smart machine: The future of work and power.* New York: Basic Books.

4

Survey Methods for Assessing Social Impacts of Computers in Health Care Organizations

Carolyn E. Aydin

Introduction

This chapter provides a guide to the use of survey methods in evaluating the potential impacts of computerized information systems on the functioning of health care organizations and the worklife of the individuals within them. In any setting, the impacts of computing go beyond the efficiency or cost-effectiveness of a system to the ways in which the technology interacts with the organization's ongoing routine policies and practices (Markus, 1984; Rice, 1987; Sproull & Kiesler, 1991; Zuboff, 1988). Because the delivery of health care requires coordination and cooperation between numerous different occupations and departments, changes in how these groups perform their work and interact with one another can have important consequences for the organization as a whole. Furthermore, the current emphasis on cost efficacy, total quality management (Sahney & Warden, 1991), and operational restructuring has increased the demand for computer systems to reduce costs and provide new and better information to administrators and health care providers. In the long term, new computer technology has the potential to change the experience and process of work as well as the structure and delivery of medical care.

To date, much of the research on computers in health care has focused on the efficiency of the systems themselves, with little attention directed toward their potential social impacts. Although research on information systems in other settings has traditionally been problem-oriented as well, there is also a significant body of research on the social impacts of computer technology (Kraemer & Danziger, 1990; Kraemer & Dutton, 1991). The present chapter draws from available studies of health care computing, as well as from research on computing in other types of organizations, to suggest potential areas for investigation and appropriate measures. The examples described were selected to illustrate specific evaluation issues and methods and are not meant to comprise a comprehensive review of the literature on computer impacts. The discussion includes the evaluation of immediate system outcomes as well as some of the work-oriented long-term impacts of new systems. Although other methodologies are mentioned, the present chapter focuses primarily on quantitative survey methods to measure system impacts.

Survey Research

Survey research, one of the most common methods used for evaluating information system impacts, involves gathering information from a sample of a population using standardized instruments (Kraemer, 1991). For scientific purposes, the intent of survey research also includes generalization to a population of individuals extending beyond the organization under study. In evaluation research, however, the sample may not be randomly selected and the population may be limited to individuals within a specific organization. Even in the case of convenience samples within a single organization, however, investigators need to take steps to ensure an adequate and representative response from individuals comprising the groups in question.

A survey or questionnaire is the primary data collection method within survey research (Kraemer, 1991). In designing any project, questionnaires should never be developed from scratch when appropriate instruments already exist (Zmud & Boynton, 1991). The use of a standard measure with established validity and reliability allows comparison of scores with other settings and spares the investigator the time-consuming process of developing a new measure (Baroudi & Orlikowski, 1988). (*Validity* may be defined as the extent to which the measure actually captures the concept it purports to measure, whereas *reliability* refers to the extent to which it is free from measurement error. See Chapter 2 in this book for a detailed discussion of research methods.)

The survey instruments described in the present chapter are drawn primarily from literature on information systems, organizations and organizational development, and work attitudes and values. The examples selected for inclusion have either been developed specifically for health care organizations or are widely used in other organizational settings with documented reliability and validity. In most cases, the instrument is included in its entirety in the chapter appendix. In other instances, references are provided to enable the investigator to obtain the instrument. This chapter is divided into sections detailing measurement strategies for: (1) user reactions to information systems and the implementation process; (2) characteristics of users that may influence their attitudes toward the system and system implementation; and (3) assessments of social impacts of computers organized into the following six dimensions: decision making, control, productivity, social interaction, job enhancement, and work environment (Kraemer & Danziger, 1990).

User Reactions to Computers and Implementation

General Measures of User Satisfaction

Assessing user satisfaction with a new computer system and the system implementation process constitutes a first step in information system evaluation. A user satisfaction survey should not be seen as a definitive evaluation; it provides a starting point for analyzing system impacts and identifying possible areas of conflict and dissatisfaction (Baroudi & Orlikowski, 1988). Research has shown that user involvement in the computer implementation process improves both use of and satisfaction with information systems (see Kraemer & Dutton, 1991, for summary information). Thus questions about the level of involvement in implementation and satisfaction with computer training are often included in user satisfaction measures. Furthermore, users who hold realistic expectations about an information system prior to implementation also tend to use the system more and be more satisfied with it (Kraemer & Dutton, 1991). However, those with unrealistically high expectations prior to system implementation may become disillusioned with the system when the final product fails to meet their expectations, emphasizing the importance of an ongoing evaluation strategy that measures user attitudes both before and after system implementation (Aydin & Rice, 1991; Lundsgaarde, Gardner, & Menlove, 1989).

User Information Satisfaction Scale. Baroudi and Orlikowski's (1988) short form of Ives, Olson, and Baroudi's (1983) User Information Satisfaction Scale is one of the few measures in the information systems literature that meets strict criteria for a well-developed survey instrument (Zmud & Boynton, 1991). The scale includes 13 paired items measuring user satisfaction with: (1) the data processing staff and services, (2) the information product, and (3) their own knowledge and involvement (see Instrument 1 in the Appendix).

The User Information Satisfaction Scale, widely used in settings outside of health care, is intended to provide the investigator with a tool to detect problems with user satisfaction and facilitate investigation of specific trouble spots pinpointed by the individual scale items. The investigator may want to compare the responses of individuals in different groups or departments on different scale components or specific items to assess how well the new computer system meets the needs of different user groups. In addition, comparative data from surveys conducted in a number of different settings are available.

Because it was designed to save time, the questions on the survey are brief. For clarity, it may be necessary to modify the questionnaire for the specific computer system or organization. The investigator may also wish to add additional items, although the changes may compromise the established validity and reliability of the instrument (Baroudi & Orlikowski, 1988).

End-User Computing Satisfaction. Doll and Torkzadeh's (1988) measure of End-User Computing Satisfaction is another of the few measures in the information systems literature meeting strict criteria for a well-developed survey instrument (Zmud & Boynton, 1991). The concept of end-user computing addresses applications in which the information users being surveyed actually use the computer terminal themselves. Thus, the measure focuses on issues such as ease of use and satisfaction with a specific computer application rather than involvement in implementation and relations with data processing staff (Doll & Torkzadeh, 1988). The measure provides Likert-type scaling as an alternative to semantic differential scaling and includes the following five factors: (1) content, (2) accuracy, (3) format, (4) ease of use, and (5) timeliness (see Instrument 2).

Doll and Torkzadeh (1989) also address the issue of user involvement in system development in the end-user computer environment. The authors hypothesize that successful involvement depends not only on the amount of involvement but also on the user's actual desire for involvement. They suggest asking system users questions describing both (1) the amount of time *actually spent* participating in specific development activities, and (2) the amount of time they wanted to spend in development activities, on a 5-point scale ranging from "a little" to "a great deal" (Doll & Torkzadeh, 1989, p. 1163).

Implementation Attitudes Questionnaire. Schultz and Slevin (1975) took a different approach, developing a comprehensive attitude measurement instrument by examining general research on organizations to determine which variables would be relevant to the implementation of information systems in the organizational environment. Their final instrument, based on factor analysis results, includes seven areas of impact (see Instrument 3). The questionnaire also includes five dependent variables measuring the respondent's likelihood of using the system and evaluation of the system's worth. Robey (1979) describes the results of several studies using the Schultz and Slevin (1975) instrument.

Adding Other Measures. The investigator can also include components of the implementation process not covered by the scales described above. Aydin and Rice (1991, 1992), for example, used items developed by Taylor and Bowers (1972) to assess (1) work group communication (i.e., discussions with co-workers and management about ways to apply or adapt the system) and (2) organizational policies (i.e., the extent to which the organization supports the system by allowing individuals time to experiment and learn more about it). (See Instrument 4.) Such organizational policies and communication support can influence the extent to which individuals develop their own methods for using the system in the process of adoption and implementation (i.e., "reinvention"; Johnson & Rice, 1984; Rogers, 1983).

Single-Item Measures. Baroudi and Orlikowski (1988) also suggest that there may be instances in which it is appropriate to employ a single-item measure of user satisfaction. Although single-item measures have been criticized for possible measurement error and lack of discriminatory power (e.g., Zmud & Boynton, 1991), research also shows that single-item global measures may be more inclusive and convenient than the summation of many facet responses (Baroudi & Orlikowski, 1988; Scarpello & Campbell, 1983).

Following this line of reasoning, Aydin and Rice (1991, 1992; Rice & Aydin, 1988, 1991) used a single-item measure in their evaluation of computerization in a student health clinic. Based on Schultz and Slevin's (1975) conclusion that an individual's cost-benefit evaluation was one of the most useful measures of perceived system success, respondents were asked to indicate their level of agreement (on a 7-point scale ranging from "strongly disagree" to "strongly agree") with the following question: "The new information system is worth the time and effort required to use it." In addition to the single-item measure, two additional questions were added after the computer was implemented asking respondents to rate the extent to which the system increased (1) the ease of performing the department's work and (2) the quality of the department's work (see Instrument 5). The three items together comprise a short global scale combining a general cost-benefit evaluation with an evaluation of the system's contribution to a department's work (Aydin & Rice, 1991; Davis, 1989).

Measuring User Adaptation

Kjerulff, Counte, Salloway, and Campbell (1981) adopted a different approach to user satisfaction by developing three instruments to assess employee attitudinal and behavioral adaptation to computerization. Employees themselves completed the Use Scale and the Change Scale while supervisors completed the Behavioral Scale for each employee using the computer (see Instrument 6). Study results described the relationship of these measures to other standardized measures such as cognitive structure, role conflict, and role ambiguity (Counte, Kjerulff, Salloway, & Campbell, 1983; see Cook, Hepworth, Wall, & Warr, 1981, for additional job measures such as role conflict and ambiguity). Findings for the Use Scale, for example, indicated that greater difficulty in using the system was reported by employees who faced more ambiguity in their jobs, had a negative orientation toward change and little desire for routine or structure, and a history of working at a number of different hospitals.

Situation-Specific User Satisfaction Measures

Kaplan and Duchon's (1987) investigation of a computer system's impact on work in clinical laboratories illustrates another approach to measuring user satisfaction. Rather than using a general satisfaction measure, Kaplan and Duchon (1987) designed an instrument to measure specific expectations, concerns, and perceived changes related to the impact of the computer system on laboratory work. Although the items may not be applicable to all systems, the questionnaire (Instrument 7) should guide investigators in developing similar situation-specific measures. The survey form also included open-ended items such as:

"What important changes do you think the computer system has caused?" and "In what ways has the computer system affected how the labs and technologists are treated by others in the Medical Center?" Kaplan and Duchon used the instrument in combination with both standardized measures of other job dimensions (see section on job enhancement below) and qualitative measures of system impacts.

Level of System Use

Level of system use can also indicate user satisfaction with an information system, especially when system use is discretionary (Hendrickson et al., 1992; Safran, Slack, & Bleich, 1989; Slack, 1989). Even with mandatory systems, however, user satisfaction with the system may determine how well they use it. How frequently an individual uses the system can also affect attitudes toward the system. Nonusers or infrequent users, for example, may not be familiar enough with a new system to realize its strengths and shortcomings. Frequent users, however, may report changes in their daily work such as an increased workload or new communication with other workers to discuss system functions and issues (Aydin & Rice, 1992).

Measuring system use often requires system-specific questionnaire items. Schultz and Slevin (1975), for example, asked prospective users to indicate the probability that they would use the computer system (see dependent variables on Instrument 3 in the Appendix). Anderson, Jay, Schweer, and Anderson (1986) asked physicians to respond to items such as: "How frequently do you *personally* use MIS to retrieve patient lists?" and "How frequently do you *personally* use MIS to enter medical orders?" using the following scale: 5 = "several times a day," 4 = "daily," 3 = "several times a week," 2 = "weekly," 1 = "less than weekly, but occasionally," and 0 = "never." Aydin and Ischar (see Chapter 11 of this book) asked nurses "When medications are entered on the computer for the patients you are assigned to care for, what percent of these are entered within two hours after the order is written?" on a scale of 0%, 10%, 20%, and so on. System use can also be monitored through online tracking of how frequently individuals log on to the system and/or how long they use it each time they log on (Hendrickson et al., 1992; Safran, Slack, & Bleich, 1989; Slack, 1989). Online tracking can also provide measures of communication relationships among users or how individuals used common features of the system (see Chapter 6 of this book).

Characteristics of Individual Users

The characteristics of individual users can help system implementers predict individual attitudes toward an information system. Individual attributes are those such as age, occupation, education, job tenure, previous computer experience, prior attitudes toward computers in general, and personality variables such as cognitive style, learning style, orientation toward change, or cognitive structure. Outcomes, however, are not always predictable. Age, job tenure, and previous computer experience, for example, have been shown to lead to both positive and negative attitudes in different settings. For example, although individuals who have worked in an organization for many years often find change difficult, Counte et al. (1983) found individuals who had a history of working in a larger number of hospitals had greater difficulty in using a new system. Although less computer experience may predict negative attitudes, the lack of standardization between computer systems may also make it difficult for experienced computer users to adapt to a new system. Measuring these background factors enables the investigator to either eliminate them or document their influence when investigating reasons for computer-related problems and issues.

Personality Factors

This section addresses user personality traits and the implementation of information systems. Whereas copyright restrictions do not permit publication of the measures themselves, specific references are provided at the end of the chapter to obtain copies of the measures.

Cognitive Style/Learning Style. Beginning in the 1970s, a number of investigators began to focus on traits such as cognitive style as an issue in the design of information systems (e.g., Keen & Morton, 1978; Kilmann & Mitroff, 1976; Mason & Mitroff, 1973). "Cognitive styles represent characteristic modes of functioning shown by individuals in their perceptual and thinking behavior" (Zmud, 1979, p. 967). Most models distinguish between an individual's analytic, systematic approach to problem solving and a more intuitive, global approach as the two main types of cognitive style. Overall, this line of research has had limited success, with generally inconclusive findings regarding information systems design and use (Benbasat, 1989; Bostrom, Olfman, & Sein, 1990; Huber, 1983). Recent meta-analytic findings indicate that the impact of cognitive style on implementation success is relatively small, with a stronger impact on user attitudes than on user performance (Alavi & Joachimsthaler, 1992).

In the health care arena, for example, Aydin (1987) found a relationship between cognitive style, as measured by the short form of the Myers-Briggs Type Indicator (Myers & McCaulley, 1985), and self-reported use of a newly implemented order entry system. Results showed "feeling types" reported that they used the computer less than did "thinking types." Subsequent studies, however, found no relationship between cognitive style and self-reported use (Aydin & Ischar, Chapter 11 of this book; Aydin & Rice, 1991).

Cognitive style or learning style may, however, be important in the design of effective training for computer users (Bostrom, Olfman, & Sein, 1990). Bostrom, Olfman, and Sein (1990) recommend giving the Kolb Learning Style Inventory (Kolb, 1976) to potential trainees and using the results to ensure accommodating the mix of individuals in the group. Summers (1990) makes a similar recommendation for educating nurses. A series of experiments on field-dependence/independence (i.e., the degree to which an individual can isolate or differentiate patterns from a complex field) also resulted in recommendations for information system components to make disembedding easier to perform (Benbasat, 1989).

Orientation Toward Change/Cognitive Structure. Approaching personality traits from a different perspective, Counte et al. (1983, 1987) asked users to complete two personality subscales from the Jackson Personality Research Form (Jackson, 1967): orientation toward change and cognitive structure. The first subscale measures general acceptance of change; the second measures a need for order and structure in one's life (Counte et al., 1983, 1987). Results showed that employees who had a negative orientation toward change of any kind and little desire for routine or structure in their daily lives had greater difficulty in using the new computer system. Since personality is, by definition, not highly subject to change, the authors concluded that individuals who are less adaptable may need more time and support during training and implementation (Counte et al., 1987).

Attitudes Toward Computers in Health Care

Measuring general attitudes toward computers in health care can also help predict individual reactions to a specific computer system. Anderson, Jay, Schweer, and Anderson (1986) developed a physician questionnaire covering the perceived desirability of a number of computer applications to medicine and the potential effects of computers on medical practice (see Instrument 8). Results showed that physicians recognized the potential of computers to improve patient care, but were concerned about the possibility of increased governmental and hospital control. The physicians' attitudes significantly affected the extent to which they used a computer-based hospital information system.

Aydin and Ischar (see Chapter 11 of this book) adapted three items from the same scale to create a short form predicting nurses' attitudes toward computerization. Items asked respondents for their level of agreement on a scale of 1 to 7 (1 = "strongly disagree," 4 = "neutral or uncertain," 7 = "strongly agree") with statements that "Hospital computer applications will: improve the technical quality of care, reduce costs of medical care, and allow nurses more time for patients." Responses to the three statements were added to form a scale (reliability coefficient alpha = .80). Results showed that attitudes toward health care computing in general predicted attitudes toward the specific computer system being evaluated. Attitudes toward the specific system, in turn, predicted self-reported system use.

Social Impacts of Computers

The preceding sections of this chapter have covered instruments to assess user satisfaction with a computer system, as well as some of the individual traits and attitudes that may help predict user satisfaction. The following sections suggest ways to measure the impacts on worklife that may be experienced by computer users. Impacts are divided into the six dimensions cited by Kraemer and Danziger (1990, p. 594) as the most commonly identified impacts of computing on work:

1. Decision making—the capacity to formulate alternatives, estimate effects, and make choices
2. Control—the power relations between different actors
3. Productivity—the ratio of inputs to outputs in the production of goods and services
4. Social interaction—the frequency and quality of interpersonal relationships among co-workers
5. Job enhancement—the skill variety and job domain
6. Work environment—the affective and evaluative orientations of the worker toward the setting of work

Since much of the research has been conducted outside of health care, each section begins with a brief summary of findings in other settings, followed by examples of research in health care along with suggestions for measurement and additional research.

Decision Making

Kraemer and Danziger (1990, p. 594) define *decision making* as "the capacity to formulate alternatives, estimate effects, and make choices." Results of research in other settings indicate that, although computers provide workers with higher quality and more accessible information for decision and action, expert systems that actually make decisions or aid human decision makers remain elusive. In health care, decision support systems may aid in diagnostic decision making as well as interpret, alert, and make therapeutic suggestions. Langton, Johnston, Haynes, and Mathieu (1993, p. 629), in their review of prospective studies that use control groups, assert that very little of the literature focuses on evaluating their "effects on real patients when used by clinicians in everyday practice."

One area in which the medical decision-making capabilities of computers have received considerable attention, however, involves computerization in inpatient, particularly intensive care unit (ICU), settings (Shabot & Gardner, 1993). Specifically, studies have focused on the *clinical* impacts of systems that provide clinicians with reminders, pharmacy and laboratory alerts, infectious disease monitoring, perioperative antibiotic use, and utilization assessment (e.g., Bradshaw, Gardner, & Pryor, 1989; Evans et al., 1985, Evans et al., 1986; Gardner & Evans, 1992; Gardner, Hulse, & Larsen, 1990; Larsen et al., 1989; Rind et al., 1992; Shabot, Bjerke, LoBue, & Leyerle, 1992). Chapters 9 and 10 in this book extend this literature by addressing broader social issues surrounding computers and medical decision making. Chapter 10 also includes a number of survey instruments used to evaluate the use of an expert system for the diagnosis of stroke.

Understanding the impact of computers on decision making goes beyond expert systems, however. One of the most important purposes of computerized order entry and results reporting, for example, is to provide the clinician with faster and more accessible information for clinical decision making (e.g., Connelly, Werth, Dean, Hultman, & Thompson, 1993; Pryor, Gardner, Clayton, & Warner, 1983; Safran, Slack, & Bleich, 1989). Thus the assessment of user satisfaction with the availability of information for decision making could be supplemented by measures such as the actual elapsed time between when the order is written and when the results are available to the physician for clinical decisions on patient care.

One medical center, for example, documented an average delay of 107 minutes between the time a physician wrote a TPN (total parenteral nutrition) order and the time the order was entered in the computer by the unit clerk (University of California, Irvine Medical Center, 1990). This delay was eliminated with the implementation of physician order entry. The success of the change depended, however, on physician acceptance of order entry, which may be lacking in other institutions.

In addition to the timing of information, the amount of information available can affect the decision-making ability of health care professionals (Fischer, Stratmann, Lundsgaarde, & Steele, 1980). Radiologists, for example, emphasize the importance of knowing physicians' reasons for requesting specific tests to ensure that the appropriate test has actually been ordered and to assist in their interpretation of results. An important factor in radiologists' acceptance of the PROMIS system was the ability of PROMIS to provide the radiologist with the complete patient record on demand, enhancing their decision-making capability (Fischer et al., 1980).

The complex division of tasks between departments, however, may increase the difficulty of implementing systems to transmit information from one department to another. Order entry for radiology, for example, may require that the individual entering the radiology order in the computer include the reason for the test as well. The physician, who may not enter his or her own orders, also may not have included the reason for ordering the test on the written order form. If the physician is no longer accessible when the clerk enters the order, the clerk may simply hazard a guess to fill the space so the computer will accept the order. In this case, the system has the capability to meet the radiologists' needs, but the organization of tasks and the unwillingness or inability of the physician and clerk to provide the required information may result in errors in tests performed and interpretation of films (Chamorro, 1992).

Several items designed to measure the decision-making aspects of a system are included in the Schultz and Slevin (1975) measure (see Instrument 3, especially Factor 1). (The instrument was originally pilot tested with a computer system for making advertising budgeting decisions.) User satisfaction measures may also reflect decision-making issues if radiologists, for example, indicate dissatisfaction with the information provided by the system. Follow-up to uncover specific problems then could include an audit of system use, interviews, and observation of individuals as they work with the new computer system.

Control

Kraemer and Danziger (1990) define several aspects of control that warrant consideration, including: (1) control of the individual's work by others, (2) the individual's ability to alter the behavior of others, (3) constraints imposed by the job itself such as time pressures, and (4) an increased sense of mastery over one's own work. The control aspects of computerization need not be conceived of as "zero sum," however, but can result in increased control by all groups (Attewell & Rule, 1984; Thompson, Sarbaugh-McCall, & Norris, 1989).

Research in settings outside of health care has shown that computing has had minimal impact in control over people in the work situation, perhaps because few systems to monitor employee work are actually implemented and monitoring capabilities are seldom used (Kraemer & Danziger, 1990). In the health care arena, computer systems that have the capability to either monitor or control physician ordering patterns have the potential to shift more control to institution administrators. In the example described above in which physicians began entering their own TPN orders in the computer, evaluation results showed a significant increase in physician compliance with hospital policies on the type and duration of orders. In fact, the computer was diplomatically referred to as a "teaching tool" and guidelines were printed on the computer screen where the physicians made their selections, but the end result was enforcement of physician compliance with medical center policies (University of California, Irvine Medical Center, 1990).

In a similar vein, computerized order entry and results reporting provide an opportunity for both peer review and quality assurance operations, as well as a "teaching tool" to encourage the use of practice guidelines (Shuman, 1988). How frequently these capabilities are actually used, however, remains an open question. Evaluation of these aspects of computerization may involve examination of organization policies on the use of computer information; interviews and surveys of key officials, physicians, and other administrators; and audits of changes in compliance with institutional policies and guidelines.

The adoption of a centralized system such as order entry and/or results reporting might also be considered to enhance administrative control over all departments in the organization simply because, whatever system is selected, it is likely to involve compromises on the part of individual departments to meet the needs of the organization as a whole. In fact, Aydin (1989), using interviews with key administrators and system users, found that pharmacy departments perceived a loss of control over both the database of physician orders on which they depended to perform their work, as well as their department's revenues, when nurses were assigned the tasks of order entry and computerized charting of medications. To regain at least some control, the pharmacy department in one hospital agreed to accept what they considered to be a "nursing system" only after hospital administration agreed to let them resume the pharmacy's expanded consultative role that had been eliminated during budget cuts. In another hospital, the pharmacy used system audits to demonstrate nursing errors in order entry and convince administrators that it would be cost-effective to assign pharmacy order entry to pharmacy technicians instead of to nursing, effectively shifting control of the orders database back to the pharmacy department (Kidder, Muraszko, & Shane, 1992).

Both interviews and observation of the meetings that occur during system adoption and the implementation process can provide important evaluation information on shifts in control and the negotiations that occur between the respective groups. In addition, evaluation surveys distributed both before and after system implementation might include situation-specific questions regarding the amount of control an individual or department has over specific aspects of the work situation. For example, individuals might be asked: "For each of the following decisions, please indicate how much say you actually have in making these decisions:" on a scale of "no say at all" to "a very great deal" (Moch, Cammann, & Cooke, 1983). The question would be followed by a series of items such as: "decisions about changing how you do your work," as well as situation-specific items that might be affected by computerization. Schultz and Slevin (1975) also include several items measuring impacts of computerization on control (see Instrument 3, especially Factor 1).

Finally, the use of computers also has the potential to shift the power relationship between physicians and patients. Although little research has addressed this aspect of computerization, there are at least two possible scenarios (Fitter, 1986). On one hand, the physician may consolidate his or her position as an expert by becoming better informed but releasing only decisions to the patient. On the other hand, the computer may be used to share information with patients and involve them in decision making about their health care (Fitter, 1986). Chapter 9 of this book discusses some of these issues. Survey instruments designed to measure patient perceptions of the consultation process may be used to address potential shifts in the power relationships between patients and health care professionals (e.g., Brownbridge, Herzmark, & Wall, 1985; Brownbridge, Lilford, & Tindale-Biscoe, 1988).

Productivity

Research on changes in productivity accompanying computerization in settings outside of health care indicates that there has been little displacement of workers with the increased productivity made possible by computers. Rather, the same number of workers tends to handle more work, with productivity gains from increased quality of work and reduced errors in information handling (Kraemer & Danziger, 1990). Most studies agree that the quantity of work has substantially increased, with more mixed results on the quality of work.

In the health care arena, nursing research, in particular, has focused on the impacts of computers on the time and quality of nursing work (e.g., Bradshaw, Sittig, Gardner, Pryor, & Budd, 1989). In general, results show that computers save nurses time in performing clerical activities such as filling out requisition slips and assembling charts (Staggers, 1988). Computers that manage the flow of information between nursing and ancillary departments save time for nurses, whereas systems that emphasize online charting and not communications may not save time (Hendrickson & Kovner, 1990). Also interesting, however, is the finding that the extra time available after computerization is not usually spent in direct patient care as hypothesized but is channeled into other areas, such as professional growth activities, inservice education, and management planning, or spread out across other nursing activities (Kjerulff, 1988; Staggers, 1988). In studies outside of nursing, Counte, Kjerulff, Salloway, and Campbell (1984) measured how individuals using an Admission, Discharge, and Transfer (ADT) system apportioned their time on the job before and after computer implementation. Respondents were employees in all hospital departments, most in clerical positions or lower-level supervisors, who were trained to use the system. Findings showed that system implementation decreased the amount of time employees spent helping other departments acquire information while, as expected, increasing the time spent on data processing (see Instrument 9). Andrews, Gardner, Metcalf, and Simmons (1985) also addressed work patterns, quality and content of charting, and productivity in their evaluation of a respiratory care computer system. Survey questions included asking therapists to compare the amount of time spent charting before and after computerization, as well as a number of other questions comparing manual and computerized charting (Andrews et al., 1985).

Computers also have the potential to increase the quality of information work by reducing errors. In considering nursing work, however, Hendrickson and Kovner (1990) note that few studies have been conducted to examine this effect. Instruments 3, 5, and 7 in the Appendix include some questions addressing respondent perceptions of changes in quality and service attributable to computerization in both general and laboratory settings.

Getting data into the computer in a timely, accurate, and efficient manner also remains an overriding issue in the implementation of medical information systems and especially the computerized medical record (McDonald, Tierney, Overhage, Martin, & Wilson, 1992; Whiting-O'Keefe, Whiting, & Henke, 1988). Issues surrounding the accuracy of order entry, for example, illustrate some important concerns. With computerized order entry, a clerk with limited expertise may enter orders in the database by selecting from menu options that may not match the exact terminology used by the physician (Chamorro, 1992; McDonald et al., 1992). Audit data can enable system implementers to determine the need for additional training of individual employees or entire groups. In one hospital, audit results indicated that initially 60% to 70% of the medication orders entered required changes by the pharmacy, a figure that was later reduced through training provided to clerical employees by the pharmacy department (Aydin, 1989).

Another essential measure of the productivity of today's hospitals is patient length of stay. Kjerulff (1988, p. 244) cites an experimental study in which two intensive care units were carefully matched for staffing and patient characteristics. Results showed that patients on the computerized unit had shorter lengths of stay with computerized data providing "better blood management." Although length-of-stay data should provide readily available outcome measures in most institutions, well-designed studies are needed to control for patient acuity and other variables in determining the impacts of computerization on patient care.

Social Interaction

Social interaction is defined by Kraemer and Danziger (1990, p. 594) as the "frequency and quality of interpersonal relationships among coworkers." Recent research on computer impacts has documented increased interdependence and communication between individuals and work groups connected by computers. Individuals use electronic mail to send information that would not have been sent or received without electronic mail and individuals who share common databases meet face-to-face as often as before computerization to discuss the shared system (Kraemer & Danziger, 1990).

Some of the evidence cited above comes from research in health care organizations. Aydin (1989), for example, showed that dependence on a common database and shared tasks can increase interdependence and cooperation between departments (see also Connelly et al., 1993; Ouellett, Sophis, Duggan, Driscoll & Priest, 1991; and Pryor et al., 1983). Anderson and Jay (1985) used network analysis (see Chapter 6 of this book) to study social interactions between health care professionals as predictors of system use. Results showed that physicians' location in a communication network had a significant effect on the adoption and utilization of a hospital information system independently of background and practice characteristics. In a smaller organization, Aydin and Rice (1992) focused specifically on the communication aspects of implementing a new clinic scheduling system. Findings showed that workers created new contacts and learned more about the work of computer users in other parts of the organization. These increases in communication also have implications for productivity when combined with findings that indicate that the more co-workers an individual talks to about the new technology, the more productive he or she is likely to be using the new system (Papa, 1990).

New patterns of communication between workers may not all be positive, however. New task arrangements can also create new problems or continue old conflicts in new guises (see Chapter 12 of this book). Kaplan (1987) highlighted interdepartmental issues in her study of the implementation of a laboratory computer system. Although respondents agreed that the computer system made results available more quickly, some laboratory workers felt a loss of contact with physicians, nurses, and patients. In addition, some physicians and nurses refused to use the terminals for results inquiry. Laboratory workers felt that these physicians and nurses expected to get test results by telephone and resented being referred to terminals or to a central processing area for their information.

Both survey research and network methods, as well as interviews and audits of system use, can be used to evaluate changes in social interaction accompanying computerization. Both Schultz and Slevin (1975) and Kaplan and Duchon (1987, 1989) include questionnaire items to explore impacts of computerization on changes in communication patterns and issues (see Instruments 3 and 7). Instrument 9 also includes communication in the list of work role activities being evaluated, and Instrument 10 provides an example of a questionnaire used to collect information on respondent contacts for network analysis (see Chapter 6 of this book). Instrument 11 provides a sample measure to document changes in the frequency of telephone contacts between departments. In addition, documentation of changes in interdependence may be measured by asking employees (both before and after computer implementation) questions such as: "How much do you have to depend on each of the following people to obtain the information needed to do your work?" The question is followed by a list of individuals or departments involved in the computerization process and response categories ranging from 1 to 4, "not at all" to "very much" (Van de Ven & Ferry, 1980).

Job Enhancement

Job enhancement, in contrast to the broader concept of work environment addressed below, focuses specifically on job content, particularly the variety of different tasks and level of skills for a given job (Kraemer & Danziger, 1990). One of the early debates related to computerization concerned whether the use of computers would reduce or expand the task variety and skills associated with specific jobs. Attewell and Rule (1984), for example, note that although some investigators argue that low-level clerical jobs can largely be replaced by new technologies, others argue that even the lowest stratum of white-collar workers may benefit from retraining schemes to upgrade their jobs. According to Kraemer and Danziger (1990), most of the research indicates that, particularly for jobs that involve diverse skills, computing has enhanced workers' perceptions of their job domain.

Research on job design usually focuses on five specific components (Cummings & Huse, 1989):

1. *Skill variety*: The degree to which a job requires a range of activities and abilities to perform the work
2. *Task identity*: The degree to which a job requires the completion of a relatively whole and identifiable piece of work
3. *Task significance*: The degree to which a job has a significant impact on other people's lives
4. *Autonomy*: The degree to which a job provides freedom and discretion in scheduling work and determining methods
5. *Feedback about results*: The degree to which a job provides employees with clear and direct feedback about task performance

Hackman and Oldham (1975) developed the Job Diagnostic Survey (included in Cook et al., 1981) to measure these core job dimensions. A shorter and easier-to-use questionnaire designed to measure the same dimensions was developed by Lawler, Mohrman, and Cummings (see Instrument 12) (Cummings & Huse, 1989).

Research on computers in settings outside of health care has frequently focused on changes in these job dimensions (e.g., word processing, Johnson & Rice, 1987). In some studies, computerization has been accompanied by attempts at work redesign specifically intended to create enriched jobs high on each of the five dimensions. Other studies simply measure whether the implementation of computers has had an impact on the dimensions of workers' jobs.

Griffin (1991) studied the long-term effects of computerization and work redesign on the jobs of tellers in 38 member banks of a large bank holding corporation. Survey data was collected at four time periods: prior to implementation, 6 months after implementation, 24 months after implementation, and 48 months after implementation. Results showed different patterns for the different measures, underscoring the importance of evaluating the impacts of computerization and job changes at multiple points in time. Job satisfaction, for example, increased between Time 1 and Time 2, but returned to levels similar to Time 1 at Times 3 and 4. Individuals also perceived changes in their jobs (i.e., changes in task variety, autonomy, feedback, significance, and identity) at Time 2 and these perceptions did not diminish over the study period. Performance scores also followed a different pattern, showing no significant increase until Time 3 and maintaining that level at Time 4.

In the health care arena, the current emphasis on cost efficacy and the need to streamline work processes and retain highly trained employees has resulted in a renewed interest in job-design issues. Evaluating the impact of computerization on the skills of health care workers, however, must also consider existing job content. With the exception of some clerical workers and other particularly routine jobs, many health care occupations involve highly varied and skilled work. For these individuals, using a computer comprises one task in a workday filled with diverse tasks. Although health care professionals sometimes voice resentment at being required to take time away from patient care to learn to use a computer system (e.g., Aydin & Rice, 1991, 1992), deskilling or routinization is not usually an issue.

Recent research on computerization in health care settings has, however, addressed the issue of job redesign, using the measures described above (Kaplan & Duchon, 1989; Rice & Aydin, 1988). Neither study, however, showed that computerization had an impact on the core job dimensions of the employees under study. Further research on job dimensions in health care settings should probably focus on employees for whom using the computer constitutes a major part of their job. In the Rice and Aydin (1988) study, in particular, computer use constituted only one task in the busy workday of most employees. Kaplan and Duchon (1989), however, also suggest that the lack of findings related to core job dimensions may reflect the fact that standard job characteristic measures do not take into account differences in how individuals holding ostensibly the same jobs actually view their work.

Work Environment

The quality of the work environment focuses on broader and more evaluative responses to work, going beyond the specific dimensions examined under job enhancement to include issues such as general job satisfaction, job stress, time pressures, and the like (Kraemer & Danziger, 1990). Research results in general do indicate that computing may increase stress and time pressure for some workers. In most studies, however, results show that computing has increased workers' job satisfaction and interest in their work. Karasek and Theorell (1990) provide a detailed analysis of job-design issues and their relationship to the health and well-being of individual workers.

In an example of comprehensive longitudinal research on the impacts of computerization, Kraut, Dumais, and Koch (1989) investigated the specific job dimensions described above, as well as the overall impact of computerization on the worklives of customer service representatives in a large public utility. Results showed that computerization can have complex and profound effects on job effectiveness and employment.

The information system investigated by Kraut et al. (1989) was designed to provide recent billing information and to allow interactive updating of customers' accounts, but no intentional attempt was made to redesign jobs or to alter the range of tasks or the interactions with customers. (Similar systems are in use in billing departments in health care institutions.) Along with the introduction of the computer system, however, other changes were made that altered the office layout, disrupting familiar seating arrangements and changing the social organization of the department. Overall, results showed that the service representatives liked their jobs less after computerization. Contact with work colleagues became less frequent and less satisfying, but there was also less job pressure and service representatives believed their overall workload had been reduced. Workers also modified the technology by finding innovative ways to use the new system as well as ways to use the system for clandestine note-passing strongly discouraged by supervisors.

Kaplan and Duchon (1987, 1989), with their study of the laboratory computer system; Counte et al. (1983, 1987), studying clerical employees involved in the admission, discharge, and transfer of patients; and Aydin and Rice (1991, 1992), with their study of computerization in a student health clinic, have all conducted comprehensive longitudinal studies aimed at uncovering changes in the worklife of health care workers following the implementation of a new computer system. (See also Andrews et al., 1985; Connelly et al., 1993; and Lundsgaarde, Gardner, & Menlove, 1989.) Results of each study reflect both the approach taken by the investigators and actual impacts of computerization in the specific health care context.

Counte et al. (1983, 1987), for example, focused on individual differences to explain reactions of employees to computerization. Long-term results indicated that both personality traits and attitudes toward computers were important predictors of individual reactions. Results of studies by both Kaplan and Duchon (1987, 1989) and Aydin and Rice (1991, 1992) focused on work group issues as well as individual differences in predicting adaptation to computerization. Findings showed that, although employees cited both additional work and improvements in quality following computerization, departmental membership was an important predictor of individual reactions. In the laboratory, Kaplan and Duchon (1987, 1989) found that technologists in some laboratories focused on work increases, whereas in other laboratories they emphasized improved information flow (Kaplan, 1987). In the student health clinic, Aydin and Rice (1991, 1992) found that attitudes toward the computer system and new communication with other departments about the system varied both by department and by occupation. One of the most important predictors was the way in which work was organized within the individual departments and the negotiated assignment of the new tasks that accompanied computerization. In comprehensive studies such as these, general job satisfaction surveys can supplement the measures already described in providing important information on employee reactions to change (see Instrument 13).

Summary

In summary, the survey methods described in this chapter comprise an essential dimension in a multimethod approach to evaluating the impacts of computers on the functioning of health care organizations and the worklife of the individuals within them. The chapter and the instruments included in the chapter appendix should provide investigators with standardized instruments, as well as guidance and examples for questionnaire design where no standardized measure exists. Although not intended as a complete review of the literature, this chapter also provides investigators with an overview of topics to consider when planning any investigation of the social impacts of computers in health care organizations.

Additional Reading

Introduction

Markus (1984) provides an excellent analysis of the changes that occur in organizations with the introduction of information systems.

Survey Research

See Kraemer (1991) for a collection of detailed reviews and discussions of survey methods in information systems research. This volume also includes Zmud and Boynton's archive of over 100 instruments (although the scales themselves are not included) and Kraemer and Dutton's assessment of survey research in management information systems as well as other references on topics discussed throughout this chapter.

Cook, Hepworth, Wall, and Warr (1981) review nearly 250 scales for measuring work attitudes, values, and perceptions and include the most widely used instruments in their entirety.

User Reactions and Characteristics of Individual Users

Kraemer (1991)—see above review.

Nelson (1990) reviews the literature on individual reactions to systems and suggests a framework that includes additional measures such as job satisfaction, organizational commitment, involvement, and performance.

Alavi and Joachimsthaler's (1992) meta-analysis of the information systems literature provides important information on the relative importance of different variables with suggestions for future research.

Burkes (1991) provides a review of nurses' attitudes toward computer systems.

Social Impacts of Computers

Kraemer and Danziger (1990) provide a framework for the social impacts of computers and review the results of the most recent research.

Cummings and Huse (1989) is an excellent organization development textbook that addresses many of the organizational change issues involved in the implementation of an information system.

Hendrickson and Kovner (1990) review the literature and make recommendations for future research.

Karasek and Theorell (1990) provide a detailed analysis of job design issues and their relationship to the health and well-being of individual workers.

References

Alavi, M., & Joachimsthaler, E. A. (1992). Revisiting DSS implementation research: A meta-analysis of the literature and suggestions for researchers. *MIS Quarterly, 16,* 95-116.

Anderson, J. G., & Jay, S. J. (1985). Computers and clinical judgment: The role of physician networks. *Social Science and Medicine, 20,* 969-979.

Anderson, J. G., Jay, S. J., Schweer, H. M., & Anderson, M. M. (1986). Why doctors don't use computers: Some empirical findings. *Journal of the Royal Society of Medicine, 79,* 142-144.

Andrews, R. D., Gardner, R. M., Metcalf, S. M., & Simmons, D. (1985). Computer charting: An evaluation of a respiratory care computer system. *Respiratory Care, 30,* 695-707.

Attewell, P., & Rule, J. (1984). Computing and organizations: What we know and what we don't know. *Communications of the ACM, 27,* 1184-1192.

Aydin, C. E. (1987). The effects of social information and cognitive style on medical information system attitudes and use. In W. W. Stead (Ed.), *Proceedings of the 11th Annual Symposium on Computer Applications in Medical Care* (pp. 601-606). New York: Institute of Electrical and Electronics Engineers.

Aydin, C. E. (1989). Occupational adaptation to computerized medical information systems. *Journal of Health and Social Behavior, 30,* 163-179.

Aydin, C. E., & Rice, R. E. (1991). Social worlds, individual differences, and implementation: Predicting attitudes toward a medical information system. *Information and Management, 20,* 119-136.

Aydin, C. E., & Rice, R. E. (1992). Bringing social worlds together: Computers as catalysts for new interactions in health care organizations. *Journal of Health and Social Behavior, 33,* 168-185.

Baroudi, J. J., & Orlikowski, W. J. (1988). A short-form measure of User Information Satisfaction: A psychometric evaluation and notes on use. *Journal of Management Information Systems, 4,* 44-59.

Benbasat, I. (1989). Laboratory experiments in information systems studies with a focus on individuals: A critical appraisal. In I. Benbasat (Ed.), *The information systems research challenge: Experimental research methods* (pp. 33-48). Boston: Harvard Business School.

Bostrom, R. P., Olfman, L., & Sein, M. K. (1990). The importance of learning style in end-user training. *MIS Quarterly,* March 1990.

Bradshaw, K. E., Gardner, R. M., & Pryor, T. A. (1989). Development of a computerized laboratory alerting system. *Computers and Biomedical Research, 22,* 575-587.

Bradshaw, K. E., Sittig, D. F., Gardner, R. M., Pryor, T. A., & Budd, M. (1989). Computer-based data entry for nurses in the ICU. *M. D. Computing, 6,* 274-280.

Brownbridge, G., Herzmark, G. A., & Wall, T. D. (1985). Patient reactions to doctors' computer use in general practice consultations. *Social Science and Medicine, 20,* 47-52.

Brownbridge, G., Lilford, R. J., & Tindale-Biscoe, S. (1988). Use of a computer to take booking histories in a hospital antenatal clinic. *Medical Care, 26,* 474-487.

Burkes, M. (1991). Identifying and relating nurses' attitudes toward computer use. *Computers in Nursing, 9,* 190-201.

Chamorro, T. (1992). *Knowledge as transference in automating hospital operations.* Nursing Information Systems, Cedars-Sinai, Medical Center, Los Angeles, CA. Unpublished report.

Connelly, D. P., Werth, G. R., Dean, D. W., Hultman, B. K., & Thompson, T. R. (1993). Physician use of an NICU laboratory reporting system. In M. E. Frisse (Ed.), *Proceedings of the 16th Annual Symposium on Computer Applications in Medical Care* (pp. 8-12). New York: McGraw-Hill.

Cook, J. D., Hepworth, S. J., Wall, T. D., & Warr, P. B. (1981). *The experience of work.* New York: Academic Press.

Counte, M. A., Kjerulff, K. H., Salloway, J. C., & Campbell, B. C. (1983, Summer). Implementation of a medical information system: Evaluation of adaptation. *HCM Review, 8,* 25-33.

Counte, M. A., Kjerulff, K. H., Salloway, J. C., & Campbell, B. C. (1984). Implementing computerization in hospitals: A case study of the behavioral and attitudinal impacts of a medical information system. *Journal of Organizational Behavior Management, 6,* 109-122.

Counte, M. A., Kjerulff, K. H., Salloway, J. C., & Campbell, B. C. (1987). Adapting to the implementation of a medical information system: A comparison of short- versus long-term findings. *Journal of Medical Systems, 11,* 11-20.

Cummings, T. G., & Huse, E. F. (1989). *Organization development and change* (4th ed.). St. Paul: West.

Davis, F. D. (1989, September). Perceived usefulness, perceived ease of use, and user acceptance of information technology. *MIS Quarterly, 13,* 319-340.

Doll, W. J, & Torkzadeh, G. (1988). The measurement of end-user computing satisfaction. *MIS Quarterly, 12,* 259-274

Doll, W. J., & Torkzadeh, G. (1989). A discrepancy model of end-user computing involvement. *Management Science, 35,* 1151-1171.

Evans, R. S., Gardner, R. M., Bush, A. R., Burke, J. P., Jacobson, J. A., Larsen, R. A., Meier, F. A., & Warner, H. R. (1985). Development of a computerized infectious disease monitor (CIDM). *Computers and Biomedical Research, 18,* 103-113.

Evans, R. S., Larsen, R. A., Burke, J. P., Gardner, R. M., Meier, F. A., Jacobson, J. A., Conti, M. T., Jacobson, J. T., & Hulse, R. K. (1986). Computer surveillance of hospital-acquired infections and antibiotic use. *Journal of the American Medical Association, 256,* 1007-1011.

Fischer, P. J., Stratmann, W. C., Lundsgaarde, H. P., & Steele, D. J. (1980). User reaction to PROMIS: Issues related to acceptability of medical innovations. In *Proceedings of the 4th Annual Symposium on Computer Applications in Medical Care* (pp. 1722-1730). Washington, DC: IEEE.

Fitter, M. (1986). Evaluation of computers in primary health care: The effect on doctor-patient communication. In H. E. Peterson & W. Schneider (Eds.), *Human-computer communications in health care* (pp. 67-80). Amsterdam: Elsevier.

Gardner, R. M., & Evans, R. S. (1992). Computer-assisted quality assurance. *Group Practice Journal, 41,* 8-11.

Gardner, R. M., Hulse, R. K, & Larsen, K. G. (1990). Assessing the effectiveness of a computerized pharmacy system. In *Proceedings of the 14th Annual Symposium on*

Computer Applications in Medical Care (pp. 668-672). Los Alamitos, CA: IEEE Computer Society Press.

Griffin, R. (1991). Effects of work redesign on employee perceptions, attitudes, and behaviors: A long-term investigation. *Academy of Management Journal, 34*, 425-435.

Hackman, J. R., & Oldham, G. R. (1975). Development of the Job Diagnostic Survey. *Journal of Applied Psychology, 60*, 159-170.

Hendrickson, G., Anderson, R. K., Clayton, P. D., Cimino, J., Hripcsak, G. M., Johnson, S. B., McCormack, M., Sengupta, S., Shea, S., Sideli, R., & Roderer, N. (1992). The integrated academic information management system at Columbia-Presbyterian Medical Center. *M. D. Computing, 9*, 35-42.

Hendrickson, G., & Kovner, C. T. (1990). Effects of computers on nursing resource use. *Computers in Nursing, 8*, 16-22.

Huber, G. P. (1983). Cognitive style as a basis for MIS and DSS designs: Much ado about nothing? *Management Science, 29*, 567-579.

Ives, B., Olson, M. H., & Baroudi, J. J. (1983). The measurement of user information satisfaction. *Communications of the ACM, 26*, 785-793.

Jackson, D. (1967). *Personality research form manual.* Goshen, NY: Research Psychologists Press.

Johnson, B. M., & Rice, R. E. (1984). Reinvention in the innovation process: The case of word processing. In R. E. Rice & Associates (Eds.), *The new media* (pp. 157-183). Beverly Hills: Sage.

Johnson, B. M., & Rice, R. E. (1987). *Managing organizational innovation.* New York: Columbia University Press.

Kaplan, B. (1987). Initial impact of a clinical laboratory computer system. *Journal of Medical Systems, 11*, 137-147.

Kaplan, B., & Duchon, D. (1987). *A qualitative and quantitative investigation of a computer system's impact on work in clinical laboratories.* Unpublished manuscript.

Kaplan, B., & Duchon, D. (1989). A job orientation model of impact on work seven months post implementation. In *Proceedings of Medinfo 89: Sixth World Congress on Medical Informatics* (pp. 1051-1055). Amsterdam: North Holland.

Karasek, R., & Theorell, T. (1990). *Healthy work: Stress, productivity, and the reconstruction of working life.* New York: Basic Books.

Keen, P. G. W., & Morton, M. S. S. (1978). *Decision support systems: An organizational perspective.* Reading, MA: Addison-Wesley.

Kidder, P. A., Muraszko, J. M., & Shane, R. (1992). *Utilization of pharmacy technicians for computer medication order entry.* Paper presented at the 1992 Annual Meeting of the American Society of Hospital Pharmacists, Washington, DC.

Kilmann, R. H., & Mitroff, I. I. (1976). Qualitative versus quantitative analysis for management science: Different forms for different psychological types. *Interfaces, 6*, 17-27.

Kjerulff, K. H. (1988). The integration of hospital information systems into nursing practice: A literature review. In M. J. Ball, K. J. Hannah, U. Gerdin Jelger, & H. Peterson (Eds.), *Nursing Informatics.* New York: Springer Verlag.

Kjerulff, K. H., Counte, J. A., Salloway, J. C., & Campbell, B. C. (1981). Understanding employee reactions to a medical information system. In *Proceedings of the 5th Annual Symposium on Computer Applications in Medical Care* (pp. 802-805). Los Angeles, CA: IEEE Computer Society Press.

Kolb, D. A. (1976). *The Learning Style Inventory technical manual.* Boston, MA: McBer.

Kraemer, K. L. (Ed.). (1991). *The information systems research challenge: Survey research methods.* Boston, MA: Harvard Business School.

Kraemer, K. L., & Danziger, J. N. (1990). The impacts of computer technology on the worklife of information workers. *Social Science Computer Review, 8,* 592-613.

Kraemer, K. L., & Dutton, W. H. (1991). Survey research in the study of management information systems. In K. L. Kraemer (Ed.), *The information systems research challenge: Survey research methods* (pp. 3-57). Boston, MA: Harvard Business School.

Kraut, R., Dumais, S., & Koch, S. (1989). Computerization, productivity, and quality of work-life. *Communications of the ACM, 32,* 220-238.

Langton, K. B., Johnston, M. E., Haynes, R. B., & Mathieu, A. (1993). A critical appraisal of the literature on the effects of computer-based clinical decision support systems on clinician performance and patient outcomes. In M. E. Frisse (Ed.), *Proceedings of the 16th Annual Symposium on Computer Applications in Medical Care* (pp. 626-630). New York: McGraw-Hill.

Larsen, R. A., Evans, R. S., Burke, J. P., Pestotnik, S. L., Gardner, R. M., & Classen, D. C. (1989). Improved perioperative antibiotic use and reduced surgical wound infections through use of computer decision analysis. *Infection Control and Hospital Epidemiology, 10,* 316-320.

Lundsgaarde, H. P., Gardner, R. M., & Menlove, R. L. (1989). Using attitudinal questionnaires to achieve benefits optimization. In *Proceedings of the 13th Annual Symposium on Computer Applications in Medical Care* (pp. 703-707). Washington, DC: Computer Society of the IEEE.

Markus, M. L. (1984). *Systems in organizations.* Boston: Pitman.

Mason, R. O., & Mitroff, I. I. (1973). A program for research on management information systems. *Management Science, 19,* 475-487.

McDonald, C. J., Tierney, W. M., Overhage, J. M., Martin, D. K., & Wilson, G. A. (1992). The Regenstrief Medical Record System: 20 years of experience in hospitals, clinics, and neighborhood health centers. *M. D. Computing, 9,* 206-217.

Moch, M., Cammann, C., & Cooke, R. A. (1983). Organizational structure: Measuring the distribution of influence. In S. E. Seashore, E. E. Lawler, III, P. H. Mirvis, & C. Cammann (Eds.), *Assessing organizational change.* New York: John Wiley.

Myers, I. B., & McCaulley, M. H. (1985). *Manual: A guide to the development and use of the Myers-Briggs Type Indicator.* Palo Alto, CA: Consulting Psychologists Press.

Nelson, D. (1990). Individual adjustment to information-driven technologies: A critical review. *MIS Quarterly, 14,* 79-98.

Ouellett, J., Sophis, G., Duggan, S., Driscoll, L., & Priest, S. (1991). Automating a multiple-day medication administration record. *Nursing Management, 22,* 30-35.

Papa, M. J. (1990). Communication network patterns and employee performance with new technology. *Communication Research, 17,* 344-368.

Pryor, T. A., Gardner, R. M., Clayton, P. D., & Warner, H. R. (1983). The HELP System. *Journal of Medical Systems, 7,* 87-102.

Rice, R. E. (1987). Computer-mediated communication and organizational innovation. *Journal of Communication, 37,* 64-94.

Rice, R. E., & Aydin, C. E. (1988). *Summary report: Student health service information system study.* Los Angeles, CA: Annenberg School for Communication, University of Southern California.

Rice, R. E., & Aydin, C. E. (1991). Attitudes toward new organizational technology: Network proximity as a mechanism for social information processing. *Administrative Science Quarterly, 36,* 219-244.

Rind, D. M., Safran, C., Phillips, R. S., Slack, W. V., Calkins, D. R., Delbanco, T. L., & Bleich, H. L. (1992). The effect of computer-based reminders on the management of hospitalized patients with worsening renal function. In P. D. Clayton (Ed.), *Proceedings of the 15th Annual Symposium on Computer Applications in Medical Care* (pp. 28-32). New York: McGraw-Hill.

Robey, D. (1979). User attitudes and management information system use. *Academy of Management Journal, 22,* 527-538.

Rogers, E. M. (1983). *Diffusion of innovations.* New York: The Free Press.

Safran, C., Slack, W. V., & Bleich, H. L. (1989). Role of computing in patient care in two hospitals. *M. D. Computing, 6,* 141-148.

Sahney, V. K., & Warden, G. L. (1991). The quest for quality and productivity in health services. *Frontiers of Health Services Management, 7,* 2-40.

Scarpello, V., & Campbell, J. P. (1983). Job satisfaction: Are all the parts there? *Personnel Psychology, 36,* 577-600.

Schultz, R. L., & Slevin, D. P. (1975). Implementation and organizational validity: An empirical investigation. In R. L. Schultz & D. P. Slevin (Eds.), *Implementing operations research/management science* (pp. 153-182). New York: American Elsevier.

Shabot, M. M., Bjerke, H. S., LoBue, M., & Leyerle, B. J. (1992). Quality assurance and utilization assessment: The major by-products of an ICU clinical information system. In P. D. Clayton (Ed.), *Proceedings of the 15th Annual Symposium on Computer Applications in Medical Care* (pp. 554-558). New York: McGraw-Hill.

Shabot, M. M., & Gardner, R. M., (1993). *Decision support systems for critical care.* New York: Springer-Verlag.

Shuman, T. M. (1988). Hospital computerization and the politics of medical decision-making. In R. L. Simpson & I. H. Simpson (Eds.), *Research in the sociology of work* (Vol. 4, pp. 261-287). Greenwich, CT: JAI.

Slack, W. (1989). Editorial: Remembrance, thanks, and welcome. *M. D. Computing, 6,* 183-185.

Sproull, L., & Kiesler, S. (1991). *Connections.* Cambridge: MIT Press.

Staggers, N. (1988). Using computers in nursing. *Computers in Nursing, 6,* 164-170.

Summers, S. (1990). Attitudes of nurses toward hospital computerization: Brain dominance model for learning. In R. A. Miller (Ed.), *Proceedings of the 14th Annual Symposium on Computer Applications in Medical Care* (pp. 902-905). Los Alamitos, CA: IEEE Computer Society Press.

Taylor, J. C., & Bowers, D. G. (1972). *Survey of organizations: A machine scored standardized questionnaire instrument.* Ann Arbor, MI: Institute for Social Research, University of Michigan.

Thompson, L., Sarbaugh-McCall, M., & Norris, D. F. (1989). The social impacts of computing: Control in organizations. *Social Science Computer Review, 7,* 407-417.

TPN audits: MD order entry. (1990). Department of Nursing, University of California, Irvine Medical Center. Unpublished report.

Van de Ven, A. H., & Ferry, D. L. (1980). *Measuring and assessing organizations.* New York: Wiley.

Whiting-O'Keefe, Q. E., Whiting, A., & Henke, J. (1988). The STOR clinical information system. *M. D. Computing, 5,* 8-21.

Zmud, R. W. (1979). Individual differences and MIS success: A review of the empirical literature. *Management Science, 25*, 966-979.

Zmud, R. W., & Boynton, A. C. (1991). Survey measures and instruments in MIS: Inventory and appraisal. In K. L. Kraemer (Ed.), *The information systems research challenge: Survey research methods* (pp. 149-180). Boston, MA: Harvard Business School.

Zuboff, S. (1988). *In the age of the smart machine*. New York: Basic Books.

Appendix:
Survey Instruments

Survey Instruments

1. Short-Form Measure of User Information Satisfaction
2. End-User Computing Satisfaction
3. Implementation Attitudes Questionnaire
4. Scales Adapted from Survey of Organizations
5. Examples of Short Global User Satisfaction Measures
6. Instruments to Assess Employee Adaptation
7. Laboratory Computer Impact Study
8. Perceived Desirability of Computer Applications in Medicine
9. Work Role Activities
10. Network Survey
11. Communication Between Departments
12. Job Design Questionnaire
13. Job Satisfaction

1. Short-Form Measure of User Information Satisfaction

The purpose of this study is to measure how *you* feel about certain aspects of the computer-based information products and services that are provided to you in your present position.

On the following pages you will find different factors, each related to some aspect of your computer-based support.[a] You are to rate each factor on the descriptive scales that follow it, based on your evaluation of the factor.

The scale positions are defined as follows:

adjective X : ___ : ___ : ___ : ___ : ___ : ___ : ___ : adjective Y

      (1) (2) (3) (4) (5) (6) (7)

(1) Extremely X   (5) Slightly Y
(2) Quite X   (6) Quite Y
(3) Slightly X   (7) Extremely Y
(4) Neither X or Y; Equally X or Y; Does not apply

The following example illustrates the scale positions and their meanings:

My vacation in the Bahamas was:

restful : ___ : ___ : ___ : ___ : ___ : ___ : _X_ : hectic

healthy : ___ : _X_ : ___ : ___ : ___ : ___ : ___ : unhealthy

According to the responses, the person's vacation was extremely hectic and quite healthy.

Instructions

1. Check each scale in the position that describes your evaluation of the factor being judged.
2. Check every scale; do not omit any.
3. Check only one position for each scale.
4. Check in the space, not between spaces. This   Not this
                                                  : _X_ : ___X___ :
5. Work rapidly. Rely on your first impressions.

Thank you very much for your cooperation.

Answer Based on Your Own Feelings

1. Relationship with the EDP[a] staff

   dissonant : ___ : ___ : ___ : ___ : ___ : ___ : ___ : harmonious

   bad : ___ : ___ : ___ : ___ : ___ : ___ : ___ : good

2. Processing of requests for changes to existing systems

   fast : ___ : ___ : ___ : ___ : ___ : ___ : ___ : slow

   untimely : ___ : ___ : ___ : ___ : ___ : ___ : ___ : timely

3. Degree of EDP training provided to users

   complete : ___ : ___ : ___ : ___ : ___ : ___ : ___ : incomplete

   low : ___ : ___ : ___ : ___ : ___ : ___ : ___ : high

4. Users' understanding of systems

   insufficient : ___ : ___ : ___ : ___ : ___ : ___ : ___ : sufficient

   complete : ___ : ___ : ___ : ___ : ___ : ___ : ___ : incomplete

5. Users' feelings of participation

   positive : ___ : ___ : ___ : ___ : ___ : ___ : ___ : negative

   insufficient : ___ : ___ : ___ : ___ : ___ : ___ : ___ : sufficient

6. Attitude of the EDP staff

   cooperative : ___ : ___ : ___ : ___ : ___ : ___ : ___ : belligerent

   negative : ___ : ___ : ___ : ___ : ___ : ___ : ___ : positive

7. Reliability of output information

        high : ___ : ___ : ___ : ___ : ___ : ___ : ___ : low

        superior : ___ : ___ : ___ : ___ : ___ : ___ : ___ : inferior

8. Relevancy of output information (to intended function)

        useful : ___ : ___ : ___ : ___ : ___ : ___ : ___ : useless

        relevant : ___ : ___ : ___ : ___ : ___ : ___ : ___ : irrelevant

9. Accuracy of output information

        inaccurate : ___ : ___ : ___ : ___ : ___ : ___ : ___ : accurate

        low : ___ : ___ : ___ : ___ : ___ : ___ : ___ : high

10. Precision of output information

        low : ___ : ___ : ___ : ___ : ___ : ___ : ___ : high

        definite : ___ : ___ : ___ : ___ : ___ : ___ : ___ : uncertain

11. Communication with EDP staff

        dissonant : ___ : ___ : ___ : ___ : ___ : ___ : ___ : harmonious

        destructive : ___ : ___ : ___ : ___ : ___ : ___ : ___ : productive

12. Time required for new systems development

        unreasonable : ___ : ___ : ___ : ___ : ___ : ___ : ___ : reasonable

        acceptable : ___ : ___ : ___ : ___ : ___ : ___ : ___ : unacceptable

13. Completeness of output information

        sufficient : ___ : ___ : ___ : ___ : ___ : ___ : ___ : insufficient

        adequate : ___ : ___ : ___ : ___ : ___ : ___ : ___ : inadequate

Scoring

The values for each item range from −3 to +3 with 0 indicating neutrality. Each scale is scored by taking the average of the two items. (Some items are reverse scored to prevent respondents from marking down one column of the questionnaire.) The total score is determined by summing the scores on the 13 scales. Three subtotals (information product, EDP staff and services, and knowledge/involvement) are the averages of their component scales. The total score can range from +39 to −39 and the subtotals from +3 to −3. All of the reliabilities (Cronbach's alpha) are above .80 and the total score has a reliability of .89.

SOURCE: Reprinted with permission from J. J. Baroudi & W. J. Orlikowski (1988), "A Short-Form Measure of User Information Satisfaction: A Psychometric Evaluation and Notes on Use," *Journal of Management Information Systems, 4*, pp. 44-59.
[a]NOTE: Computer-based support includes the following: in-house computer, timesharing, service bureau, access to a remote computer, use of computer-generated reports.

2. End-User Computing Satisfaction

Scale:
  1 = Almost never
  2 = Some of the time
  3 = Almost half of the time
  4 = Most of the time
  5 = Almost always

The 12-item End-User Computing Satisfaction measure includes the following five components (Cronbach's Alpha for the 12-item scale = .92):

Factor 1: CONTENT (coefficient alpha = .89)
  C1: Does the system provide the precise information you need?
  C2: Does the information content meet your needs?
  C3: Does the system provide reports that seem to be just about exactly what you need?
  C4: Does the system provide sufficient information?

Factor 2: ACCURACY (coefficient alpha = .91)
  A1: Is the system accurate?
  A2: Are you satisfied with the accuracy of the system?

Factor 3: FORMAT (coefficient alpha = .78)
  F1: Do you think the output is presented in a useful format?
  F2: Is the information clear?

Factor 4: EASE OF USE (coefficient alpha = .85)
  E1: Is the system user-friendly?
  E2: Is the system easy to use?

Factor 5: TIMELINESS (coefficient alpha = .82)
  T1: Do you get the information you need in time?
  T2: Does the system provide up-to-date information?

SOURCE: Adapted from W. J. Doll & G. Torkzadeh (1988), "The measurement of end-user computing satisfaction." *MIS Quarterly, 12*, pp. 259-274.

3. Implementation Attitudes Questionnaire

You are asked to read each statement carefully and to circle one of the words from each following line that describes most clearly how you feel about the statement. For example:

I find the computer system interesting.

Strongly disagree   Disagree   Uncertain   Agree   Strongly agree
                                                   X

This would indicate that you agree with the statement.

Please keep in mind that what is important is your own opinion.

The computer system is presently being considered for implementation. Remember, this questionnaire is asking for *your opinion about the computer system.*

Each item implies "after the implementation," that is, this questionnaire is concerned with how you feel about each statement as it applies to the situation *after the computer system is operational.*

Each item implies that changes will occur *after the computer system* is in use. For example, the statement

"My job will be more satisfying."
        implies
"My job will be more satisfying . . . *after the computer system is in use.*"

Note: The original questionnaire included 67 items. The items listed below were interpretable in 7 factors. An additional 10 items did not load significantly on a factor or were not interpretable.

Factor List

Factor 1: PERFORMANCE—Effect on Job Performance and Performance Visibility

My job will be more satisfying.
Others will better see the results of my efforts.
It will be easier to perform my job well.
The accuracy of information I receive will be improved by the computer system.
I will have more control over my job.
I will be able to improve my performance.
Others will be more aware of what I am doing.
The information I will receive from the computer system will make my job easier.
I will spend less time looking for information.
I will be able to see better the results of my efforts.
The accuracy of my forecast will improve as a result of using the computer system.
My performance will be more closely monitored.
The division/department will perform better.

Factor 2: INTERPERSONAL—Interpersonal Relations, Communication, and Increased Interaction and Consultation with Others

I will need to communicate with others more.
I will need the help of others more.
I will need to consult others more often before making a decision.
I will need to talk with other people more.
I will need the help of others more.

Factor 3: CHANGES—Changes Will Occur in Organizational Structure and People I Deal With

The individuals I work with will change.

The management structure will be changed.

The computer system will not require any changes in division/department structure.

I will have to get to know several new people.

Factor 4: GOALS—Goals Will Be More Clear, More Congruent to Workers, and More Achievable

Individuals will set higher targets for performance.

The use of the computer system will increase profits.

This project is technically sound.

Company goals will become more clear.

My counterparts in other division/departments will identify more with the organization's goals.

The patterns of communication will be more simplified.

My goals and the company's goals will be more similar than they are now.

The aims of my counterparts in other divisions/departments will be more easily achieved.

My personal goals will be better reconciled with the company's goals.

Factor 5: SUPPORT/RESISTANCE—Computer System Has Implementation Support—Adequate Top Management, Technical, and Organizational Support —and Does Not Have Undue Resistance

Top management will provide the resources to implement the computer system.

People will accept the required change.

Top management sees the computer system as being important.

Implementing the computer system will be difficult.

Top management does not realize how complex this change is.

People will be given sufficient training to utilize the computer system.

This project is important to top management.

There will be adequate staff available to successfully implement the computer system.

My counterparts in other divisions/departments are generally resistant to changes of this type.

Personal conflicts will not increase as a result of the computer system.

The developers of the computer system will provide adequate training to users.

Factor 6: CLIENT—System Developers Understand the Problems and Work Well with Their Clients

The developers of these techniques don't understand our problems.

I enjoy working with those who are implementing the computer system.

When I talk to those implementing the computer system, they respect my opinions.

Factor 7: URGENCY—Need for Results, Even with Costs Involved; Importance to Me, Boss, Top Management

The computer system costs too much.
I will be supported by my boss if I decide not to use this model.
Decisions based on the computer system will be better.
The results of the computer system are needed now.
The computer system is important to me.
I need the computer system.
It is important that the computer system be used soon.
This project is important to my boss.
The computer system should be put into use immediately.
It is urgent that the computer system be implemented.
The sooner the computer system is in use the better.
Benefits will outweigh the costs.

Dependent Variables

1. Please circle the number on the scale below that indicates the probability that you will use the computer system.

   0   .1   .2   .3   .4   .5   .6   .7   .8   .9   1.0

2. Please circle the number on the scale below that indicates the probability that others will use the computer system.

   0   .1   .2   .3   .4   .5   .6   .7   .8   .9   1.0

3. Please circle the number on the scale below that indicates the probability that the computer system will be a success.

   0   .1   .2   .3   .4   .5   .6   .7   .8   .9   1.0

4. On the 10-point scale below indicate your evaluation of the worth of the computer system.

Not useful at all				Moderately useful					Excellent
1	2	3	4	5	6	7	8	9	10

5. Please circle the number on the scale below that indicates the level of accuracy you expect from the computer system.

Not useful at all				Moderately useful					Excellent
1	2	3	4	5	6	7	8	9	10

SOURCE: Adapted from R. L. Schultz & D. P. Slevin (1975), "Implementation and Organizational Validity: An Empirical Investigation," in R. L. Schultz & D. P. Slevin (Eds.), *Implementing Operations Research/Management Science* (New York: American Elsevier), pp. 153-182. Scales were determined by factor analysis. (Used by permission.)

4. Scales Adapted From Survey of Organizations

This section asks about learning to use the system. Use the following codes to indicate your response:

1 = Strongly disagree
2 = Disagree
3 = Slightly disagree
4 = Neutral

5 = Slightly agree
6 = Agree
7 = Strongly agree

Please indicate the extent to which you agree with the following statements:

1. I attend regular meetings where we talk about
   how to use the system. 1 2 3 4 5 6 7

2. Organizational policies generally discourage me
   from developing new procedures or uses of the system. 1 2 3 4 5 6 7

3. I receive praise for developing new ways to use the
   system to accomplish my job or to solve problems
   using the system . . .
   —from my supervisor 1 2 3 4 5 6 7
   —from my coworkers 1 2 3 4 5 6 7

4. I generally do not have time to learn or experiment
   with possible new procedures or uses of the system. 1 2 3 4 5 6 7

5. My co-workers and/or I develop new procedures
   or uses of the system. 1 2 3 4 5 6 7

6. Other people do not generally encourage me to
   experiment with new procedures or uses of the system. 1 2 3 4 5 6 7

7. I talk about ways to use the system to accomplish
   my job or solve problems . . .
   —with my supervisor 1 2 3 4 5 6 7
   —with my co-workers 1 2 3 4 5 6 7

SOURCE: Adapted from J. C. Taylor & D. G. Bowers (1972), *Survey of Organizations: A Machine Scored Standardized Questionnaire Instrument* (Ann Arbor: Institute for Social Research, University of Michigan).
NOTE: The variables were interpretable in 2 factors. Questions 1, 3, 5, and 7 comprise Factor 1—Work Group Communication About the Computer. Questions 2, 4, and 6 comprise Factor 2—Organizational Support for Implementation. Cronbach's coefficient alpha for Factor 1 when the variables were added = .88; Factor 2 = .61. See Aydin & Rice (1991, 1992) for details.

5. Examples of Short Global User Satisfaction Measures

Single-Item Measure

Use the following codes to indicate your response:

1 = Strongly disagree	5 = Slightly agree
2 = Disagree	6 = Agree
3 = Slightly disagree	7 = Strongly agree
4 = Neutral	

How much do you agree with the following statement about the system?

The new computer system is worth the time
and effort required to use it.   1 2 3 4 5 6 7

Use the following code to indicate your response:

1 = Significantly decreased	5 = Slightly increased
2 = Decreased	6 = Increased
3 = Slightly decreased	7 = Significantly increased
4 = No change, no opinion	

Overall, to what extent has the system changed these two aspects of *your own* department?

Ease of performing our department's work	1 2 3 4 5 6 7
Quality of our department's work	1 2 3 4 5 6 7

SOURCE: C. E. Aydin & R. E. Rice (1991), "Social worlds, individual differences, and implementation: Predicting attitudes toward a medical information system." (*Information and Management, 20*, 119-136).
NOTE: Single-item measure test-retest reliability on same questionnaire in different context is .73. Cronbach's alpha for three items combined is .83.

6. Instruments to Assess Employee Adaptation

Use Scale

How frequently have you had problems with the MIS since implementation?
1. All day long everyday
2. Several times a day
3. About once a day
4. Several times a week
5. Once a week or less

If you could do away with the MIS and go back to the old way of doing things, would you?

1. Yes

2. No

How frequently do you find it necessary to bypass the MIS and use the old way of doing things?

1. All day long everyday

2. Several times a day

3. About once a day

4. Several times a week

5. Once a week or less

How frequently do you feel like hitting the MIS terminal or breaking a light pen?

1. All day long everyday

2. Several times a day

3. About once a day

4. Several times a week

5. Once a week or less

6. Never

Change Scale

How has the MIS changed your job?

This MIS has made my job:

more difficult	1 7	easier
more interesting	1 7	less interesting
less stressful	1 7	more stressful
more fun	1 7	less fun
more pleasant	1 7	less pleasant

Behavioral Scale

Please rate the frequency with which this employee has exhibited the following behaviors with regard to the MIS (1 = never, 2 = occasionally, 3 = fairly frequently, 4 = very frequently):

1. Praising the MIS

2. Difficulty learning to use the MIS

3. Very cooperative with MIS personnel

4. Complaining about the MIS

5. A high level of proficiency learning to use the MIS

6. Lack of cooperation with the MIS personnel

7. Improved work performance
8. Increased absenteeism or tardiness
9. Using the MIS appropriately
10. Slowing work performance
11. Enjoying working on the MIS
12. Bypassing the MIS, i.e., using pre-MIS procedures to do things

Scoring

Use Scale: Responses to the items were summed to derive a total score. Cronbach alpha was .79.

Change Scale: Responses to items 2 through 5 were reversed and then the five items were summed to derive a total change score. Cronbach alpha was .82.

Behavioral Scale: All of the negative items are reversed and a total score computed. Cronbach Alpha was .80.

SOURCE: K. H. Kjerulff, M. A. Counte, J. S. Salloway, & B. C. Campbell (1981), "Understanding employee reactions to a medical information system," in *Proceedings of the Fifth Annual Symposium on Computer Applications in Medical Care (pp. 802-805).* Los Angeles, CA: IEEE Computer Society Press.

7. Laboratory Computer Impact Survey

The next set of questions asks about how things have changed since the introduction of the laboratory computer system. Please base your answers on what it is like now, not on how it was when the computer system was installed. Please answer as best as you can, even if you weren't here when the computer was installed.

External Communication (coefficient alpha = .62; mean response = 3.37)
The computer makes it easier to route samples to the appropriate laboratory.
Computerized lab records aid communication between the lab and other personnel.
The computer system improves the relationship between the labs and other medical personnel.

Service Outcomes (coefficient alpha = .84; mean response = 3.13)
We provide better service because of the computer.
We should have gotten a computer system a long time ago.
The computer helps make the labs better managed.
Overall, reports from my lab are more accurate now than before the computer was installed.
Test reports are more accurate because they have to be entered into the computer.
Because of the computer there is better interpretive information provided with test reports.

Personal Intentions (coefficient alpha = .53; mean response = 4.30)
I plan to avoid using the computer system as much as possible. (R)

I plan to use the computer system as much as possible.

Personal Hassles (coefficient alpha = .86; mean response = 2.68)

The number of phone calls I answer has increased.

Since the computer was installed my work is more satisfying than it used to be. (R)

The computer makes it harder to meet all the demands placed on me.

Because of the computer I now have more work to do.

The computer has changed my job from being a technologist to being a clerk.

My responsibilities have increased because of the computer.

Our work is slowed down because we have to do data entry.

We have to find ways around the computer in order to get our work done.

Increased Blame (coefficient alpha = .87; mean response = 2.71)

People call the lab now with more problems and questions that I wish I didn't have to deal with.

Since the computer was installed people in the labs are getting blamed for problems that aren't really their fault.

Doctors and nurses complain to us more now that we have the computer.

We now do a lot of work CPA (specimen intake) did.

We get blamed for CPA's mistakes.

The computer people run the labs now.

Doctors and nurses cooperate with us less than they did before the computer.

I don't think doctors and nurses like the computer system.

The computer system causes ill will toward the labs.

Response Scale: Range from 1 to 5: 1 = Strongly disagree, 3 = Neutral, 5 = Strongly agree. (R) indicates reverse scoring.

SOURCES: B. Kaplan & D. Duchon (1987), *A qualitative and quantitative investigation of a computer system's impact on work in clinical laboratories* (unpublished manuscript); B. Kaplan & D. Duchon (1989), "A job orientation model of impact on work seven months post implementation," in *Proceedings of Medinfo 89: Sixth World Congress on Medical Informatics* (pp. 1051-1055). Amsterdam: North-Holland.
NOTE: Questions concerning personal intentions were adapted from Kjerulff et al. (1982), "Predicting employee adaptation to the implementation of a medical information system," in *Proceedings of the Sixth Annual Symposium on Computer Applications in Medical Care* (pp. 392-397). Silver Springs, MD: IEEE Computer Society.

8. Perceived Desirability of Computer Applications in Medicine

As the use of computers in medicine increases, it is reasonable to expect both positive and negative consequences from these uses. Although the manner in which any of these applications is implemented may influence their desirability, we are interested in your assessment of the overall desirability of the uses, independent of any specific implementation.

The following are various actual or potential applications of computers to medicine. Please indicate how desirable for the field of medicine you feel the following applications are by indicating your response on the following scale:

5 = Very desirable (VD)
4 = Desirable (D)
3 = Neutral (N)
2 = Undesirable (U)
1 = Very undesirable (VU)

Factor I: Patient Care

1. Medical information systems (MIS) such as the Technicon system currently implemented at Methodist Hospital
2. Computerized patient disease registries (e.g., tumor registries)
4. As a source of results of clinical trials, studies, and case reports. The results could be accessed online at a terminal and relevant information printed
5. Outpatient monitoring with a device such as a Holter monitor, for example
6. Computerized storage of permanent medical records to replace the current paper system. The record would then be accessible through a computer terminal
11. The computer as a source of summaries of published papers so a physician could scan them at a terminal to assess the relevance of papers to his practice

Factor II: Medical Decision Making

3. To provide a probability estimate of whether the correct diagnosis has been made given the patient's clinical data
7. Permit access to a database that provides probability estimates of side effects and morbidity of various treatment options
8. Permit access to a database that provides the probability of a successful outcome for various treatment options

Factor III: Physician Substitute

9. For use in continuing medical education as an alternative to traveling to classes and seminars. Lectures would be presented on videotape and certification exams taken on a microcomputer
10. A computer system where the patient would sit down at a computer terminal and enter his or her medical history in response to questions presented on the screen
12. A system where allied health personnel would do the initial diagnostic work-up on a patient and enter the information into a computer. On the basis of this information, the computer program would recommend whether the patient's symptoms warrant seeing the physician or not
13. For use as a physician substitute to provide diagnosis and treatment recommendations for use by paramedical personnel. For example, MYCIN is a program designed to advise nonexperts in the selection of antibiotic therapies for infectious diseases

Perceived Effects of Computers on Medical Practice

We are also interested in the consequences you anticipate as the use of computers as diagnostic and therapeutic aids in medicine increases. Please indicate how strongly you agree or disagree with the following statements by indicating your response on the following scale:

5 = Strongly agree (SA)
4 = Agree (A)
3 = Undecided (U)
2 = Disagree (D)
1 = Strongly disagree (SD)

Clinical Computer Applications:

Factor I: Cost and Quality

Will slow the rising rate of hospital costs by permitting easier monitoring of tests and procedures recommended by physicians

Will slow the rising rate of hospital costs by reducing the need for some clerical and ancillary personnel

Will improve the technical quality of health care by making available to the physician current information about optimum tests, procedures, and treatment plans

Will make health care more generally available by reducing overall costs

Will improve the quality of medical education through computer-based instruction, which allows medical students to learn and review material at their own speed and convenience

Will be assigned the more tedious and time-consuming tasks allowing physicians to devote more time and attention to the patient as a person

Factor II: Physician Autonomy

Will increase government control of physicians' practices because physicians' practices and their decisions may be more easily monitored as computerized record-keeping increases

Will increase hospital control of physicians' practices because physicians' decisions and practices may be more easily monitored

Will threaten personal and professional privacy because computerized records may be less secure

Will result in serious legal and ethical problems as the use of medical diagnostic and decision-making programs by physicians increases

Factor III: Physician's Role

Will probably be hard for physicians to learn to use

Will result in reliance on cookbook medicine and diminish physician judgment

Will depersonalize medical practice

Will alienate physicians from their patients because of electronic gadgetry

Will result in less efficient use of physician time because using a computer tends to be very time-consuming

Will threaten the physician's self-image as a decision maker if computers become a diagnostic aid

Will diminish the patient's image of the physician if the physician is seen using a diagnostic aid

Will tend to reduce patients' satisfaction with the quality of health care that they perceive they receive

Will be based on quantifiable information while qualitative information will be ignored

Factor IV: Medical Manpower

Will reduce the need for paraprofessionals

Will reduce the need for primary care physicians

Will reduce the need for specialists

Factor V: Organization

Will result in allied health personnel performing some duties now performed by physicians

Will cause a shift in medical education from an almost exclusive emphasis on the physical and biological sciences toward an emphasis on the social and psychological aspects of health care

Will reduce the primary care physician's reliance on specialists

Will embody value-judgments concerning therapy that may not be readily apparent to the physician-user of the system

Will decentralize health care by allowing physicians access to sophisticated medical technology normally available only at hospitals

Will make it necessary (through passwords) to limit access to diagnostic and therapeutic programs only to physicians specially trained in their use

SOURCE: J. G. Anderson, S. J. Jay, H. M. Schweer, & M. M. Anderson (1986), "Why Doctors Don't Use Computers: Some Empirical Findings," *Journal of the Royal Society of Medicine, 79*, pp. 142-144.

9. Work Role Activities

Each subject is asked how they spent their time yesterday (in hours and minutes). They are also asked if that time period was a typical working day: Very typical, Somewhat typical, Not at all typical. The proportion of time on each activity is calculated by summing their total work time in minutes and dividing the reported minutes spent on each activity by that sum. Data are collected before and after implementation of a computer system: Before implementation, 6 months after implementation, 1 year after implementation.

Activities:
Talking on the telephone
Filling out forms
Talking with patients and families
Extraneous paperwork
Helping other departments acquire information
Talking with co-workers
Data processing
Traveling around the hospital
Attendance at meetings

SOURCE: M. A. Counte, K. H. Kjerulff, J. C. Salloway, & B. C. Campbell (1984), "Implementing Computerization in Hospitals: A Case Study of the Behavioral and Attitudinal Impacts of a Medical Information System," *Journal of Organizational Behavior Management, 6,* pp. 109-122.

10. Network Survey

This question is a little different. Your answers will help describe how some jobs are related to other jobs. Again, we assure you that your answers will be kept completely confidential. Please indicate: *How frequently, on the average, do you have significant discussions with other SHS personnel about how you accomplish your work?* For each person, please circle the number that best indicates the frequency of those discussions:

0 = Not once in the past year
1 = Once a month or so
2 = Several times a month
3 = Every week
4 = Several times a week
5 = Every day
6 = Several times a day

The names and units of all personnel are listed in alphabetical order in the first two columns. For example:

Personnel	Unit	Never	Month	Times/Mo.	Week	Times/Wk.	Day	Times/Day
Jones, J.	Lab	0	1	2	3	4	5	6
Smith	Admin	0	1	2	3	4	5	6
West	Clinic	0	1	2	3	4	5	6
Etc.								

SOURCE: R. E. Rice & C. E. Aydin (1991), "Attitudes Toward New Organizational Technology: Network Proximity as a Mechanism for Social Information Processing," *Administrative Science Quarterly, 36,* pp. 219-244.

11. Communication Between Departments

This survey asks you to think about communication between your area and other departments in the medical center. Please circle only one answer *on each line*. All responses will be CONFIDENTIAL.

How often do you usually speak to someone from each of the following departments on the telephone?

	Many Times a Day	A Few Times a Day	Once a Day	A Few Times a Week	Once a Week	Never
Admitting	6	5	4	3	2	1
Radiology	6	5	4	3	2	1
Etc.						

(Add additional departments to list)

SOURCE: C. E. Aydin, *Computerized Order Entry in a Large Medical Center: Evaluating Interactions Between Departments* (see Chapter 12 of this book).
NOTE: Test-retest reliabilities for Admitting = .79, Radiology = .80, from beginning to end of 3-hour class on order entry.

12. Job Design Questionnaire

Here are some statements about your job. How much do you agree or disagree with each?

1 = Strongly disagree	5 = Slightly agree
2 = Disagree	6 = Agree
3 = Slightly disagree	7 = Strongly agree
4 = Undecided	

My job:

1. provides much variety   1 2 3 4 5 6 7
2. permits me to be left on my own to do my own work   1 2 3 4 5 6 7
3. is arranged so that I often have the opportunity to see
   jobs or projects through to completion   1 2 3 4 5 6 7
4. provides feedback on how well I am doing as I am
   working   1 2 3 4 5 6 7
5. is relatively significant in our organization   1 2 3 4 5 6 7
6. gives me considerable opportunity for independence
   and freedom in how I do my work   1 2 3 4 5 6 7
7. gives me the opportunity to do a number of
   different things   1 2 3 4 5 6 7
8. provides me an opportunity to find out how
   well I am doing   1 2 3 4 5 6 7
9. is very significant or important in the broader
   scheme of things   1 2 3 4 5 6 7
10. provides an opportunity for independent thought
    and action   1 2 3 4 5 6 7
11. provides me with a great deal of variety at work   1 2 3 4 5 6 7

12. is arranged so that I have the opportunity to
    complete the work I start   1 2 3 4 5 6 7
13. provides me with the feeling that I know whether
    I am performing well or poorly   1 2 3 4 5 6 7
14. is arranged so that I have the chance to do a job from
    the beginning to the end (i.e., a chance to do the
    whole job)   1 2 3 4 5 6 7
15. is one where a lot of other people can be affected
    by how well the work gets done   1 2 3 4 5 6 7

Scoring

Skill variety: Questions 1, 7, 11
Task identity: Questions 3, 12, 14
Task significance: Questions 5, 9, 15
Autonomy: Questions 2, 6, 10
Feedback about results: Questions 4, 8, 13

A total score for each job dimension is computed by adding the responses for the three items for a total score ranging from 3 (low) to 21 (high).

SOURCE: T. G. Cummings & E. F. Huse (1989), *Organization Development and Change* (4th ed., St. Paul, MN: West), p. 92. Reprinted by permission of T. Cummings, University of Southern California.

13. Job Satisfaction

Use the following codes to indicate your response:

1 = Strongly dissatisfied
2 = Dissatisfied
3 = Neutral or No opinion
4 = Satisfied
5 = Strongly satisfied

How satisfied are you with:

The nature of the work you perform?   1 2 3 4 5
The person who supervises you—your organizational superior?   1 2 3 4 5
Your relations with others in the organization with whom you   1 2 3 4 5
    work—your co-workers?
The pay you receive for your job?   1 2 3 4 5
The opportunities that exist in this organization for   1 2 3 4 5
    advancement—with promotion?

Scoring

Sum into one global job satisfaction index.

Test-retest reliability over 14 days for individual items involving 36 secretaries ranged from .71 to .73; for overall sum, .83. Convergent validity correlations, compared to Job Descriptive Index (JDI) and Minnesota Importance Questionnaire (MSQ) for 308 public utility employees and 96 middle managers of a transport company were from .59 to .80. (See Cook et al., 1981, for details of JDI and MSQ.) Discriminant validity showed 100% of directional comparisons and Kendall's W showed .72 to .90 for patterns across different items by methods. Criterion validity showed nearly identical correlations as JDI to task structure, group cohesiveness, and supervisory consideration.

SOURCE: C. Schriesheim & A. Tsui (1981), *Development and Validation of a Short Satisfaction Measure for Use in Survey Feedback Interventions* (paper presented at the Academy of Management Western Region Meeting, April 1981).

5

Experimental Research Methods for Evaluating Health Care Information Systems

James G. Anderson
Stephen J. Jay

Introduction

The major purpose of this chapter is to outline how experimental research methods can be used to evaluate health care information systems. Experimental research methods are characterized by the following: The research is conducted in a laboratory or an applied setting. If possible, subjects are assigned to treatment and control groups on a random basis. One or more independent variables are manipulated by the investigator (an *independent variable* is a variable that is manipulated by the investigator, such as the provision of clinical reminders to the physicians). As far as possible, control is exercised over other variables that might affect the outcome. One or more dependent variables or outcomes are measured (e.g., whether the physician responds to the clinical reminder) (Fromkin & Streufert, 1976; Stone, 1978). Three different types of experimental research strategies are discussed and illustrated: laboratory experiments, quasi-experiments or field experiments, and computer simulation experiments. These approaches differ in the amount of control the investigator has over subjects, the research setting, and the generalizability of the findings to real-world organizational environments.

Each of these research strategies is designed to provide answers to research questions as validly and economically as possible. Research questions are stated as specific hypotheses to be empirically tested. The research design specifies which variables to manipulate, the type and number of observations to be made, and how the data are to be analyzed.

Before the investigator can conclude that the experimental variable or condition has caused the outcome, a number of other reasons for the relationship between the independent and dependent variable must be ruled out. Change in the outcome measure may have occurred even in the absence of the experimental manipulation. *Internal validity* refers to the confidence that the investigator has that the experimental variables or interventions caused the observed changes in the outcome measures (Campbell & Stanley, 1966).

The research design helps the investigator control the variance of the outcome measures due to various sources. First, the investigator must conduct the research so that the experimental and control conditions are as different from one another as possible. This is necessary in order to detect whether or not experimental and control conditions have significantly different effects on the dependent variable or outcome measure. Second, the design attempts to control for the influence of extraneous variables that may also affect the outcome measures. This usually involves choosing homogeneous subjects, random assignment of subjects to experimental and control groups, matching subjects on important characteristics, and incorporating selected extraneous variables into the research design as attributes. Third, the research design attempts to minimize error variance. These fluctuations in the level of the outcome measures are due to individual difference among the subjects and to errors of measurement (Kerlinger, 1986). The ways the research design controls the variance of the outcome measure determine the internal validity of the study.

In designing experimental research there is a trade-off between the need to control the various factors that may affect the outcome measure and thus are threats to the internal validity of the study and the desire to generalize the study's findings beyond the immediate experimental situation (Mason, 1989). Control is usually achieved by isolating certain aspects of the process to be investigated and manipulating some of those aspects in a systematic fashion in a carefully designed artificial environment or setting.

This concern of the investigator for generalizability of the research findings has been termed the *external validity* of the research by Campbell and Stanley (1966). Some of the questions that need to be asked are: How well does the experiment describe the real process that is being investigated? How valid are the operational measures of the independent and dependent variables? To what population of subjects can

TABLE 5.1 Comparison of Different Research Strategies on Control and Generalizability

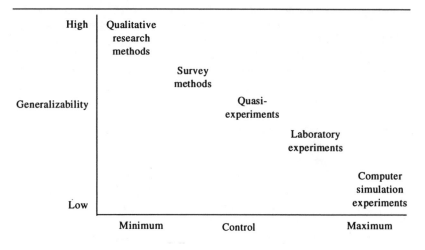

the results be generalized? How representative is the experimental setting of the actual organizational setting of the information system?

In general, the research strategies discussed in this chapter and earlier ones vary in the amount of control that the investigator exercises over the variable or variables whose effects are being studied, the subjects who participate in the study, and the setting in which the study is undertaken. These methods also vary significantly in the generalizability of research findings to real organizational settings. Table 5.1 compares several major research methods on these two dimensions.

Computer simulation experiments, which involve the manipulation of mathematical or logical models of the phenomenon under investigation, permit the most control over the research environment and the factors or variables whose effects are being studied. However, computer models are high-level abstractions of the process under investigation and lack important features of the actual organizational settings. Thus, the generalizability of the findings from such models needs to be carefully established.

Experiments in laboratory situations share similar characteristics. They accord the investigator manipulative control over variables under investigation and control over extraneous factors that may influence the outcomes, but they, too, omit important features of the real-world environment.

Quasi-experiments can be performed when the system being evaluated cannot be adequately studied in a laboratory setting. Although this research design does not allow the investigator to control many of the extraneous factors that may affect the outcome measures, it does provide findings that are more generalizable to the actual organizational setting when alternative explanations for the findings can be ruled out.

Finally, surveys (see Chapter 4 of this book) and qualitative methods (see Chapter 3), if designed appropriately, produce the most generalizable findings because they involve systematic study of individuals and/or organizational units in natural settings (Jenkins, 1985).

Laboratory experiments should always include qualitative research methods as well. Qualitative methods can be used to illuminate the context in which the experiment is conducted. These approaches may uncover situational factors and site-specific influences that help the investigator to validly interpret the experimental results or to account for unexplained and inconsistent outcomes. The use of complementary qualitative techniques is especially important when conducting quasi-experimental studies in which there is less control over the experimental setting and the investigator may be unable to randomly assign subjects to treatment and control groups (Cook & Campbell, 1979).

Laboratory Experiments

Laboratory experiments permit the investigator to completely determine the nature and timing of the experimental or independent variables. Also, a great deal of control can be exercised over extraneous variables that may threaten the internal validity of the study. This is usually accomplished by performing the study in a research environment that is isolated from the usual organizational setting. Also, experimental variables or conditions can be systematically manipulated under controlled conditions that largely eliminate the effects of extraneous variables that might also affect the outcome measures (Kerlinger, 1986).

Even though a high degree of control over the experimental setting can be exercised in the laboratory, several threats to internal validity still exist. Subjects are aware of the nature of the study. Also, the researcher's expectations and cues may affect the subjects response (Argyris, 1980; Cook & Campbell, 1979; Fromkin & Streufert, 1976; Orne, 1962). Another major weakness of laboratory experiments has to do with external validity. Laboratory environments are artificial and lack the reality of organizational settings. Usually only a few variables can be included. Also, effects of experimental variables are generally weaker in the laboratory than in real life. Consequently, the range of situations to which the findings are applicable are limited (Stone, 1978).

Laboratory experiments may serve a number of purposes. They may be used to test specific features of an information system while it is under development. Gould (1985) describes how a series of small individual changes can be made and evaluated using small groups of subjects and laboratory experiments.

A second major purpose of laboratory experiments is to test predictions from theories or inferences from other studies about the effects of information systems under controlled, unconfounded conditions. Furthermore, laboratory experimental methods can be used to design and carry out a series of experiments by manipulating a few critical variables at a time. The cumulative findings of these studies may provide important insights into the impacts of information systems (Benbasat, 1989a).

Benbasat (1989b) reviews information system experiments on individual decision makers. A series of studies examined the effects of user characteristics and individual differences on individual performance and attitudes toward information systems. Variables studied included decision making or cognitive style, personality variables, and demographic characteristics. Another set of studies reviewed involved experiments comparing information presentation formats. A more recent set of experimental studies has investigated the influence of decision-support systems on decision performance (for reviews, see Benbasat & Nault, 1990; Sharda, Barr, & McDonnell, 1988).

Laboratory experiments can also be used to study the effects of information systems on small group activities and performance. DeSanctis (1989) suggests three reasons why this line of research is important. First, work groups are the basic unit of organizations in which individuals exchange information, coordinate efforts, and provide support and motivation for one another. Second, group decision-support technology increasingly is being utilized in organizations. Its impact on group interaction and performance needs to be evaluated (Kraemer & King, 1988). Third, information systems could be designed to support group activities and functions other than providing structured information.

Small groups in organizations serve many purposes, for example, information exchange, social involvement, political representation, coordination of individual efforts, and conflict resolution. These functions are performed through interpersonal exchange of information, as well as of goods and services. Information systems have the potential to significantly influence the structure and functioning of these work groups (Goodman, 1986). DeSanctis (1989) suggests that the introduction of an information system alters the amount, type, and meaning of information and the networks through which it is exchanged. It is critical that investigators attempt to better understand how these organizational interventions bring about changes in group structure, tasks, goals, and power relationships.

DeSanctis (1989) suggests that another important function of laboratory experiments is to ask "What if" questions. Applications and system designs tested in the laboratory may then be put into practice. Some examples of this are the development of automated planning methods that can be used by groups within the organization (Nunamaker, Applegate, & Konsynski, 1987), the development of information systems as a medium for conflict resolution (Poole, Homes, & DeSanctis, 1988), and interpersonal influence (Zigurs, Poole, & DeSanctis, 1988).

When combined with qualitative process analysis techniques, laboratory experiments can provide a great deal of detailed data for developers and evaluators of information systems. Process analysis examines the sequence of behavioral and cognitive activities involved in the use of information systems. These methods include discourse coding to classify the events that take place; behavior ratings applied to audio tapes, videotapes, computer logs, and so on; information analysis based on interviews with subjects; and prompted reviews in which users are interviewed as they review their actions and decisions (DeSanctis, 1989). These methods have been used to analyze both individual (Todd & Benbasat, 1987) and group (Poole et al., 1987; Zigurs et al., 1988) use of information systems.

Physician Response to Computer Reminders

McDonald et al. (1984) provide an example of an experimental study designed to determine the effect of clinical reminders provided by the Regenstrief Medical Record System. The computerized medical record contained physician-authored rules that can remind physicians of patient conditions that need attention. These reminders include preventive care (e.g., occult blood testing); prophylactic treatment (e.g., use of beta blockers to prevent sudden death after myocardial infarction); and active treatment (e.g., treatment of congestive heart failure). The computer system used these rules to review each patient's computerized medical record the day before each visit.

Physicians assigned to the experimental or treatment group received computer-based reminders on patients assigned to them in a general medicine clinic. Physicians assigned to the control group did not receive reminders for their patients. There were no significant differences between patients cared for by physicians in the experimental and control groups with respect to the number of clinic visits or hospitalization during the study period. The dependent or outcome measure was the physician's rate of response to the clinical indications that stimulated the computer reminders. The 61 physicians assigned to the experimental group who received reminders responded to 49% of these indications. The 54 physicians assigned to the control group that did not receive computer reminders responded to only 29% of the indications. The investigators concluded that computer reminders had a strong and persistent effect on patient care.

Other studies by Tierney, McDonald, and their colleagues (1987, 1988, 1990, 1993) of the effect of providing computer-based information on physicians' orders for diagnostic tests provide excellent examples of the application of experimental research designs.

Study of the Training Effects of ILIAD, a Diagnostic Expert System

Another example of this research strategy is provided by a study of ILIAD's (a diagnostic expert system) ability to teach medical students better diagnostic and problem-solving skills (Turner et al., 1991). The subjects were 75 third-year medical students in the 1990-1991 class at the University of Utah. After an initial orientation with ILIAD, students were required to complete one simulated training case and one test case each week for 5 weeks.

Ten different simulated test cases with diagnostic problems were created. Five cases represented relatively prevalent or Common cases (e.g., myocardial infarction); five represented Uncommon cases (e.g., multiple sclerosis). Each week, all students received a test case that had the same final diagnosis as the previous week's learning case (Trained) or an unrelated case (Untrained). Students alternated between Trained and Untrained cases. Four different dependent variables were used: (1) errors of the final diagnostic hypotheses, (2) completeness of the workup, (3) cost of the workup, and (4) the average hypothesis score.

Students experienced significantly fewer diagnostic errors on Trained than on Untrained cases. The difference between Common and Uncommon cases was not significant. Results for the cost variable indicated that subjects completed the workups with lower cost in the Trained than the Untrained conditions. The investigators concluded that the findings support their hypothesis that the problem-solving performance of medical students can be improved through experience with ILIAD's simulated patients.

Quasi-Experiments

Quasi-experiments are studies conducted in an actual organizational environment where certain variables are systematically manipulated. At the same time, the investigator exercises as much control over the variable and the experimental conditions as is feasible. Control, however, is rarely, if ever, as thorough as in laboratory experiments (Kerlinger, 1986). This research strategy is particularly useful because many aspects of the interaction of information systems with individuals and work groups in the organizational setting cannot be adequately studied in the laboratory.

Quasi-experiments are a compromise between laboratory experiments and surveys and unobtrusive qualitative research techniques. A major difference between these approaches is the degree to which the investigator is able to incorporate randomness and experimental control into the investigation (Blackburn, 1987; Caporaso, 1973; Stone, 1978). Campbell and Stanley (1966) point out that there are many research situations in which a quasi-experimental design can be used to guide the assignment of individuals or groups to experimental and control conditions, the scheduling of the experimental manipulation, and the collection and analysis of data. In carrying out the study, the investigator attempts to preserve as many of the features of a laboratory experiment as possible.

Lack of control over many variables that may contaminate the effects of the experimental manipulation is a major weakness of quasi-experiments. Frequently the investigator must work with intact groups and cannot randomly assign individuals to experimental and control groups. Also, there are usually many environmental factors over which there is little or no control because the study is conducted in a natural organizational setting. When random assignment is not possible, it is essential that multiple groups be used and measures be taken before and after the experimental intervention is introduced. This permits the investigator to assess differences in the magnitude of any changes that take place between treatment and control groups (Zmud, Olson, & Hauser, 1989).

There are several major advantages of this research strategy. First, quasi-experiments provide a useful means of answering practical questions and testing theories about the impact of information systems. In general, the more natural the setting for the study, the more generalizable the findings to the real organizational environment. A second advantage is that quasi-experiments can be used to study complex social and organizational processes that are difficult to study in the laboratory. Third, experimental effects are usually stronger in a quasi-experiment than in the laboratory. This is partly due to the fact that studies that are per- formed in the actual operational setting are not viewed as artificial by participants (Blackburn, 1987; Cook & Campbell, 1979; Kerlinger, 1986; Stone, 1978).

Despite the advantages of this methodological approach, a recent review of the information system, communication, and organizational behavior literature revealed only seven studies that have used quasi-experimental methods. These are reviewed by Zmud et al. (1989).

Evaluation of the Implementation of the HELP System

Lundsgaarde, Gardner, and Menlove (1989) provide an example of the use of quasi-experimental research design that was used to evaluate the implementation of the HELP system (Kuperman, Gardner, & Pryor, 1991) at the McKay-Dee Hospital in Ogden, Utah. The purpose of the evaluation was to measure the performance of the system and to assess provider attitudes toward the future expectations regarding the new computerized system. The evaluation effort was formative in that it was designed to facilitate the adoption and utilization of the system.

The study design used was a quasi-experiment. Clinical and ancillary units within the McKay-Dee Hospital that were not automated during the initial implementation phase and wards at the LDS Hospital that had been automated earlier were designated as control units. They were compared to experimental units at the McKay-Dee Hospital that were to receive the HELP system. The hypothesis was that implementation and utilization of the new computerized clinical system would result in significant benefits to patient care. Questionnaires were designed and administered to providers before and after implementation of the computerized medical information system.

Results from the pre-implementation data were used to identify barriers to implementation and to find effective ways to overcome them. In general, all three categories of providers, physicians, nurses, and staff indicated a preference for training by colleagues using actual clinical data. As a result arrangements were made for McKay-Dee Hospital professionals to visit their counterparts at the LDS Hospital for tutorial sessions with the HELP system. Also, all subgroups of potential users agreed on priorities of system features. The greatest interest was evidenced in alerts, warnings about potentially dangerous situations such as medication interactions or critical laboratory results; rapid communication of tests results from laboratories and ancillary services; cost reduction through elimination of duplicate tests; and redundant data entry.

Modifying Physicians' Order Entry Patterns

A recent study by Anderson, Jay, Perry, and Anderson (1990) utilized a quasi-experimental design or a field experiment to change the way that physicians enter orders into a hospital information system. This study appears in this book as Chapter 13. The model of change that motivated the study was based on social network theory (see Chapter 6 of this book). This theory holds that individuals who share similar positions in the interpersonal network of an organization will largely interact with the same group of individuals. As a result, they will share similar beliefs, attitudes, and behavior. Both interaction and competition among these individuals will motivate them to adopt an innovation soon after their colleagues who share similar positions in the organization do so.

Based on this model, a quasi-experiment was carried out at Methodist Hospital of Indiana, a 1120-bed private teaching hospital that had implemented a TDS HC4000 hospital information system. Written medical orders could be entered into the system by unit secretaries or physician assistants using generic menus built into the system software. As an alternative, physicians could create personal order sets tailored to their specific patients. It was hypothesized that use of these order sets would result in fewer transcription errors, decreased clerical work, and faster laboratory results reporting.

For the study, 109 physicians on the following hospital services were selected as the experimental group: cardiovascular disease, general surgery, obstetrics and gynecology, and orthopedic surgery. Ten other services with 231 physicians were selected as a control group. STRUCTURE, a network analysis program, was used to analyze information system data on consultation networks among physicians on the experimental services. Influential physicians were identified on these services and meetings were held to inform them of the advantages of using personal order sets for order entry into the medical information system.

Data on system use were collected on all services both before and at two points after the experimental treatment. It was hypothesized that if the influential physicians increased their system use, other physicians and personnel on the experimental services would also increase their usage.

The results of the study indicated that there were significant differences between the experimental and control groups. In general, a greater number of orders per patient were entered on the experimental services using personal order sets. Also, there were significant differences among the hospital personnel who entered medical orders into the hospital information system. The most orders were entered by unit secretaries; the least by physicians. Also, the use of personal order sets on the experimental services by physicians, unit secretaries, and physician assistants increased significantly over time. The results of the study suggest that interventions that utilize communication networks among physicians are an effective means of influencing physicians and other hospital personnel in the way they use a medical information system.

Modifying Physicians' Test Ordering Behavior

A second quasi-experiment was conducted by Anderson, Jay, Zimmerer, Farid, and Anderson (1990) to evaluate the use of structured order forms designed to be used with a medical information system to reduce the ordering of unnecessary outpatient tests. The study was performed in two outpatient clinics at Methodist Hospital of Indiana. Structured order forms were developed containing explicit criteria for ordering the following common tests: (1) urinalysis, (2) complete blood count (CBC), (3) and chemistry-23. The forms required physicians to indicate a reason for ordering the test. Data were collected from the laboratory information system during a 9-month baseline period and a 2-month intervention period. Differences in test ordering were examined between the baseline and intervention periods, between second- and third-year residents, and between the Adult Ambulatory Care Center, staffed by internal medicine residents, and the Family Practice Center, staffed by family practice residents.

Test ordering rates for chemistry-23 remained fairly constant in both clinics during the two periods. Use of the order form appears to have had no significant effect on the ordering of this test battery. However, the rate of CBCs ordered declined significantly on both clinics during the 2-month intervention period. Also, the number of urinalyses ordered in the family practice clinic decreased significantly during the intervention period. Overall, the reduction in tests that resulted from the use of structured order forms resulted in cost savings of $4,000 for the 2-month period.

Computer Simulation Experiments

Computer simulation experiments involve the manipulation of mathematical and logical models that describe the behavior of individuals and the organization in response to an information system (Naylor, 1969; Naylor, Balintfy, Burdick, & Chu, 1966). The principal difference between this methodology and laboratory or quasi-experiments is that the experiment is conducted with a mathematical model of the system rather than in the actual organizational setting or with a laboratory representation of it.

Simulation offers an excellent means of studying the operational effectiveness of an information system. Using a model, the system can be studied without interfering with the actual operation of the system or the organizational environment. Moreover, simulation models can be used to study the complex interaction of patients, staff, facilities, services, and information so integral to health care organizations.

Computer simulation models have the highest level of internal validity. Independent and dependent variables and their relationships are included in the model. Extraneous variables that threaten the interpretation of the results from laboratory and field experiments are relegated to random error terms. The weakness of this approach lies in the generalizability of the results to real organizational settings. Consequently, it is important that investigators validate their models before basing decisions on the results of experiments with the simulation. Validation is generally performed by determining how well the simulated values of dependent variables compare with historical data. A second approach is to determine the accuracy with which the simulation model predicts the behavior of the system in future time periods (Naylor et al., 1966).

An example of this research methodology is reviewed below. It involves medical order entry into a medical information system.

Simulation of Order Entry

Anderson et al. (1988) developed a computer simulation model to represent the process by which medical orders were entered into the medical information system at Methodist Hospital of Indiana. The model was constructed using INSIGHT, a general purpose, discrete event simulation language (Roberts, 1983). The model is graphically represented in Figure 5.1 using standard symbols used by the program. The symbols represent nodes. The nodes are connected to form a network that represents the sequence of activities involved and the resources

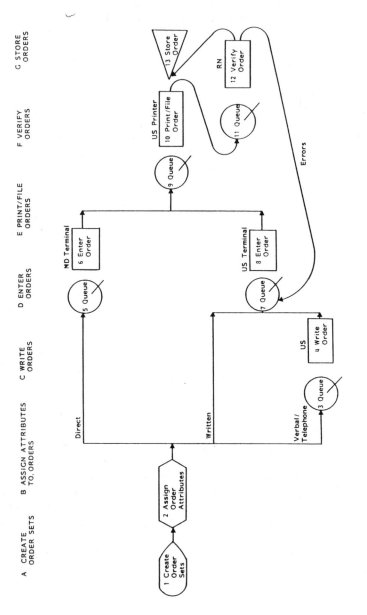

Figure 5.1. Computer Simulation Model: Physician Use of a Hospital Information System
SOURCE: Reprinted by permisson of the American Medical Informatics Association from Anderson et al. (1988).

128

required to process medical orders on a hospital unit. When resources such as a computer terminal are not available, order entry may be delayed.

The model was used to perform computer simulation experiments to estimate the effects of different modes of order entry on the systems' performance and on errors in order entry. An initial control run replicated the existing conditions on the hospital units. Written orders accounted for 95% of the medical orders; verbal or telephone orders were 2%. Physicians directly entered only 3% of the orders into the information system. The first experimental run assumed that physicians used personal order sets to directly enter 50% of their own orders into the information system. The second experimental run assumed 50% of the medical orders were entered by unit secretaries using personal order sets. The third run assumed physicians and unit secretaries between them entered 50% of the orders using personal order sets.

When both physicians and unit secretaries used personal order sets to enter medical orders into the information system, the average time to implement orders was reduced by nearly half. Moreover, the average time that orders were delayed because of the unavailability of a computer terminal or personnel was reduced from 30.7 minutes to 15.6 minutes. Also, time involved in order entry was reduced by a third and errors in order entry by more than a third.

The results of this experiment were used to perform a cost-benefit analysis. Under the initial conditions it was estimated that order entry throughout the hospital required 112 FTE unit secretaries. The annual cost in salaries and fringe benefits was over $2 million per year. The computer simulation experiments predicted that the same volume of medical orders could be processed using personal order sets by 77 FTE unit secretaries, an annual savings of 35 FTEs and $630,000. Also, the number of errors in order entry could be reduced by 83%.

Another computer simulation experiment was performed on the order entry process using a network model programmed with SLAM (Pritsker, Sigal, & Hammesfahr, 1989). Anderson, Jay, Cathcart, Perry, and Anderson (1989) used a computer model to evaluate the results of changing the way in which medical orders were entered into the medical information system. As in the earlier simulation, a control run replicated the existing conditions on nursing units. Initially, unit secretaries entered 82% of the medical orders into the information system. Seventy-nine percent of the orders were entered using the generic menus that are part of the information system. For the experimental run it was assumed that an additional 10% of the orders were entered using physicians' personal order sets.

Although the time spent in order entry remained the same, the volume of orders entered increased 16% under the experimental conditions. Much of the increased volume was due to a significant decrease in delays. The average time that orders spent waiting until a unit secretary was available to enter and print, and file, orders decreased by 71% and 44%, respectively. At the same time, the average delay until an RN was available to verify orders increased 36%. Quality of patient care also was affected. The increased use of personal order sets reduced errors in order entry by over 25%. This may also help to account for the increase in the volume of orders processed by unit secretaries.

Conclusion

This chapter describes and illustrates the use of experimental research methods to evaluate health care information systems. We have discussed issues concerning the amount of control the investigator has over subjects in the research setting and the generalizability of the research findings to real-world organizational environments.

Experimental methods permit the investigator to test predictions drawn from theory or other studies under controlled conditions and thus generate reliable knowledge about causal relations among variables. In general, this approach provides a methodology that can be used to establish associations or relationships among variables, to discover the temporal order of causes and effects, and to eliminate rival plausible explanations for changes that are observed in the dependent measure. Even in organizational settings where true experiments cannot be conducted, this methodology can be used to guide research and evaluation.

Experimental research methods provide unique and important analytical tools that can be used to evaluate health care information systems. These methods facilitate our ability to explain the effects or impacts of our interventions within health care organizations. In general, there are a number of different ways to achieve control in order to make causal inferences concerning interventions. Subject selection, random assignment, and manipulation represent only a few of these approaches. Analytical controls and quasi-experimental research designs provide additional tools that can be used to eliminate rival explanations for results observed in field settings. Each of the research methods discussed and illustrated employs mixtures of manipulative and analytical control that can be used to draw inferences concerning the impact of health care information systems.

Additional Reading

Basic Concepts

Bailar and Mosteller (1992) provide an excellent readable guide to the application of statistics to studies of health care.

Laboratory Experiments

Volume 2 of the Harvard Business School Research Colloquium on The Information Systems Research Challenge (Benbasat, 1989a) contains a series of papers that discuss the use of laboratory experiments to generate information about the use and impact of computer-based information systems. Papers in this volume by Benbasat (1989b) and DeSanctis (1989) review experiments involving individual decision makers and small group research, respectively.

Campbell and Stanley (1966), Fromkin and Streufert (1976), and Kerlinger (1986) provide excellent discussions of the nature of laboratory experiments, their strengths and weaknesses in comparison with other research methods, and threats to the internal and external validity of research studies.

Quasi-Experiments

Cook and Campbell (1979) provide an overview of quasi-experimental designs and analytical techniques that can be used in field settings.

Zmud, Olson, and Hauser (1989) provide a summary and critique of seven field experiments involving computer-based information systems.

Computer Simulation Experiments

Naylor and others (Naylor et al., 1966; Naylor, 1969) provide a good introduction to the design of computer simulation experiments. Anderson and others (1988, 1989) provide examples of this research strategy for studying the use of a hospital information system.

References

Anderson, J. G., Jay, S. J., Cathcart, L., Clevenger, S. J., Kassing, D. R., Perry, J., & Anderson, M. M. (1988). A computer simulation of physician use of a hospital information system. In W. E. Hammond (Ed.), *Proceedings of the AAMSI Congress 1988* (pp. 114-118). Washington, DC: American Association for Medical Systems and Informatics.

Anderson, J. G., Jay, S. J., Cathcart, L., Perry, J., & Anderson, M. M. (1989). Evaluating physician use of a hospital information system. In W. E. Hammond (Ed.), *Proceedings of the Eighth Annual AAMSI Congress 1989* (pp. 52-56). Washington, DC: American Association for Medical Systems and Informatics.

Anderson, J. G., Jay, S. J., Perry, J., & Anderson, M. M. (1990). Diffusion of computer applications among physicians: A quasi-experimental study. *Clinical Sociology Review, 8*, 116-127.

Anderson, J. G., Jay, S. J., Zimmerer, J. B., Farid, R. S., & Anderson, M. M. (1990). Evaluation of an intervention aimed at modifying physician test-ordering behavior. In R. A. Miller (Ed.), *Proceedings of the 14th Annual Symposium on Computer Applications in Medical Care* (pp. 683-687). Los Alamitos, CA: IEEE Computer Society Press.

Argyris, C. (1980). *Inner contradictions of rigorous research.* New York: Academic Press.

Bailer, J. C., III, & Mosteller, F. (1992). *Medical uses of statistics.* Boston, MA: NEJM.

Benbasat, I. (Ed.). (1989a). *The information systems research challenge: Experimental research methods* (vol. 2). Boston, MA: Harvard Business School.

Benbasat, I. (1989b). Laboratory experiments in information systems studies with a focus on individuals: A critical appraisal. In I. Benbasat (Ed.), *The information systems research challenge: Experimental research methods* (vol. 2, pp. 33-47). Boston, MA: Harvard Business School.

Benbasat, I., & Nault, B. R. (1990). An evaluation of empirical research in managerial support technologies. *Decision Support Systems, 6*, 203-226.

Blackburn, R. S. (1987). Experimental design in organizational settings. In J. Lorsch (Ed.), *Handbook of organizational behavior* (pp. 126-139). Englewood Cliffs, NJ: Prentice Hall.

Campbell, D., & Stanley, J. (1966). *Experimental and quasi-experimental designs for research.* Chicago: Rand McNally.

Caporaso, J. A. (1973). Quasi-experimental approaches to social sciences: Perspectives and problems. In J. A. Caporaso & L. L. Roos, Jr. (Eds.), *Quasi-experimental approaches: Testing theory and evaluating policy* (pp. 3-38). Evanston, IL: Northwestern University Press.

Cook, T. D., & Campbell, D. T. (1979). *Quasi-experimentation: Design and analysis issues for field settings.* Boston: Houghton Mifflin.

DeSanctis, G. (1989). Small group research in information systems: Theory and methods. In I. Benbasat (Ed.), *The information systems research challenge: Experimental research methods* (vol. 2, pp. 53-82). Boston, MA: Harvard Business School.

Fromkin, H. L., & Streufert, S. (1976). Laboratory experimentation. In M. D. Dunette (Ed.), *Handbook of industrial and organizational psychology* (pp. 415-465). Chicago: Rand McNally.

Goodman, P. S. (1986). *Designing effective work groups.* San Francisco: Jossey-Bass.

Gould, J. D. (1985). How to do psychological research on person-computer issues. *Proceedings CHI '85 Conference* (pp. 41-43). New York: Association for Computing Machinery.

Jenkins, A. M. (1983). *MIS design variables and decision making performance: A simulation experiment.* Ann Arbor, MI: UMI Research Press.

Jenkins, A. M. (1985). Research methodologies and MIS research. In E. Mumford, R. Hirschheim, G. Fitzgerald, & T. Wood-Harper (Eds.), *Research methods in information systems* (pp. 103-117). Amsterdam: North Holland.

Kerlinger, F. N. (1986). *Foundations of behavioral research* (3rd ed). Chicago: Holt, Rinehart & Winston.

Kraemer, K., & King, J. (1988). Computer-based systems for group decision support: Status of use and problems in development. *Computing Surveys, 20,* 115-146.

Kuperman, G. J., Gardner, R. M., & Pryor, T. A. (1991). *HELP: A dynamic hospital information system.* New York: Springer Verlag.

Lundsgaarde, H. P., Gardner, R. M., & Menlove, R. L. (1989). Using attitudinal questionnaires to achieve benefits optimization. In *Proceedings of the 13th Annual Symposium on Computer Applications in Medical Care* (pp. 703-708). Washington, DC: IEEE Computer Society.

Mason, R. O. (1989). MIS experiments: A pragmatic perspective. In I. Benbasat (Ed.), *The information systems research challenge: Experimental research methods* (vol. 2, pp. 3-20). Boston, MA: Harvard Business School.

McDonald, C. J., Hui, S. L., Smith, D. M., Tierney, W. M., Cohen, S. J., Weinberger, M., & McCabe, G. P. (1984). Reminders to physicians from an introspective computer medical record: A two-year randomized trial. *Annals of Internal Medicine, 100,* 130-138.

Naylor, T. H. (1969). *The design of computer simulation experiments.* Durham, NC: Duke University Press.

Naylor, T. H., Balintfy, J. L., Burdick, D. S., & Chu, K. (1966). *Computer simulation techniques.* New York: Wiley.

Nunamaker, J. F., Applegate, L. M., & Konsynski, B. R. (1987). Facilitating group creativity with GDSS. *Journal of Management Information Systems, 3,* 5-19.

Orne, M. T. (1962). On the social psychology of the psychological experiment: With particular reference to demand characteristics and their implications. *American Psychologist, 17,* 776-783.

Poole, M. S., Folger, J. P., & Hewes, D. E. (1987). Analyzing interpersonal interaction. In E. Roloff & G. R. Miller (Eds.), *Interpersonal processes* (pp. 220-256). Newbury Park, CA: Sage.

Poole, M. S., Holmes, M., & DeSanctis, G. (1988). Conflict management and group decision support systems. In *Proceedings of the Second Conference on Computer-Supported Cooperative Work.* New York: Association for Computing Machinery.

Pritsker, A. A. B., Sigal, C. E., & Hammesfahr, R. D. J. (1989). *SLAM II: Network models for decision support.* Englewood Cliffs, NJ: Prentice Hall.

Roberts, S. D. (1983). *Simulation modeling and analysis with INSIGHT.* Indianapolis, IN: Regenstrief Institute for Health Care.

Sharda, R., Barr, S. H., & McDonnell, J. C. (1988). Decision support system effectiveness: A review and an empirical test. *Management Science, 34,* 139-159.

Stone, E. (1978). *Research methods in organizational behavior.* Glenview, IL: Scott Foresman.

Todd, P., & Benbasat, I. (1987). Process tracing methods in decision support systems research: Exploring the black box. *MIS Quarterly, 11,* 493-512.

Tierney, W. M., McDonald, C. J., Hui, S. L., & Martin, D. K. (1988). Computer predictions of abnormal test results: Effects on outpatient testing. *JAMA, 259,* 1194-1198.

Tierney, W. M., McDonald, C. J., Martin, D. K., Hui, S. L., & Rogers, M. P. (1987). Computerized display of past test results: Effect on outpatient testing. *Annals of Internal Medicine, 107,* 569-574.

Tierney, W. M., Miller, M. E., & McDonald, C. J. (1990). The effect on test ordering of informing physicians of the charges for outpatient diagnostic tests. *NEJM, 322,* 1499-1504.

Tierney, W. M., Miller, M. E., Overhage, J. M., & McDonald, C. J. (1993). Physician inpatient order writing on microcomputer workstations: Effects on resource utilization. *JAMA, 269,* 379-383.

Turner, C. W., Lincoln, M. J., Haug, P., Williamson, J. W., Jessen, S., Cundick, K., & Warner, H. (1991). ILIAD training effects: A cognitive model and empirical findings. In P. D. Clayton (Eds.), *Proceedings of the 15th Annual Symposium on Computer Applications in Medical Care* (pp. 68-72). New York: McGraw-Hill.

Zigurs, I., Poole, M. S., & DeSanctis, G. (1988). A study of influence of computer-mediated group decision making. *MIS Quarterly, 12,* 625-644.

Zmud, R. W., Olson, M. H., & Hauser, R. (1989). Field experimentation in MIS research. In I. Benbasat (Ed.), *The information systems research challenge: Experimental research methods* (vol. 2, pp. 97-111). Boston, MA: Harvard Business School.

6

Social Networks and Health Care Information Systems

A Structural Approach to Evaluation

Ronald E. Rice
James G. Anderson

Introduction

Users' attitudes toward information systems have considerable influence on the diffusion and success of such systems (Lucas, 1981). Early expectations may not be met and use of the system may decline over time. Adoption may be uneven across departments and occupations. Physicians and nurses may resist the implementation of a new computer system if it negatively affects their status, autonomy, or traditional staff relations (Anderson, Jay, Schweer, & Anderson, 1986; Brenner & Logan, 1980; Counte, Kjerulff, Salloway, & Campbell, 1987).

Although some changes brought about by the implementation of a new medical information system may be negative, others may be positive. For example, the use of remote terminals may decrease face-to-face communication among users and require new types and distributions of cognitive and technical skills among employees. At the same time, such systems may also allow integration of activities and knowledge across databases, departments, and temporal boundaries. They may

AUTHOR'S NOTE: The first author would like to thank Dr. Carolyn Aydin for her considerable contributions, the members of the Student Health Service for their participation, and Dr. M. Lynne Markus for helping to initiate the SHS study.

also provide opportunities for development of new skills and upward job mobility (Hirschheim, 1985; Johnson & Rice, 1987; Markus, 1984; Olson & Lucas, 1982).

Three Structural Aspects of Health Care Organizations

Adoption and utilization of computer-based information systems and attitudes toward them and their effectiveness all involve three underlying structural aspects of organizations: interdependency, interaction, and integration. These organizational characteristics become particularly salient in health care organizations and will be discussed below.

Interdependency

Fundamental tensions exist in health care settings because of differentiation and interdependency. Health care employees belong to different social worlds (medical and nonmedical), occupations (nurses, physicians, administrators, clerical workers, medical technicians), and departments (medical records, women's health), yet their work requires considerable interdependence across these boundaries. Few medical care tasks can be performed without the cooperation of one or more departments (Aydin & Rice, 1992).

At the same time, such boundaries may result in different understandings of overall systems and organizational processes. For example, although physicians in different departments in the same hospital are all likely to be concerned with treating patients, physicians and nurses working in the same department will share common concerns related to the specific tasks, norms, values, and language of that department (Tushman & Scanlan, 1981). Thus, exchange of information and understanding of roles may be asymmetric and insufficient across some departmental boundaries, creating conflict and struggles for power and access to resources (Olson & Lucas, 1982, p. 845).

Interaction

However, interaction within and across boundaries represents opportunities for gaining greater understanding of specialized but interdependent information and sharing of resources, leading to cooperation and coordination (Aydin, 1989; Donnellon, Gray, & Bougon, 1986; Hackman, 1983, p. 1457; Kimberly & Evanisko, 1981; McCann & Galbraith, 1981; Van de Ven, 1986; Van Maanen & Barley, 1985). Further, interpersonal interaction with patients and other health care workers is often a primary professional motivation for workers in health settings (Mauksch, 1972). Moreover, communications among medical practitioners affect the rate of adoption and diffusion of medical technology. Research has demonstrated that the structure of these communication networks determines which physicians are likely to be early or late adopters of new drugs (Coleman, Katz, & Menzel, 1966; Stross & Harlan, 1979) and a hospital information system (Anderson & Jay, 1985a, 1985b; Anderson, Jay, Schweer, & Anderson, 1987; Anderson, Jay, Schweer, Anderson, & Kassing, 1987).

Integration

By providing geographically dispersed access to common and interrelated medical information, medical information systems can help to create a "virtual office" (Giuliano, 1982), with boundaries related to task and information flow rather than to traditional functional departments, occupations, and spatial proximity (Rice, 1987). Integrated medical information systems that create common databases thus require health care departments to cooperate, altering interdependencies and interactions across departmental and occupational boundaries. For example, how nurses enter drug information into a system will affect how the pharmacy department provides services and manages its billing (Aydin, 1989). These interdependencies necessitate standardized forms, terminology, and policies and procedures, possibly requiring considerable interdepartmental coordination, negotiations, and conflict (Cook, 1985). This integration may reduce dependence on other departments for access to information, possibly reducing conflict (Hage, Aiken, & Marrett, 1971; Olson & Lucas, 1982). Such technological requirements and mediation of interaction can also reinforce these boundaries by isolating workers from interpersonal interactions, by routinizing tasks, and by requiring the development of specialized skills and norms.

Thus there is a complex and subtle interplay of structural differences involving interdependencies and interaction that are affected by the introduction of medical information technology. Kaplan (1986, 1989), for example, noted differences in definitions of the technologists' role in different clinical laboratories in the same medical center. Barley (1986) reported that the first use of body scanners in the radiology departments of two hospitals resulted in new boundaries between the various technological subunits but with different patterns of change in each hospital. Lundsgaarde, Fischer, and Steele (1981) evaluated user acceptance of a computerized problem-oriented medical record system designed to enhance communication among health care professionals on a general medical ward. Nurses and ancillary personnel readily accepted and used the system because it led to an expansion of their professional roles, whereas physicians refused to cooperate in using the system because it was more time-consuming than the manual system and they feared that it would disrupt traditional staff relations.

Basics of Social Network Analysis

Fundamental Concepts

Typically, studies of the implementation of computer-based information systems have focused on their impact on individual's attitudes, work roles, and levels of utilization. However, understanding the effects of introducing a new medical information system into an organization requires an approach that also considers patterns of social relations— such as interaction, interdependence, and integration—rather than focusing solely on individuals. Social network analysis provides both conceptual and analytical tools that can be used in evaluating these other impacts of information systems.

Social network analysis is the study of patterns of relations among a set of people, departments, organizations, and so on. For example, physicians form networks of other physicians with whom they consult in providing patient care. Within these networks some physicians, departments, and such are more extensively connected to other individuals or units than are others. The purpose of social network analysis is to detect the presence of structure or patterns of relations using empirical data; to explain the occurrence of different structures in different types of organizations, settings, or organizational units; and to analyze the effects that network structure or location in the network have on individual members' attitudes, behavior, and performance (Knoke & Kuklinski, 1982).

This methodological approach presumes that individuals are embedded in social networks and structures and thus that their attitudes, norms, and behaviors are influenced through (1) direct and indirect exposure to other network members' behavior, attitudes, and influences; (2) access to resources in those networks; and (3) their position in the network structure (Burt, 1980; Davis, 1966; Hackman, 1983, p. 1455; Laumann & Marsden, 1979; Riley & Riley, 1972; Rogers & Kincaid, 1981; Salancik & Pfeffer, 1978; Wellman, 1983). In general, it is hypothesized that the structure of relations among individuals or units and their location in the network have important behavioral, perceptual, and attitudinal consequences both for individual members and for the system as a whole (see also Rice, Grant, Schmitz, & Torobin, 1990; Williams, Rice, & Rogers, 1988; and Chapter 11). Such influence may take many forms. For example, innovation diffusion studies have found that individuals who are prominent in these networks are more likely to adopt the innovations sooner and to influence others; whereas those on the periphery are likely to be influenced later in the diffusion process or not at all. Prominent members are those who are extensively involved in the network, thus giving them greater access to the flow of information (Knoke & Burt, 1983).

Relationships

Social network analysis is performed on relational, positional, or spatial data that provide information about the existence or strength of relationships among members of the network (Davis, 1984; Dow, 1988; Erickson, 1988; Johnson, 1988; Rice, 1992). Relational data indicate the extent to which network members interact directly and indirectly with one another (Rogers & Kincaid, 1981). An example is one in which a physician consults another physician about a patient or a new drug or procedure.

Individuals are *positionally* proximate to the extent that they occupy the same roles in a group or organization and thus share the same sets of obligations, status, and expectations. There are various forms of positional proximity. Adherents of the *structural equivalence* form argue that two individuals may have similar attitudes because they have *similar* relationships with the *same* other individuals. These individuals not only share common patterns of interactions with others in the organization but also share common attributes, attitudes, and socialization experiences (Burt, 1980, 1987). For example, two primary care physicians may consult with the same group of specialists but not with one another. *Organizational position* can be conceptualized as similar patterns of information and control relations among horizontally and vertically differentiated jobs (Dow, 1988).

Individuals may be *spatially* proximate, without necessarily being relationally or positionally proximate. Such proximity may occur when individuals with similar tasks are placed together or have common problems or client flow. This spatial proximity in turn produces similar exposure/inaccessibility to others, events, resources, and other aspects of the workplace (Hackman, 1983). For example, a study discussed later in this chapter measured the walking distance between each pair of employees of a student health service. Finally, any or all of the three types of network data may describe relationships among *individuals* or *groups*.

Data Collection

Network analysis depends on the availability of relational, positional, or spatial data—that indicate relations or similarities among members. Once collected, these data are typically organized in a matrix in which rows and columns represent individuals, departments, or organizations that have relations with one another. The simple binary presence or absence of relationships, or scalar measures of the frequency, strength, or value of relationships, are represented by numbers in the appropriate cells of the matrix. This square matrix is generally termed an *adjacency matrix*. Relationships may be symmetric (such as when two physicians report that they each communicate with the other "several times a day") or asymmetric (such as when a generalist physician refers patients to a specialist physician, but not vice versa).

An example of relational data is shown in Figure 6.1. Referrals of patients among 24 physicians who comprise a private group practice are shown. A number in a cell of the matrix indicates the number of different types of professional relations between the two physicians.

Other forms of relational data that are not square matrices can be converted into such matrices and analyzed using social network techniques. For example, a typical table in a report might indicate the number of different modules of a medical information system used by physicians on the medical staff (see Table 6.1a). In this case, the rows represent physicians and the columns represent the modules. This matrix is commonly called an *incidence* or *event matrix*. We can derive two square adjacency matrices from this original table or incidence matrix. In one resulting matrix, the rows and columns represent physicians, and the cell values indicate the number of modules of the medical information system used in common by each pair of physicians (see Table 6.1b), which is one indicator of how similar the physicians are. In the second resulting matrix (see Table 6.1c), the rows and columns represent the modules, and the cell values indicate how many physicians use various combinations of the information system modules. Most techniques used to analyze network data involve the direct manipulation of the square adjacency matrices, although the incidence matrices may also be directly analyzed.

Network data may be collected through various methods, such as by providing respondents with a complete roster of all other members in

Initiating Physician[a]	Responding Physician[b]																							
	A	B	C	D	E	F	G	H	I	J	K	L	M	N	O	P	Q	R	S	T	U	V	W	X
A	–	0	0	1	3	1	3	1	3	1	2	1	0	1	2	0	3	1	0	0	1	1	3	2
B	1	–	0	0	0	1	1	0	2	1	0	1	2	0	0	1	1	0	1	0	0	0	0	1
C	3	0	–	1	0	3	0	3	3	2	0	2	2	1	0	2	1	4	1	1	2	1	0	2
D	3	3	0	–	0	2	0	0	3	2	0	3	3	0	0	0	0	3	1	3	3	2	0	0
E	4	3	1	1	–	3	1	3	3	1	3	1	3	1	1	3	2	1	3	1	1	1	2	1
F	0	0	2	1	1	–	0	0	1	1	1	1	1	1	0	0	1	2	1	2	2	0	0	2
G	2	3	0	0	0	2	–	0	3	0	1	0	1	0	0	1	0	1	1	0	1	0	1	3
H	0	1	1	2	0	0	0	–	2	2	2	1	1	3	0	1	0	0	0	0	1	0	0	0
I	2	0	2	0	0	3	0	1	–	2	2	1	1	1	0	0	2	1	1	2	0	0	1	2
J	3	3	3	1	1	2	1	3	4	–	4	3	3	1	1	3	2	1	3	1	2	1	2	2
K	1	0	0	0	1	1	0	1	2	1	–	1	0	1	0	0	2	2	0	0	0	0	2	0
L	2	3	3	2	2	3	1	3	3	2	1	–	3	3	0	2	2	2	3	3	3	4	0	2
M	1	2	1	1	1	1	2	2	2	2	0	2	–	2	1	2	2	1	2	2	0	3	2	2
N	3	1	3	1	3	3	2	4	4	3	4	3	3	–	0	3	3	1	2	3	3	3	3	2
O	1	0	0	0	1	0	0	0	1	0	0	0	0	0	–	0	1	0	1	1	0	0	1	1
P	0	3	0	0	0	1	2	0	1	1	1	0	1	1	0	–	1	1	1	1	2	1	1	0
Q	3	1	1	1	3	1	1	1	2	1	2	1	1	1	2	2	–	1	2	1	1	1	3	1
R	0	1	2	0	2	3	1	3	3	0	3	1	2	0	0	2	1	–	0	1	2	1	0	2
S	1	2	1	1	1	2	2	1	2	2	2	2	2	2	1	3	2	2	–	1	2	2	2	3
T	0	0	1	1	0	2	1	0	2	0	2	0	2	0	0	2	0	0	0	–	0	0	0	4
U	3	1	2	2	2	3	1	3	3	2	3	4	2	1	1	3	2	2	3	3	–	2	3	3
V	1	1	0	2	0	2	0	0	1	0	1	2	1	0	0	0	1	1	0	0	2	–	1	0
W	2	1	1	0	1	2	0	0	2	0	2	0	2	0	0	2	1	0	2	0	0	0	–	2
X	1	3	1	0	0	2	2	0	1	1	1	1	2	0	1	1	1	1	0	3	1	1	0	–

Figure 6.1. Physician Network—Number of Different Types of Professional Relations Among 24 Physicians Who Are Members of the Group Practice

[a]Initiating Physician: Physician who refers patient or consults with colleagues.
[b]Responding Physician: Physician to whom patient is referred.

the system and asking them to check off the frequency, strength, importance, or ranking of each other member, possibly on several types of

TABLE 6.1 Incidence Matrix and the Two Adjacency Matrices Derived From It

a. Incidence Matrix Indicating Which Medical Information System Modules Are Used by Each Physician

Physician	*Admission Discharge Transfer*	*Order Entry Results Reporting*
A	1	1
B	1	1
C	1	0

b. Adjacency Matrix: The Number of System Modules Used in Common by Each Pair of Physicians

2 = Physician	A	B	C
A	2	2	1
B	2	2	1
C	1	1	1

c. Adjacency Matrix: The Number of Physicians Using Each Combination of System Modules

System Modules	*Admission Discharge Transfer*	*Order Entry Results Reporting*
Admission Discharge Transfer	3	2
Order Entry Results Reporting	2	2

relations, or by asking respondents to list those with whom they interact. Other forms of network data exist, such as snowball samples, nominations, observations, and reports by respondents of perceived relationships among others. An example of snowball sampling is provided in Chapter 9 of this book, in which users of a computerized decision support system were asked to identify other users.

Different forms of network data may also be collected by a system's computer itself, such as the number, length, content, and timing of messages sent among a set of system users (Rice, 1990). System data have been used in studies of medical information systems to identify the attending and consulting physicians for each patient, time elapsed between system implementation and a physician's first use, and varieties of usage, such as obtaining patient lists or laboratory results or entering and retrieving medical orders (regardless of whether entered directly by the physician or indirectly for the physician by other hospital personnel) (Anderson, Jay, Schweer, Anderson, & Kassing, 1987).

Finally, any form of network data can be analyzed with respect to a wide variety of network characteristics, as described next.

Analytic Techniques and Measures

Network analysis can provide descriptive and inferential insights into a wide variety of topics: (1) individual *roles* such as isolates, members of groups such as cliques; (2) the existence and relative positions of those *groupings* in the overall network; (3) *relationships* such as strength, direction, reciprocation, and stability of interactions such as patient referrals; and (4) the overall *structure* of the network such as hierarchies and status rankings. Network indices may be *measured* at the individual or group level and subsequently *analyzed* at the individual or group level. In the "Applications" section below, a number of social network measures and analytical techniques will be illustrated.

Applications

The following sections provide two summary examples of how network approaches have been used to study issues of adoption and use, attitudes, and interdepartmental communication. The first study explored how physicians' positions in the referral and consultation network predicted their adoption and utilization of a medical information system (see Anderson & Jay, 1985a, 1985b; Anderson, Jay, Schweer, & Anderson, 1987; and Anderson, Jay, Schweer, Anderson, & Kassing, 1987, for details). This study also evaluated an experimental program that identified and used physicians who were influential in the referral and consultation networks to increase physicians' use of the medical information system (Anderson, Jay, Perry, & Anderson, 1990). The second study examined the influence of network and occupational groupings on the use of and attitudes toward an integrated medical records system at a student health service and subsequent changes in cross-departmental information exchange (see Aydin & Rice, 1991, 1992, and Rice & Aydin, 1991, for details).

Influence of Physician Networks on System Adoption and Utilization

Study Site and Data

Setting. This study was conducted at Methodist Hospital of Indiana, a private teaching hospital. The hospital had installed the Technicon medical information system that had been upgraded to the TDS HC4000 system, accessible by remote terminals throughout the hospital. At the time that the study was undertaken, the information system supported the following applications: patient registration, admission/discharge/ transfer, laboratory, pharmacy, radiology, nursing services, order entry, and results reporting. The system provides communication between hospital services, physicians, and nursing services. During the patient's hospitalization, it serves as a computerized medical record. It collects, organizes, and presents clinical data in order to improve the management of patient care. Physicians with computer codes can retrieve patient information and enter medical orders directly into the system (Anderson, 1992a, 1992b).

In a preliminary study, a questionnaire was used to collect relational data from 24 physicians in a group practice. Physicians were asked to indicate which physicians they referred patients to, consulted with, discussed professional matters with, and took calls for. Self-reported measures of system use were also obtained (see Anderson & Jay, 1985a). In the second phase of the study a questionnaire was used to collect information on physician attitudes toward medical computer applications from 644 physicians on the hospital's medical staff (77% completed the instrument—see Anderson et al., 1986). At three points in time over a 1-year period, the medical information system tapes were accessed to obtain data on physicians' use of the system and relational data indicating the attending and all consulting physicians for each patient (Anderson, Jay, Schweer, Anderson, & Kassing, 1987).

Measures. (a) *Individual attributes.* Individual attributes measured included physician's age, specialty, board certification, number of hospital admissions during the last 6 months, professional activities (0 = no professional or administrative activities, 1 = routine participation on hospital committees, 2 = major activities such as chairman of a hospital committee or officer of a medical society), and medical education (whether or not a physician was involved in training house staff). (b) *Attitudes toward medical computer systems.* This was measured as the degree to which the physician was concerned that computers are likely to reduce professional autonomy (from 1 = little or no concern to 5 = a great deal of concern). (c) *Adoption and use of the system.* Time to adoption was measured as the time that elapsed between the date the hospital information system was implemented and the date the physician voluntarily underwent training to use the system. Two measures of utilization were the proportion of each physician's medical orders that were entered directly by a physician using a terminal over a period of 6 days, and the sum of the frequency of physician use of the system to obtain patient lists, retrieve and print laboratory results, and enter and retrieve medical orders.

(d) *Network measures*. First, densities were computed to describe relations among subgroups of physicians. *Density* is the number of relations or ties between pairs of network members (e.g., physicians) divided by the total number of possible ties. Values range from 0 to 1.0 if each member (e.g., physician) is directly connected to all other network members. Second, centrality scores (ranging from 0 to 1) were calculated to describe the degree to which information and resources are dispersed throughout the group or centered around a few individuals. In more centralized networks, a few individuals will have high scores while the majority will have low scores. Third, a measure of the physician's predominant role in the network of sending, relaying, or receiving patients and information was computed as the ratio of the number of interactions the physician initiated to those that were initiated by colleagues. Fourth, multiplexity was measured as the proportion of group members with whom a physician had more than one type of relationship. Finally, a measure of prestige was calculated, ranging from 0 (no one consulted the physician) to 1 (all other physicians on the service consulted the physician).

Influence of Physician Network Position

A blockmodel analysis and multidimensional scaling of the relational data among the set of 24 physicians were used to analyze how the physician's position in the referral and consultation network influenced adoption and use of the system (see Anderson & Jay, 1985a). The blockmodel analysis identified groups of physicians who had similar patterns of referrals, consultations, discussions, and on-call coverage with the other physicians in the group practice. Next, relations among these groups of physicians were analyzed. Finally, multidimensional sealing was used to represent the relations among the physicians graphically (Scott, 1991).

CONCOR, a network program that iteratively correlates the rows (and or columns) of an adjacency matrix to identify structurally equivalent positions and hierarchically clusters (Johnson, 1967) the final correlation matrix, was applied to the rows of the four matrices that indicated the professional relations among the physicians. Physicians were considered structurally equivalent, or members of a group, if their pattern of relations with other physicians was similar, as portrayed in Figure 6.2. Figure 6.3 represents the densities of professional relations among the groups. A circle or a line linking two groups indicates that the density of relations among physicians in a group or between two groups of physicians is greater than the density of the total network.

The results suggest a refinement of the center-periphery pattern of relations observed among other groups of professionals. These studies found that professionals are generally informally organized around a central group of influentials who direct and control the flow of information and resources to colleagues (Cole & Cole, 1973; Crane, 1972). Figure 6.3 suggests that two central cohesive groups are linked to the other groups of physicians. The physicians in Group 1 act as gate-keepers in referring patients and consulting with physicians in the other three groups. Physicians in Group 2 appear to initiate discussions on professional matters with all of the other groups.

An examination of the shared attributes and network characteristics of physicians who make up the groups supports this relational structure (see Figure 6.4). Physicians in Group 1 are older and more active in professional activities. They are centrally involved in the professional networks as evidenced by their scores on the indices of centrality, multiplexity, and network role. They initiate almost 1.5 times as many referrals, consultations, and discussions with other physicians as they receive. This may account for their lower number of hospital admissions. Most of the physicians in this group obtained their computer codes and underwent training to use the system at about the same time. They are also the heaviest users of the medical information system: during the 6-day period studied, they directly entered 45% of their own medical orders into the system.

The second group consists of younger physicians with large private practices. They admitted the most patients to the hospital. They too adopted the medical information system into their clinical practice soon after its implementation and used it to enter about 25% of their medical orders during the study period. Physicians in Groups 3 and 4 on the periphery of the network were slow to adopt the system and two physicians never applied for a computer code. These physicians infrequently used the system for order entry.

The network with its groups of structurally equivalent physicians can also be represented spatially through multidimensional scaling, as shown in Figure 6.5. The multidimensional scaling spatially represents the relations among network members in three dimensions. The four major groups that were identified by the CONCOR clustering program emerge as well-determined clusters. The general location of Group 2 between Groups 1 and 3 is consistent with the intermediary role that this group of physicians plays in clinical consultations and discussions.

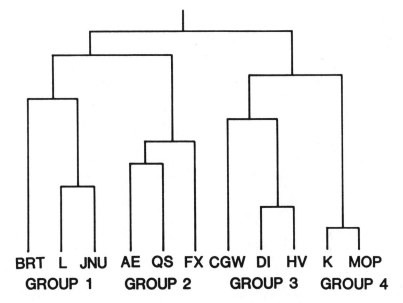

Figure 6.2. Hierarchical Clustering of 24 Physicians Into Four Structurally Equivalent Groups. Physicians in each group have similar patterns of relations with all other physicians in the network. (See Note 1.)

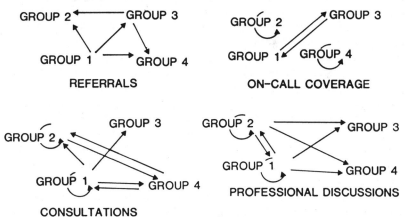

Figure 6.3. Relations Among the Four Structurally Equivalent Groups of Physicians. A circle or a line linking two groups indicates that the density of relations among physicians in a group or between two groups of physicians is greater than the density of the total network. (See Note 1.)

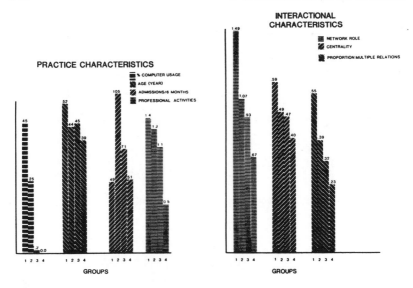

Figure 6.4. Attributes and Network Characteristics of Physicians in the Four Groups (See Note 1.)

Also, the relative position of individual physicians in the three-dimensional space helps to illuminate the role that they play in the network. For example, physician N is located at the center of Group 1. Analysis of his attributes indicates that he plays a central role in referrals and consultations among physicians in the network.

In the second phase of the study, physicians on each hospital service with similar consultation patterns were identified. Figure 6.6 portrays one network that indicates the relationships among groups of the 51 physicians on general surgery. Five of the six groups of physicians are cliques. They frequently consult other group members in providing patient care. The groups also form a hierarchy. Physicians in Group 3 are consulted by members of all other groups. In turn, physicians in Groups 1 and 2 are consulted by those in Groups 4, 5, and 6. Physicians in Group 6 are not consulted at all by their colleagues.

Table 6.2 contains information about attributes, adoption, and utilization of the medical information system by each group of physicians. Physicians in Groups 1, 2, and 3, who are consulted most often, are the youngest and the most involved in the graduate medical education program. Practice patterns also differ significantly among the groups. Physicians in Group 3, who are at the center of the consultation network, admit the most patients to the hospital, were among the earliest to begin

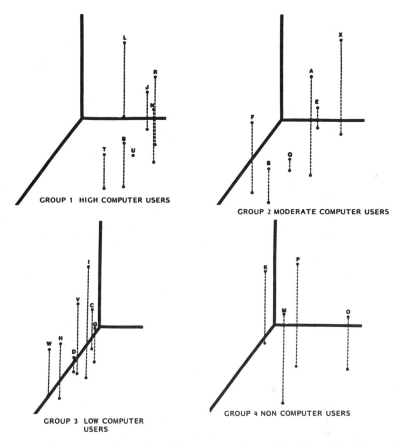

Figure 6.5. Three-Dimensional Representation of the Physician Network Resulting From the KYST Multidimensional Scaling Program. The four groups of physicians identified by the CONCOR clustering program are represented separately in order to illustrate their relative location in three-dimensional space. (See Note 1.)

using the medical information system, and use it most frequently in their clinical practice. They also express the least concern about the potential effect of computer systems on their professional autonomy. In contrast, physicians in Groups 5 and 6 who are more peripherally located in the network admit fewer patients, were the slowest to adopt the medical information system, use it less frequently in their clinical practice, and fear a loss of autonomy as a result of the introduction of computers into medicine.

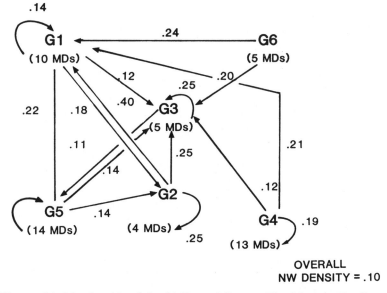

Figure 6.6. Membership of the 51 General Surgery Physicians in Six Groups. Physicians in each group have similar patterns of relations with all the other physicians in the network.

SOURCE: Reprinted by permission of Springer-Verlag from Anderson & Jay (1987).

Influencing Physician Use
of the Medical Information System

The final phase of the study implemented and evaluated an experimental program that explicitly used a network-based approach to increase physician use of the medical information system (see Anderson et al., 1990). The study used a quasi-experimental design and appears as Chapter 13 of this book. The results of the study suggest that network approaches are an effective means of influencing physicians' and other medical personnel's use of a medical information system.

Organizational Adaptation
to a Medical Information System

Study Site and Data

Setting. The case study summarized here involves the implementation of a vendor's multi-application medical records information system at the student health service (SHS) of a major urban university. A year

TABLE 6.2 Mean Attributes, Adoption, and Utilization for Each Group of Physicians: General Surgery ($n = 51$)

Group	Age	Prestige	Board Certification	Admissions	Medical Education	Attitude	HIS Adoption	HIS Use
1	33	0.23	0.30	2.20	1.00	3.14	0.33	2.46
	(0.33)*	(0.50)	(1.61)	(1.78)	(0)	(0.32)	(1.73)	(0.29)
2	38	0.18	0.50	4.43	1.00	2.83	0	2.73
	(0.38)	(0.51)	(1.15)	(1.54)	(0)	(0.13)	(0)	(0.35)
3	34	0.19	0.20	7.17	1.00	2.75	1.00	3.23
	(0.26)	(0.68)	(2.24)	(1.61)	(0)	(0.20)	(0)	(0.39)
4	41	0.12	0.62	6.79	0.75	3.77	2.25	2.63
	(0.27)	(0.41)	(0.82)	(1.12)	(0.62)	(0.18)	(0.85)	(0.52)
5	43	0.09	0.50	3.95	0.11	3.25	3.89	1.98
	(0.31)	(0.96)	(1.04)	(1.32)	(3.00)	(0.26)	(1.02)	(0.84)
6	46	0.0	0.80	4.0	0.33	4.00	4.00	1.67
	(0.34)	(0)	(0.56)	(1.58)	(1.73)	(0.35)	(0.90)	(0.85)
Total	40	0.13	0.49	4.69	0.56	3.35	2.52	2.46
	(0.31)	(0.81)	(1.03)	(1.41)	(1.09)	(0.26)	(1.19)	(0.52)
F-ratio	1.32	6.65	1.17	0.71	4.96	1.74	1.32	0.75
p<	0.27	0.0001	0.34	0.62	0.004	0.15	0.29	0.59

*Coefficient of variation

SOURCE: Reprinted by permission of Springer-Verlag from Anderson & Jay (1987).

151

after the first system module was implemented, many system functions were operating to: (1) schedule appointments and generate encounter forms (which were printed out by the computer system for each patient's visit and served as "triggers" for most other SHS activities), (2) enter codes for diagnoses and services performed, (3) reconcile written encounter forms with data entered in the computer, and (4) generate reports. Questionnaires, structured interviews, observations, and archival data were collected several months before the system was implemented (Time 1), several months after implementation had begun (Time 2), and approximately 1 year after the second survey (Time 3). Of the approximately 110 full- and part-time employees, 88 were still employed at Time 3; 74 of these employees (84%) completed both the Time 1 and Time 3 questionnaires.

Measures. (a) *Departments and occupations.* Individuals belonged to 1 of 11 departments and 1 of 5 professional occupations, according to organizational records. (b) *Attitude toward the system.* A single-item attitude question asked the extent to which the system was worth the time and effort required to use it (with values from 1 = strongly disagree to 7 = strongly agree). A "combined attitude scale" was also computed by creating factor scores from (1) the residuals of the single item regressed on the same question measured at Time 1 (to control for autocorrelation between Time 1 and Time 3) and (2) two Time 3 questions concerning the extent to which the system changed the ease of doing the department's work and the quality of that work (with values from 1 = significantly decreased to 7 = significantly increased). (c) *Usage of the system.* A 6-point scale ranged from "0" for respondents who never used the system at all, to "1" for those who never used the terminals but did (1) provide information to it, (2) use information from it, or (3) use reports from it, up to "5" for respondents who used the terminals "most of the day." (d) *Archival measures of occupational, organizational and spatial location.* The system trainer, who was also head of SHS's medical records, provided a detailed personnel roster, a formal organizational reporting chart, and a floor plan indicating each employee's location.

Differences Between Departments and Occupations

A traditional analysis testing for differences in the means of various attitudes over time, and between occupations and departments, found that the single-item attitude measure was positive but decreased significantly from 6.02 (agree) to 5.27 (between slightly agree and agree) nearly 2 years later ($p<.01$). Table 6.3 shows that, overall, the mean of

TABLE 6.3 Combined Attitude Scale Toward Computers by Occupation and Department

	N	*Mean*	*SD*
Occupation[a]			
Administrators	6	.77	.37
MDs	5	−1.19	.79
RNs	10	−.34	1.19
Other medical	15	−.14	1.03
Office/clerical	25	.25	.81
F-ratio		4.14**	
Department[b]			
Finance/personnel	8	.29	.80
Primary care	15	−.01	1.12
Women's health	7	−1.08	.92
Specialty clinics	5	−.23	1.47
Medical records	8	.43	.56
Lab	5	−.52	.90
Health education	5	.41	.44
F-ratio		2.28*	

SOURCE: Adapted from Aydin & Rice (1991).
[a] A posteriori Duncan multiple range tests show that (1) MDs differed significantly from Office/Clerical and Administrators and Other Medical, and (2) RNs differed significantly from Administrators.
[b] Includes departments with at least five employees responding to both Time 1 and Time 3 questionnaires. A posteriori Duncan multiple range tests show that Women's Health differed significantly from Primary Care, Finance/Personnel, Health Education, and Medical Records.
*$p<.05$; **$p<.01$.

the Time 3 combined attitude scale differed significantly for the five occupations, with physicians significantly more negative. The mean also differed significantly across departments, with Women's Health employees having significantly less positive attitudes ($p<.05$).

Influence of Network Structure on Attitudes

However, a social network analysis provides different kinds of results.

Network Data. A network roster on the Time 2 questionnaire asked respondents to circle "How frequently, on the average, do you have significant discussions with [each listed] other personnel about how you accomplish your work?" using a scale of 0 = not once in the last year, 1 = once a month or so, 2 = several times a month, 3 = every week, 4 = several times a day, 5 = every day, 6 = several times a day. The final usable adjacency matrix was 62×62. The cell values of this matrix were then squared, to approximate the number of times per month person i interacted with person j (e.g., "every day" is approximately 25 days per month, and $5^2 = 25$). Weak relations (less than 4^2, or "once a week") were dropped. When a symmetric matrix was necessary, the mean of the (i,j) and (j,i) value was used in each cell. The result was the *relational matrix*. The initial data for the *spatial matrix* was simply the pairwise walking distance between each pair of SHS employees, based on the floor plan.

Although analyzed in the full study, positional proximity and structural equivalence results are not reported here.

Network Influence. For individual-level *overall relational proximity*, frequency of interaction with all those with whom the individual communicated was used. *Relational groups* were identified by the NEGOPY network analysis program. Individual-level *overall spatial proximity* was measured by the squared, then reversed spatial matrix. Hierarchical clustering was used to identify *spatial clusters*.

Figures 6.7 and 6.8, portray, respectively, the relational groupings mapped onto the floor plan and the spatial clusters mapped onto the floor plan, each noting the groupings with highest and lowest mean combined attitudes and usage level. Such visual analyses are useful in locating areas of similar attitudes or usage, as well as boundaries between different attitudes and usage, and showing the relationships among relational and spatial network groupings.

For the individual-level analyses, for each respondent, the combined attitude score of each proximate other (whether relational, positional, or spatial) was multiplied by that other's proximity score (along with the extent to which the respondent felt that the opinion of one's co-workers or one's supervisor was important), then averaged over all proximate others for that respondent. For the group-level analyses, the mean of each member's combined attitude was calculated for each group or cluster.

Individual-Level Results. Based on several regressions, the best individual-level network-based predictors of an individual's combined attitude toward the system were the (1) mean attitude of one's co-workers (each weighted by the frequency of relational interaction with them, but not by importance of co-workers' opinions), and the (2) attitude of one's positional supervisor (weighted by importance of opinion). The variance explained ranged from 17% to 28%.

Group-Level Results. Results from an analysis of variance (ANOVA) show that there was an overall significant difference between the attitude

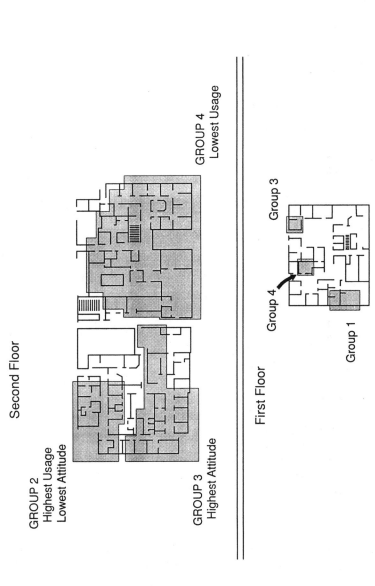

Second Floor

GROUP 2
Highest Usage
Lowest Attitude

GROUP 3
Highest Attitude

GROUP 4
Lowest Usage

First Floor

Group 3

Group 4

Group 1

Figure 6.7. Relational Groups Mapped Onto SHS Floor Plan Showing Groups With Highest and Lowest Attitudes and Highest and Lowest Computer Usage.

155

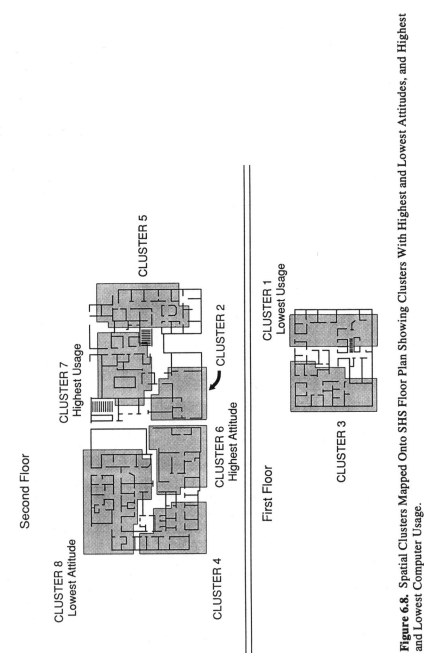

Figure 6.8. Spatial Clusters Mapped Onto SHS Floor Plan Showing Clusters With Highest and Lowest Attitudes, and Highest and Lowest Computer Usage.

means of the *four relational groups*. The group with the most positive attitude toward the system (Group 3) consisted primarily of cashier, billing, and upper-level administrative personnel. The least positive group (Group 2) consisted primarily of finance and personnel em-ployees and some administrators, and it had the highest level of use. As Figure 6.7 shows, these two groups are located next to each other, so spatial proximity cannot be playing a large role in similarity of attitudes.

There was no overall difference in average attitude about the system across the nine *spatially proximate clusters*, though there was an overall difference in system usage. The lowest usage occurred in the spatial subset consisting of radiology (Cluster 1), and the highest usage occurred in the spatial cluster of medical records personnel (Cluster 7), who were part of the relational group showing the lowest overall usage. The two spatial clusters with the highest (Cluster 6) and lowest (Cluster 8) com-bined attitudes toward the system are also located next to each other.

Influence of Occupational Relations on Attitudes

Although occupational membership plays some role in differences in attitudes toward, and use of, the system, we cannot yet say whether oc-cupational membership represents a form of network influence.

So, to identify within- and cross-occupational relations, a 5×5 occupation-by-occupation matrix was aggregated from the 62×62 relational matrix. Each occupation's row and column values were then divided by the number of members of that occupation to create the proportional density of within-occupation and cross-occupation com-munication relations. Then an *image matrix* was created by dichotomiz-ing each cell value into "1" if the value was higher than the overall average density of interaction (3.76) or '0' otherwise. Table 6.4 shows the density matrix and the image matrix.

Compared to the average level of communication interaction at SHS, MDs receive information from RNs but do not otherwise communicate with the rest of SHS or even among themselves. Administrators occupy a central place by communicating reciprocally with RNs and office/ clerical staff, all three of whom also communicate within their own occupations. Other medical staff (radiologists, pharmacy) basically communicate only with themselves. The most central occupation in the SHS network, the administrators, has the most positive attitude.

From a *relational* perspective, the density matrix indicates that only the physicians talk with themselves more than they do with any other occupation (although this is still less than the average level of interac-tion). The other medical workers, nurses, and administration all talk

TABLE 6.4 Density Matrix, Image Matrix, and Mean Combined Attitude Score for the Five Occupational Categories at SHS

Occupation	N	Density Matrix					Image Matrix				
		MD	OM	RN	AD	CL	MD	OM	RN	AD	CL
Physicians	6	**2.77**	1.94	2.45	2.28	.47	**0**	0	0	0	0
Other medical	15	3.50	**3.93**	1.92	5.08	2.04	0	**1**	0	0	0
Nurses	12	4.85	3.60	**8.19**	12.83	3.42	1	0	**1**	1	0
Administration	6	3.28	3.11	5.41	**3.33**	7.12	0	0	1	**0**	1
Clerical	29	1.24	1.20	2.26	4.13	**3.99**	0	0	0	1	**1**
Mean combined Attitude Score		−1.19	−.14	−.34	77	.25					
F-ratio = 4.14, $p<.01$											

SOURCE: Adapted from Aydin & Rice (1991).

with at least one other occupation proportionally more frequently than they do with their own occupation (though they each talk with themselves more than the average overall interaction level). Although 78% (48) of all the individuals did interact within their own occupation at a level at least equal to their average interaction with *all* other individuals (a rather minimal criterion), the communication density within each occupation (the diagonal value) is less than 50% of the total communication density for the respective row. These results indicate that we cannot consider occupations as *relational* groups.

Conclusion

This chapter demonstrates how social network analysis can be used in evaluating responses to and the impact of medical information systems. Both are influenced by characteristics of the organization's structure and by relationships—whether relational, positional, or spatial—among individuals and organizational units. The distinguishing characteristic of this approach to evaluation is that it uses information about the professional's location in organizational and professional networks and his or her relations with other professionals as well as individual attributes to understand adoption, diffusion, use, and attitudes toward a medical information system.

Additional Reading

Network Analysis

A wide variety of network analysis methods, computer packages, and measures exist (Alba, 1982; Berkowitz, 1982; Burt, 1980; Burt & Minor, 1983; Fombrun, 1982; Freeman, 1979; Marsden & Lin, 1982; Monge & Contractor, 1988; Rice & Richards, 1985; Richards & Rice, 1981; Rogers & Kincaid, 1981; Tichy, 1981; Wellman & Berkowitz, 1988). Knoke and Kuklinski (1982) and Scott (1991) provide excellent readable introductions to social network analysis.

Network Analysis Programs

In the United States, the three most-used network analysis packages are these:

1. UCINET IV (a wide-ranging suite of menu-driven programs and functions), obtainable from Dr. Stephen Borgatti, Analytic Technologies, 306 S. Walker St., Columbia, SC 29205; Bitnet: NO40016@UNIVSCVM.

2. STRUCTURE (a suite of programs emphasizing structural equivalence), obtainable from Dr. Ronald S. Burt, Center for the Social Sciences, 420 West 118th St., 8th floor, Columbia University, New York, NY 10027.

3. NEGOPY (a single program using a relational, graph-theory approach), obtainable from Dr. William Richards, Department of Communication, Simon Fraser University, Burnaby, British Columbia, CANADA, V5A 1S6; Bitnet: WRICHARD@WHISTLER.SFU.CA.

4. Also available is a companion program called FATCAT (Fat Categorical data) for cross-comparing network/relational data with attribute/categorical data. Also well known in Europe is Gradap (Graph Definition and Analysis Package), a suite of programs more similar to the familiar SPSS package than the other network analysis programs. It is available for about $500 from iec ProGAMMA, Kraneweg 8, 9718 JP, Groningen, The Netherlands.

Note

1. Figures 6.2 to 6.5 are reprinted by permission of JAI Press, Inc. (publishers of *The Sociological Quarterly*) and by permission from Pergamon Press Ltd (publishers of *Social Science & Medicine*) from Anderson & Jay (1985c, 1985a).

References

Alba, R. (1982). Taking stock of network analysis: A decade's results. *Research in the sociology of organizations, 1*, 39-74.

Anderson, J. G. (1992a). Information systems, medical. In A. Kent & J. G. Williams (Eds.), *Encyclopedia of microcomputers* (vol. 9, pp. 39-65). New York: Marcel Dekker.

Anderson, J. G. (1992b). Computerized medical record systems in ambulatory care. *Journal of Ambulatory Care Management, 15*, 1-8.

Anderson, J. G., & Jay, S. J. (1985a). Computers and clinical judgment: The role of physician networks. *Social Science and Medicine, 20*(10), 969-979.

Anderson, J. G., & Jay, S. J. (1985b). Physician utilization of computers: A network analysis of the diffusion process. In L. Frederiksen & A. Riley (Eds.), *Computers, people and productivity* (pp. 21-36). New York: Haworth Press.

Anderson, J. G. & Jay, S. J. (1985c). The diffusion of medical technology: Social network analysis and policy research. *The Sociological Quarterly, 26*(1), 49-64.

Anderson, J. G., Jay, S. J., Perry, J., & Anderson, M. M. (1990). Diffusion of computer applications among physicians: A quasi-experimental study. *Clinical Sociology Review, 8*, 116-127.

Anderson, J. G., Jay, S. J., Schweer, H. M., & Anderson, M. M. (1986). Why doctors don't use computers: Some empirical findings. *Journal of the Royal Society of Medicine, 79*, 142-144.

Anderson, J. G., Jay, S. J., Schweer, H. M., & Anderson, M. M. (1987). Diffusion and impact of computers in organizational settings: Empirical findings from a hospital. In G. Salvendy, S. L. Sauter, & J. J. Hurrell, Jr. (Eds.), *Social, ergonomic and stress aspects of work with computers* (pp. 3-10). New York: Elsevier.

Anderson, J. G., Jay, S. J., Schweer, H., Anderson, M., & Kassing, D. (1987). Physician communication networks and the adoption and utilization of computer applications in medicine. In J. G. Anderson & S. J. Jay (Eds.), *Use and impact of computers in clinical medicine* (pp. 185-199). New York: Springer Verlag.

Aydin, C. E. (1989). Occupational adaptation to computerized medical information systems. *Journal of Health and Social Behavior, 30*, 163-179.

Aydin, C., & Rice, R. E. (1991). Social worlds, individual differences, and implementation: Predicting attitudes toward a medical information system. *Information and Management, 20*, 119-136.

Aydin, C., & Rice, R. E. (1992). Bringing social worlds together: Information systems as catalysts for interdepartmental interactions. *Journal of Health and Social Behavior, 33*, 168-185.

Barley, S. R. (1986). Technology as an occasion for structuring: Evidence from observations of CT scanners and the social order of radiology departments. *Administrative Science Quarterly, 31*, 78-108.

Berkowitz, S. (1982). *An introduction to structural analysis: The network approach to social research*. Toronto, Canada: Butterworths.

Brenner, D., & Logan, R. (1980). Some considerations in the diffusion of medical technologies: Medical information systems. In D. Nimmo (Ed.), *Communication yearbook* (vol. 4, pp. 609-623). New Brunswick, NJ: Transaction Press.

Burt, R. (1980). Models of network structure. *Annual Review of Sociology, 6*, 79-141.

Burt, R. (1987). Social contagion and innovation: Cohesion versus structural equivalence. *American Journal of Sociology, 92*(6), 1287-1335.

Burt, R., & Minor, M. (Eds.). (1983). *Applied network analysis.* Newbury Park, CA: Sage.

Cole, J. R., & Cole, S. (1973). *Social stratification in science.* Chicago: University of Chicago Press.

Coleman, J. S., Katz, E., & Menzel, H. (1966). *Medical innovation: A diffusion study.* Indianapolis, IN: Bobbs-Merrill.

Cook, M. (1985). The impact of a patient care information system on the organization. In K. J. Hannah, E. J. Guillemin, & D. N. Conklin (Eds.), *Nursing uses of computer and information science* (pp. 161-165). Amsterdam: Elsevier.

Counte, M. A., Kjerulff, K. H., Salloway, J. C., & Campbell, B. C. (1987). Implementing computerization in hospitals: A case study of the behavioral and attitudinal impacts of a medical information system. In J. G. Anderson & S. J. Jay (Eds.), *Use and impact of computers in clinical medicine* (pp. 224-237). New York: Springer Verlag.

Crane, D. (1972). *Invisible colleges: Diffusion of knowledge in scientific communities.* Chicago: University of Chicago Press.

Davis, J. (1966). Structural balance, mechanical solidarity, and interpersonal relations. In J. Berger, M. Zelditch, Jr., & B. Anderson (Eds.), *Sociological theories in progress* (Vol. 1, pp. 74-101). Boston: Houghton Mifflin.

Davis, T. (1984). The influence of the physical environment in offices. *Academy of Management Review, 9*(2), 271-283.

Donnellon, A., Gray, B., & Bougon, M. G. (1986). Communication, meaning, and organized action. *Administrative Science Quarterly, 31*, 43-55.

Dow, G. (1988). Configurational and coactivational views of organizational structure. *Academy of Management Review, 12*(1), 53-64.

Erickson, B. (1988). The relational basis of attitudes. In B. Wellman & S. Berkowitz (Eds.), *Social structures: A network approach* (pp. 99-121). New York: Cambridge University Press.

Fombrun, C. (1982). Strategies for network research in organizations. *Academy Management Review, 7*, 280-291.

Freeman, L. (1979). Centrality in social networks: Conceptual clarification. *Social Networks, 1*, 215-239.

Giuliano, V. (1982). The mechanization of office work. *Scientific American, 247*(3), 148-165.

Hackman, J. R. (1983). Group influences on individuals. In M. D. Dunnette (Ed.), *Handbook of industrial and organizational psychology* (pp. 1455-1525). New York: John Wiley.

Hage, J., Aiken, M., & Marrett, C. (1971). Organizational structure and communications. *American Sociological Review, 36*, 860-871.

Hirschheim, R. A. (1985). *Office automation: A social and organizational perspective.* New York: Wiley.

Johnson, B. M., & Rice, R. E. (1987). *Managing organizational innovation: The evolution from word processing to office information systems.* New York: Columbia University Press.

Johnson, J. D. (1988). On the use of communication gradients. In G. Goldhaber & G. Barnett (Eds.), *Handbook of organizational communication.* Norwood, NJ: Ablex.

Johnson, S. (1967). Hierarchical clustering schemes. *Psychometrika, 32*, 241-253.

Kaplan, B. (1986). Impact of a clinical laboratory system: Users' perceptions. In *Medinfo 86: Sixth World Congress on Medical Informatics* (pp. 1057-1061). Amsterdam: Elsevier Science Publishers B. V.

Kaplan, B., & Duchon, D. (1989). A job orientation model of impact on work seven months post implementation. In *Medinfo 89: Sixth World Congress on Medical Informatics* (pp. 1051-1055). Amsterdam: North Holland.

Kimberly, J., & Evanisko, M. (1981). Organizational innovation: The influence of individual, organizational and contextual factors on hospital adoption of technological and administrative innovations. *Academy of Management Journal, 24*, 689-713.

Knoke, D., & Burt, R. S. (1983). Prominence. In R. S. Burt & M. J. Minor (Eds.), *Applied network analysis* (pp. 195-222). Newbury Park, CA: Sage.

Knoke, D., & Kuklinski, J. (1982). *Network analysis.* Newbury Park, CA: Sage.

Laumann, E., & Marsden, P. (1979). The analysis of oppositional structures in political elites: Identifying collective actors. *American Sociological Review, 44*, 713-732.

Lucas, H., Jr. (1981). *Implementation: The key to successful information systems.* New York: Columbia University Press.

Lundsgaarde, H. P., Fischer, P. A., & Steele, D. J. (1981). *Human problems in computerized medicine.* University of Kansas Publications in Anthropology, No. 13. Lawrence: University of Kansas.

Markus, M. L. (1984). *Systems in organizations: Bugs and features.* Boston, MA: Pitman.

Marsden, P., & Lin, N. (Eds.). (1982). *Social structure and network analysis.* Newbury Park, CA: Sage.

Mauksch, H. O. (1972). Patient care as a perspective for hospital organization research. In B. S. Georgopoulos (Ed.), *Organization research on health institutions* (pp. 159-172). Ann Arbor: Institute for Social Research, University of Michigan.

McCann, J., & Galbraith, J. R. (1981). Interdepartmental relations. In P. C. Nystrom & W. H. Starbuck (Eds.), *Handbook of organizational design, vol. 2: Remodeling organizations and their environments* (pp. 60-84). New York: Oxford University Press.

Monge, P., & Contractor, N. (1988). Measurement techniques for the study of communication networks. In C. Tardy (Ed.), *A handbook for the study of human communication: Methods and instruments for observing, measuring, and assessing communication processes* (pp. 107-138). Norwood, NJ: Ablex.

Olson, M., & Lucas, H., Jr. (1982). The impact of office automation on the organization: Some implications for research and practice. *Communications of the ACM, 25*(11), 838-847.

Rice, R. E. (1987). Computer-mediated communication and organizational innovation. *Journal of Communication, 37*(4), 65-94.

Rice, R. E. (1990). Computer-mediated communication system network data: Theoretical concerns and empirical examples. *International Journal of Man-Machine Studies, 30*, 1-21.

Rice, R. E. (1993). Using network concepts to clarify sources and mechanisms of social influence. In G. Barnett & W. Richards, Jr. (Eds.), *Advances in communication network analysis* (pp. 43-52). Norwood, NJ: Ablex.

Rice, R. E., & Aydin, C. (1991). Attitudes towards new organizational technology: Network proximity as a mechanism for social information processing. *Administrative Science Quarterly, 36*, 219-244.

Rice, R. E., Grant, A., Schmitz, J., & Torobin, J. (1990). Individual and network influences on the adoption and perceived outcomes of electronic messaging. *Social Networks, 12*(1), 27-55.

Rice, R. E., & Richards, W., Jr. (1985). An overview of network analysis methods and programs. In B. Dervin & M. Voigt (Eds.), *Progress in communication sciences* (vol. 6, pp. 105-165). Norwood, NJ: Ablex.

Richards, W., Jr., & Rice, R. E. (1981). NEGOPY network analysis program. *Social Networks, 3*(3), 215-223.

Riley, J., & Riley, M. (1972). Sociology: An approach to human communication. In R. Budd & B. Ruben (Eds.), *Approaches to human communication* (pp. 356-382). New York: Spartan.

Rogers, E. M., & Kincaid, L. (1981). *Communication networks: Toward a new paradigm for research.* New York: Free Press.

Salancik, G. R., & Pfeffer, J. (1978). A social information approach to job attitudes and task design. *Administrative Science Quarterly, 23*, 224-252.

Scott, J. (1991). *Social network analysis: A handbook.* Newbury Park, CA: Sage.

Stross, J. K., & Harlan, W. R. (1979). The dissemination of new medical information. *Journal of the American Medical Association, 241*, 2822-2824.

Tichy, N. (1981). Networks in organizations. In P. Nystrom & W. Starbuck. (Eds.), *Handbook of organizational design* (vol. 2, pp. 225-249). New York: Oxford University Press.

Tushman, M. L., & Scanlan, T. J. (1981). Boundary spanning individuals: Their role in information transfer and their antecedents. *Academy of Management Journal, 24*, 289-305.

Van de Ven, A. H. (1986). Central problems in the management of innovation. *Management Science, 32*, 590-607.

Van Maanen, J., & Barley, S. R. (1985). Cultural organization, fragments of a theory. In P. J. Frost, L. F. Moore, M. R. Louis, C. C. Lundberg, & J. Martin (Eds.), *Organizational culture* (pp. 31-53). Beverly Hills, CA: Sage.

Wellman, B. (1983). Network analysis: Some basic principles. In R. Colins (Ed.), *Sociological theory 1983* (pp. 155-200). San Francisco: Jossey-Bass.

Wellman, B., & Berkowitz, S. (Eds.). (1988). *Social structures: A network approach.* New York: Cambridge University Press.

Williams, F., Rice, R., & Rogers, E. M. (1988). *Research methods and the new media.* New York: Free Press.

7

Cost-Benefit Analysis of Medical Information Systems

A Critique

Gerald L. Glandon
Tracy L. Buck

Introduction

The importance of information systems and related services to the health care industry has been substantial both in terms of internal operations and in terms of relations external to the health care delivery organization. Internally, information systems support continued efforts to improve efficiency by assisting managers in obtaining useful cost information. The new generation of information systems has begun and will continue to move from primarily financial applications to "clinical decision-support systems" (Kerr & Jelinek, 1990). As a result, organizations have an improved ability to monitor and intervene with those clinical processes and providers supplying substandard care.

From an external perspective, appropriate information system acquisition and use today assists executives with a variety of important strategic planning activities that collectively influence the effectiveness of the institution. The inability to make appropriate corporate decisions about information technology acquisition today may put an institution behind its competitors for at least the next decade and perhaps forever. Analysts from other industries suggest that making use of information systems to shape strategy may enhance competitive performance and success (Cole, 1985). In some cases, the inability to adopt the new technology may signal the end of a hospital as an independent entity as its competitive position erodes. Porter (1985) argues that an organization must engage in activities that fundamentally transform the structure of the industry, significantly alter the position of the firm's products, or formulate new corporate opportunities to gain competitive advantage. Further, this acquisition signifies that an institution has participated in the early phases of an information technology explosion with almost no parallel.

Information technologies are costly and change rapidly, however. Thus there appears to be almost no end to the dollars that can be devoted to this investment. Because the dollars spent on information technology have alternative uses, such as clinical technologies and manpower, care must be exercised in the these budget allocations. Increasing financial stress and accountability puts pressure on managers to make the "right" decisions regarding the breadth and depth of information technology acquisition.

Despite the importance of these decisions from strategic (effectiveness) and operational (efficiency) perspectives, a review of the "state of the art" cost-benefit analyses (CBA) or cost-effectiveness analyses (CEA) of HIS in 1988 revealed several severe shortcomings (Glandon & Shapiro, 1988). The review also identified specific barriers to the appropriate, comprehensive evaluation of hospital information systems. This chapter briefly updates the review of CBA and CEA of information systems. It directly addresses the impediments identified by developing a paradigm for information system evaluation designed to aid those wishing to conduct this type of analysis for their institution.

Background

Health Care Environment

Costs

The health care environment can be characterized as one filled with change and stress. This condition is a primary factor in the demand for information systems, but it also makes the manager hesitant to commit financial resources without justification. Health care expenditures increased nationally at an annualized rate of 11.0% from 1970 to 1990 (Levit, Lazenby, Cowan, & Letsch, 1991). These expenditure increases have occurred for nearly all components of the health care delivery system, with some notable exceptions. The largest single component of health care expenditures was for hospital services, which was 43.7% of total health care expenditures in 1990, up 11.1% per year from 1970. Prescription drugs increased less rapidly than other components during the period (9.1%) and expenditures for nursing home services (11.9%) and home health services (21.1%) increased at particularly rapid rates (Levit, Lazenby, Cowan, & Letsch, 1991).

Even after controlling for general inflation and the increase in the population (annualized rates of 5.3% and 0.9%, respectively), real per capita expenditures have increased at a 4.8% annual rate versus a 2.2% real per capita rate of increase in gross national product. As a result, the United States now spends 12.2% of its GNP on health care expenditures, up from 7.4% in 1970. These increases are much more rapid than those of any other industrialized country (Graig, 1991).

Government and Business Responses

These high and persistent annualized increases in health care expenditures prompted government and private payers to adopt almost any program that could control costs. The federal government instituted prospective payment for hospitals in 1983. This program regulated the hospital price level for Medicare cases and provided an incentive for hospitals to improve efficiency. The results are mixed with respect to both cost and quality (Altman & Garfink, 1990; Rogers et al., 1990). The change in the form of hospital payment did create a "conflict of incentives" between the hospital management and its medical staff (Glandon & Morrisey, 1986). This conflict has given hospital management a financial incentive to understand physician practice patterns and utilization of hospital resources. An interesting potential effect from the point of view of information systems is that payment reform may influence an institution's likelihood of purchasing health care technology (Anderson & Steinberg, 1984).

As policy analysts look for the "cause" of increasing costs of medical care, several characteristics of the system raise questions about its efficiency and effectiveness. First, high variability in utilization of reasonably standardized procedures across geographic areas makes one question the standards of care that are being observed (Folland & Stano, 1990). Second, rigorous analysis indicates that there is a substantial amount of inappropriate care being delivered (Leape et al., 1990). Third, apparent low levels of efficiency and effectiveness of health care institutions have given rise to a revolution in thinking about the management and delivery of care. Although the names may be different, total quality management or continuous quality improvement programs have become important cornerstones in most health care institutions. Rapid increases in health expenditures along with these potential system problems have also resulted in a variety of controls by private payers. The potential of cost controls to limit the purchase of medical technology generally has been recognized for some time (Warner, 1978).

Information Needs

The changes in the health care delivery process, the increased competition for patients, and the resultant regulatory and cost containment responses by business have increased the need for information technology. Information technology is required to assist the hospital, physician, and other providers in making accurate strategic, administrative, and operational decisions:

- Strategic decisions involve an information base that is both internal and external to the institution. Assessing the market and regulatory environment, identifying and appraising the competition, and institutional planning all require access to information on the management of the institution as well as system or market information.

- Administrative decisions require predominantly internal information that spans multiple components of an organization. This level of decision making requires knowledge of external factors but concentrates on the internal needs.

- Operational needs consist of the clinical and financial systems currently in place to meet the patient care quality, employee management, reimbursement, and contracting needs. Emphasis is on monitoring and reporting clinical quality, paying employees, and determining and lowering the cost of care. These needs will continue as long as health care institutions continue to exist. The financial information needs, in particular, will continue as long as Medicare, Medicaid, and commercial payers seek relief from increasing health care expenses.

The need for information systems has increased as existing demands have continued and major new initiatives regarding total quality have generated a demand for new and better information. The movement toward an emphasis on the role of institutional total quality management on clinical quality has been a major motivator for more breadth and depth of information reporting. Recently published articles suggest the efficacy of information systems in the quality function (Janssen, Viste, & Gituck, 1990; Weissman, Mossel, Haimet, & King, 1990).

Barriers to Evaluation of Information Systems

Little in the way of formal cost-benefit or cost-effectiveness analyses has been published for information systems generally. Although hospital information systems have received attention, a comprehensive review published in 1988 revealed few studies (Glandon & Shapiro, 1988). The studies that did exist, in general, suffered from a variety of methodological flaws. More important, analyses of information systems now must consider more than applications to hospitals. The rapid growth of ambulatory surgery, medical group practice, and managed care has created an increased need for information systems outside of the acute care hospital. Although many lessons regarding evaluation may be transferable, there are different information needs and perhaps more complex impediments in these alternative health care delivery sites. A comprehensive review of cost-benefit or cost-effectiveness analyses of medical information systems must incorporate both traditional inpatient and alternative applications.

The Glandon and Shapiro (1988) study discovered three primary reasons that hospitals spend large amounts of money on information technology without detailed CBA or CEA in advance and also fail to evaluate these systems once implemented. First, much of this technology is acquired or developed for its own sake (technology for technology's sake). At least during the period of predominantly cost-based reimbursement, hospitals bore no financial consequences for keeping up with the Joneses with regard to HIS. Physicians, nurses, and administrative staff all believed that the technology had some potential for improving clinical or administrative practice and thus supported adoption. None of these groups faced the cost consequences of the decision, thus adoption was not generally an issue.

Second, most of the institutions that faced the HIS decision had some constraints regarding the cost of the evaluation itself. Many administrators may have surmised that this complex, interdependent technology could not be effectively evaluated at an acceptable cost. The range and type of benefits and costs involved in HIS technology defy simple measurement and validation. Often the evaluation requires a significant amount of highly valued staff time and/or hiring expensive consultants. Furthermore, if intuition indicates that most participants want the technology irrespective of the cost findings, it would be difficult for most administrators to justify the cost of the evaluation.

Third, once implemented, much of the reason for the cost analysis is no longer relevant. Economists call this *sunk cost* or "water under the bridge." It is highly unlikely that an adverse finding from a retrospective study would prompt the hospital to "undo" the technology. Consequently, why conduct the study? In addition, some administrators may not want to risk documenting and publicizing what may in retrospect be a mistake.

The question that remains to be addressed concerns the likely future of information system cost-benefit and cost-effectiveness evaluations. Cost concerns brought on by prospective payment and other programs may direct the focus of information technology assessment onto the demonstration of cost-effectiveness (Steele, 1989). As a result, CBA and CEA methods will likely become more commonly known and used. However, the evaluation of the emerging technologies may become more difficult. Early applications considered first-order effects such as the reduction of clerical labor. In the future, the objectives of information technology may include higher-order effects, such as marketing, research, and image promotion, that are more difficult to evaluate.

Cost-Benefit/Cost-Effectiveness Analyses

Overview

The complex literature on cost-benefit analysis (CBA) and cost-effectiveness analysis (CEA) in health care has been well developed (see Doubilet, Weinstein, & McNeil, 1986; Frank, 1981; Fuchs, 1980; Hellinger, 1980; Warner & Luce, 1982; Weinstein & Stason, 1977). In addition, a number of researchers have applied this methodology to health care issues in recent years (Drazen, Feeley, Metzger, & Wolfe, 1980; Foote & Erfurt, 1991; Mauskopf, Bradley, & French, 1991; Trahey, 1991; Tsevat, Wong, Pauker, & Steinberg, 1991; Veluchamy & Saver, 1990; Weeks, Tierney, & Weinstein, 1991). Therefore this chapter will not develop the methodology in detail nor will it review past applications. However, it is important to outline the motivation for and the key steps of these analyses.

CBA and CEA constitute procedures for improving rational decision making. Although not exactly the same, these two techniques differ only slightly. CBA assigns dollar values to the costs and benefits of a proposed investment. CEA differs only in that certain beneficial consequences of a program or technology are evaluated in nonmonetary terms, for example, "lives saved." Both techniques build on the basic microeconomic models of individual and firm decision making. These models assume that individuals maximize their utility and firms maximize profits and that decisions made by both are "rational" in the sense that they are consistent with those objectives.

Although prices serve as a mechanism or signal for allocating goods and services to the most highly valued (optimal) use in many markets, external resource allocation rules may be required if prices do not exist. Government (Warner & Luce, 1982) first used these techniques for such projects as river and harbor development, flood control/irrigation, and later, national defense programs, where markets did not exist to ensure provision of an optimal quantity of these goods or services by the private sector. In the absence of market prices, CBA and CEA provided a set of rules to help the government decide what, how, and for whom to produce (Warner & Luce, 1982; Weisbrod, 1983).

Cost-benefit analysis can apply to investment decisions or internal resource allocation decisions by individual firms even though the firm may operate in a conventional market. Firms rarely use prices for internal transactions of goods and services. Therefore management needs an analysis method to help decide which investment decisions are beneficial to the firm's production process and which are not. When deciding to adopt a proposed program or technology one might ask, Does it increase or decrease benefits and does it increase or decrease costs? If both costs and benefits increase or both costs and benefits decrease, formal cost-benefit or cost-effectiveness analysis is required. Under these conditions, the decision to invest depends on whether the increase in benefits exceeds the increase in costs.

Key Steps in CBA and CEA

Performance of either CBA or CEA requires the analyst to follow standard research evaluation protocols, with a few major differences in emphasis. Eight key evaluation elements, drawn from the literature (Glandon & Shapiro, 1988; Warner & Luce, 1982), must be addressed in conducting CBA and CEA.

1. Identify Study Objectives

As with most evaluations, identifying the key objectives represents the crucial means of both limiting and defining the study. For example, is the client seeking information to assist in pre-implementation decision making (feasibility analysis) or to review the impact of investments already made (post-implementation audits)? The objectives specified by the client (hospital, clinic, HMO, etc.) may also cause problems. In many cases, the objectives may be poorly defined. The key objectives may be indirect and removed from the direct application of the information system; thus analysts may use intermediate or proxy objectives. Although this operational necessity is understandable, it makes one wonder if the system ever did accomplish its real intent. For example, a clinical information system may be designed to improve the quality of care delivered at an institution. Because many factors may influence overall quality, the evaluation of the system may be conducted in terms of its ability to deliver standardized reports in a timely and accurate manner. Similarly, an executive information system (EIS) may be designed to enable senior management to make more effective decisions so that the institution can maintain or increase its market share. Because many other factors can influence this outcome, the analyst may justify an EIS based on its ability to deliver specified information to the senior executive regardless of whether the appropriate decisions are made.

2. Specify Alternatives

A comprehensive list of alternatives must be developed to ensure consideration of relevant options for addressing the underlying problem. Although too many alternatives can increase the complexity of the evaluation problem, too narrow a focus may lead the investigator to ignore key solutions. Warner and Luce (1982) provide the example of ignoring prevention programs when analyzing conventional clinical intervention approaches to cancer control. Consideration of alternatives is particularly important because neither CBA nor CEA evaluates programs in a vacuum. Rather, programs are viewed relative to all other *reasonable* investments (including "nontechnological" solutions) designed to further the firm's and/or society's objectives.

Specifying alternatives is also important for information system evaluation. The relevant alternative to a proposed information system application is almost never "no system." Analysts must consider the next most sophisticated option to make a valid comparison. For example, cost accounting systems based on standard costs may provide more accurate information regarding the financial consequences of treating different types of patients. This may be used in program evaluation, contracting, and program planning. However, the alternative is usually cost estimates based on cost-to-charge ratios, which, although less accurate, do provide some information concerning patient costs. The alternative is not the complete absence of patient-specific cost information.

3. Develop a Framework for Analysis

The health care delivery system can be viewed as a production process. This framework for analysis treats labor, machines, supplies, and information systems as specific inputs that, combined in a precise manner, produce measurable output. Thus, the information system alternatives under consideration represent different "production technologies." In essence this implies that the analyst must understand what function the information system is intended to accomplish to fully grasp how the technology performs. Economists call this *modeling the production process.*

4. Measure Costs

Program costs represent the portion of the cost-benefit or cost-effectiveness equation that is usually considered first. Although the process of identifying and tallying program costs may at first appear to be a simple accounting problem, cost-estimation actually presents both theoretical and empirical challenges. For example, economists typically consider the *opportunity cost* concept in assessing costs. The opportunity cost of a resource used in a particular program equals the value of the next best application of that resource. Although opportunity costs and accounting costs do not necessarily differ, opportunity costs become an issue when "free resources," which do not appear on an accountant's books, are employed in a production process. For example, volunteers used to transport patients may appear to be free. However, if these volunteers could have performed far more valuable alternative duties, they are costly when used to transport patients.

Also, the scope of the costs included in the analysis may greatly affect evaluation findings. Cost calculations should include not only the direct HIS equipment purchase price but also indirect costs such as training costs, the cost of resultant employee turnover, and the costs of programs designed to facilitate and measure realization of potential benefits.

Finally, the relevant time frame for pre- and post-implementation cost measurement must be defined, otherwise costs that are incurred prior to and at some time not immediately following HIS implementation may be ignored inappropriately.

A review of cost evaluations of information systems reveals nine key components of cost applied to hospital settings: hardware, software, supplies, data processing department personnel, maintenance, training, installation and implementation, depreciation, and cost of capital. These are unevenly included, however, as potential cost elements and few studies include elements from each.

5. Measure Benefits

Benefits identification and measurement represents the other key component of CBA or CEA evaluation. The scope of benefits to be included must be defined carefully. Particularly in the health care field, in addition to firm-specific benefits, societal gains such as lives saved, morbidity reduced, or function restored may need to be considered (Hu & Sandifer, 1981). Since many of these benefits are rarely priced and transacted in a market, they do not lend themselves to measurement by simple accounting systems. Assigning a value to life or to improved function represents a major economic challenge and the primary reason that "social" CBA and CEA is performed. Also, as for cost measurement, the determination of the time period for measurement of benefits accruing from an investment may influence evaluation results.

For summarization purposes, benefits can be grouped into two distinct categories: direct financial and quality benefits. *Direct financial* benefits include eight separate categories: personnel (actual reduced, diverted, potential, increase avoided), forms and supplies, equipment, data processing or service costs, lost charges (gross), charge capture, accounts receivable, and inventory carrying costs. Although all of these are potentially important, savings in personnel may constitute the most important component (Drazen et al., 1980). However, these benefits are also the most difficult to realize or at least to document that they are realized (Glandon & Shapiro, 1988). It appears to be difficult for institutions to actually reduce the number of FTEs despite the introduction of information technology that operations engineers indicate reduce work requirements.

Quality and other benefits also consist of nine distinct categories: increased patient care time, reduced order errors, faster order completion, increased satisfaction (physician, nursing and clinical staff, administration), spotting clinical problems, reduced repeat tests or orders, better documentation, better facility use, and management reports and decision support. These benefits may be important but generally have an indirect, time delayed, and uncertain effect on an institution.

For example, the objectives of a sophisticated patient care information system may include an increase in admissions or market share. The system may increase physician satisfaction with the patient care treatment process by making ordering of tests easier, improving access to patient information, and generally reducing time and effort leading to increased physician referrals to the institution. Thus physician satisfaction is an intermediate outcome that might be used because it is relatively easy to assess. Improved physician satisfaction is only of value to an institution, however, if admissions actually increase because the satisfied physicians refer more patients and/or tell about the system. The difficulty with using admissions or market share is that physicians may have increased referrals to the institution even without the system, or referrals may decrease in spite of the system.

6. Life Cycle/Discounting

Typically, projects have start-up costs that occur primarily in an early period, operating costs that continue over time, and, possibly, major periodic maintenance or enhancement costs that should be anticipated at various points in the project's life cycle. Benefits generally accrue over time. To compare the costs of an information system with benefits, both of which are realized at different points in time, all dollar figures must be converted to a value at a particular point in time. Most analysts discount benefits and costs to the present.

Discounting raises two key questions that the evaluator must consider. First, what is the appropriate time over which the information system is expected to be operational? Second, what is the rate at which benefits and costs should be discounted? In other words, what is the premium at which one would exchange goods today for goods to be received next year? Once a discount rate and project life cycle (n years) are selected, the stream of benefits and costs that result can be reduced to a discounted present value using the following equations:

$$PVB = B_0 + B_1/(1 + r_1)^1 + B_2/(1 + r_2)^2 + \ldots + B_n/(1 + r_n)n$$
$$PVC = C_0 + C_1/(1 + r_1)^1 + C_2/(1 + r_2)^2 + \ldots + C_n/(1 + r_n)n$$

PVB and PVC represent the discounted present value of benefits and costs, respectively. B_i and C_i represent the net benefits and costs accrued in the ith year and r_i is the discount rate in the ith year (usually assumed equal for all years). Because the discount rate is positive, benefits received and cost accrued in the future are worth less than benefits received today in present value terms.

7. Uncertainty

By their nature, CBA and CEA require analysts to deal with uncertain events, for example, estimates of: the value of life or restored function, the certainty of benefits realization, operating costs of a program, life cycle, discount rates, and so on. The sensitivity of evaluation results to the accuracy of estimates of uncertain variables should therefore be considered.

8. Equity

Applications of CBA or CEA should consider the equity of the distribution of costs and benefits. Because these analyses usually apply to social programs, a divergence between who bears the costs and who reaps the benefits can be as important to decision makers as the total level of costs and benefits. However, equity may be an issue with respect to the evaluation of information systems by the firm as well. This importance may be classified under the heading of political reality. If the operating units or organizational constituencies (e.g., private practice medical staff, nursing staff) benefit from a program but do not shoulder a portion of its cost, they will likely eagerly support its implementation. However, if the system increases their work or effort level but generates benefits or savings to other components of the organization, they will likely oppose the system. The assessment of equity may be important when trying to determine the ultimate feasibility of an information or any other system.

Findings of Existing Studies

Nineteen studies were sufficiently comprehensive to be evaluated overall and with respect to eight key parameters. This section will also present a limited review of new CBA or CEA studies.

Overall

The 1988 review concluded that "despite the wide variety of systems evaluated, the numerous study settings, and the diverse methods, most studies concluded that hospital information systems were beneficial" (Glandon & Shapiro, 1988). Eight of the 10 studies that were amenable to CBA or CEA formats found that benefits exceeded cost. In fact, some reported benefits at 4 to 5 times costs. Even those studies reviewed that did not conform to direct CBA or CEA formats (i.e., used return on investment, cost savings per patient, or net present value) generally indicated that the information systems studied were beneficial. Of the 2 studies that found that benefits were less than costs, 1 appeared, on the surface, to be the most objective because the results came from a federal government evaluation conducted by investigators not employed by the hospital involved.

Objectives

With respect to study objectives, six of the studies were designed to justify the proposed expenditure, whereas the remainder were conducted after the fact to justify or confirm the wisdom of the investment. Only three of the studies looked beyond direct economic benefits. These studies examined a variety of other factors but did not attempt to put dollar estimates on these benefits (Barrett, Barnum, Gordon, & Pesut, 1975; Huff & Bond, 1970; Wolfe, 1986).

Sponsorship

Study sponsorship was examined to confirm the objectivity of the studies. Twelve of the 19 studies were conducted by the institution that implemented the information system. Only 4 of the studies were funded by the government and conducted on systems outside of government control (Barrett et al., 1975; Barrett, Hersch, & Caswel, 1979; Gall & Norwood, 1977; Huff & Bond, 1970). One study (Technicon, 1975) was sponsored by a commercial HIS vendor.

Alternatives

The majority of studies reviewed appears to generally view information systems as a "zero-one" proposition, without consideration of alternatives to the scope (departmental or functional applications) or the level of sophistication of the information processing technology employed. Further, with some exceptions (Arenson & London, 1979; Barrett et al., 1975; Gall & Norwood, 1977; Hubbell, 1984; Moore, 1982; Wolfe, 1986), the studies did not provide adequate descriptions of the system being evaluated. Most of the studies compared (actual or predicted) post-implementation costs and benefits with those prior to installation but did not consider alternatives. There were no comparisons of "make-buy" alternatives to the information system or, with one exception (Carter, 1984), alternative system vendors.

Costs

This literature generally did not adequately document the derivation of system costs, with only seven studies providing detailed cost information. Some studies recognized broadly considered costs but presented only select categories. Further, a number of these studies presented costs, benefits, and net benefits on an annualized basis (Anser Analytic Service, 1982; Carter, 1984; Hubbell, 1984; Moore, 1982;

Napoli & Russo, 1982; Shapin, 1979; Wolfe, 1986). Most ignored salvage value of equipment; they generally failed to discuss the "lease-buy" decision; and all but Carter (1984) failed to document selection, acquisition, and implementation costs. This last finding is interesting because many authors asserted (Lauesen, Young, & Kennedy, 1982; Minch, 1982) that a large proportion of the benefits required significant management effort and planning to realize.

Benefits

The literature fails to present a systematic, generalizable, and consistently sound approach to benefit measurement and valuation. Most studies concentrated on monetary benefits and ignored nonmonetary benefits. The studies generally considered a narrowly defined set of benefits in the formal cost-benefit or cost-effectiveness analysis. Analyses ranged from a concentration on only 1 benefit (Kim & Schmitz, 1975) to a formal consideration of 20 types of benefits (Lauesen & Kennedy, 1980). These benefits ranged from qualitative to quantitative. Only Anser Analytic Service (1982) attempted to assign monetary value to less directly financial benefits. A related problem was the potential that many of the personnel benefits included may be illusory. The four categories identified—actual reductions, diverted, potential, and increase avoided—cover the type of benefits that may accrue, but only the first category represents savings due to staff reductions that actually occurred and are attributable to automation.

Life Cycle

The studies generally did not discuss the assumptions involved in selection of a relevant life cycle. Some studies (Hubbell, 1984) avoided the issue by simply presenting results for the first "X" years of operation, or on an annual basis (Napoli & Russo, 1982), without indicating an actual life cycle estimate. Other studies merely stated the life cycle selected but provided no rationale for the time period selected.

Inflation/Discounting

The CBA and CEA studies we evaluated generally did not demonstrate consistently adequate treatment of the issues related to inflation and discounting. Some studies ignored the issue entirely (Arenson & London, 1979; Napoli & Russo, 1982); others (Hubbell, 1984) used a rate of inflation for wage rates but did not appear to discount the benefit stream; some studies (Kim & Schmitz, 1975; Shapin, 1979) utilized multiple discount rates.

Uncertainty

There was minimal use of sensitivity analysis in the literature to deal with uncertainty. When employed, only one (of several assumptions) was tested.

New Findings

Since that review, there have been analyses involving the costs or benefits of information systems in health care but no large-scale, comprehensive evaluation. There is no evidence that analysts have performed and reported evaluations of large-scale information systems nor have they performed a full-scope analysis. Apparently no researchers have invested the time and effort to fully document a comprehensive range of relevant information system benefits or to fully document the costs of selection, purchase, implementation, and follow-up of the information system in question. Although many published papers appear to be reporting on CBA or CEA, their content is disappointing (Gellman, 1989; MacKenzie, 1989; Sinclair, 1991).

Despite this lack of empirical progress, some interesting changes in evaluations have occurred. Analysts and practitioners facing the decision to purchase and implement an information system have began to recognize the need for comprehensive cost-benefit evaluations. For example, Westlake (1983) delineated many of the prospects and problems faced when evaluating an automated data processing system for a clinical laboratory. In a hypothetical example, he outlined the steps involved in performing a cost-effectiveness study of a laboratory information system including: discussions of the objectives, specifying alternatives, understanding the production process, estimating costs, estimating revenue, and discounting problems. He also identified four obstacles to cost analyses that indicate a significant degree of sophistication in analysis. Specifically, he recognized that the beneficial effects of laboratory systems are numerous, often intangible, and may not even ensue because of external factors.

Similarly, Zielstorff (1985) summarized the need for cost-benefit analyses of computer systems in nursing. She concluded, however, that because these systems generally are not designed exclusively for nursing, and involve many other components of the delivery system, their benefits are diffuse (i.e., accrue to others within the organization) and difficult to measure.

As mentioned above, we have little confidence in the validity and generalizability of the cost-benefit findings with respect to hospital information systems. Only two studies, Barrett et al. (1979) and Schmitz (1974), found that benefits were less than costs. Furthermore, the negative findings by Barrett et al. (1979) were from the study that appeared most objective on the surface, an evaluation sponsored by the federal government in which the investigators were not employed by the hospital involved.

Problems With Cost Evaluations of Information Systems

The same problems found in the earlier review of hospital information systems appear to apply today. These problems will be restated, emphasizing the current needs to evaluate information systems. First, most studies had serious *questions of objectivity*. With only three exceptions, the studies had been conducted by the HIS user or vendor. Furthermore, few of the studies appeared in peer-reviewed journals. Although the origin of the evaluator and the source of the publication does not necessarily invalidate the findings, it certainly calls into question the objectivity of the evaluations. Second, the analyses suffered from *methodology problems* when compared to conventional CBA or CEA. Specifically, the studies failed to: adequately specify, measure, and validate costs of HIS; identify, define, and estimate HIS benefits; control for confounding variables by appropriate modeling; and handle technical estimation issues such as inflation, discounting, and uncertainty. These problems with methodology may have many explanations but may not be easily rectified because of the inherent difficulty in evaluating information systems.

Third, at the time of the review, most of the studies had become *seriously out of date*. Almost half of the studies found and reviewed were published in the 1970s. With the rapid changes observed in information systems technology in the mid to late 1980s, these evaluations may have been conducted on what is now obsolete information system technology.

Fourth, although the studies reviewed differed in geographic location and in time, almost all of the studies had been conducted at a *single hospital* with particular HIS technology. This fact renders the findings not generalizable to the total hospital market.

Finally, few of the studies attempted an evaluation of the HIS from beyond the *perspective of an individual institution*. Despite the major role government plays in the financing of health care, the social benefits and costs of this HIS intervention were not considered.

As a result of these shortcomings in the "state of the art," the empirical findings of the net benefits of HIS should be seriously questioned. Little can be drawn from these findings except to maintain that efforts should be directed toward helping hospital managers design and implement evaluations of information systems.

An Analysis Paradigm for Information Systems

Defining Health Care Information Systems

In the most general sense, an information system is merely a process for collecting, processing, and disseminating information in an organization. This process utilizes staff, policies, and procedures and may include varying degrees of automation. An information system that makes extensive use of computer hardware and software is called a *computer-based information system* (O'Brien, 1982).

Part of the difficulty in information systems evaluation lies in these systems' bewildering range of scope (size), functionality, and system configuration. Information systems in health care include hospitalwide comprehensive information systems covering a wide range of functions in both clinical and administrative areas as well as ancillary systems and stand-alone departmental systems. Multi-institutional arrangements create complex information systems structures that may utilize local clinical and ancillary functions as well as distributed financial and other informational reporting functions. The varying degrees of integration make each of these systems unique, whether they are institutional or multi-entity, thus confounding the evaluation process.

Our task becomes one of defining information systems in a way that makes use of commonalities yet allows for differences across institutional settings. This framework can then be used as the basis for identifying where information systems goals and objectives impact the organizational benefits and costs. One approach is to define categories of information systems and describe their information requirements. This will assist those attempting CBA or CEA in deciding the scope of evaluation that is most appropriate and feasible.

There are many methods of categorizing information systems within health care organizations (Austin, 1988; Drazen et al., 1980; Krobock, 1984; Malec, 1991). Although all have strengths and weaknesses, for this analysis a three-category method has been adopted to describe information systems in an organization. These three categories corresponding to information requirements are *operational systems*, *administrative systems*, and *strategic planning systems*.

Operational systems are essentially transactional. This means that they handle internal, day-to-day, real-time information processing tasks. These systems are typically utilized at the staff and line supervisor level. Examples include admission, discharge, and transfer (ADT); census reporting; inventory control; and financial systems such as general ledger and accounts payable.

Administrative systems consist of control reporting and operational planning systems. Control reporting systems are used to compare actual versus targeted results, and operational planning systems are used to identify resources necessary to support organizational activities (Austin, 1988; Hicks, 1990). Examples of control reporting systems may include case mix, incomplete chart reporting, absence and turnover control, and revenue statistics. Examples of operational planning systems may include care planning, patient scheduling, wage and salary planning, and capital spending. These types of systems are also commonly referred to as *management information systems* or *decision-support systems* and tend to rely mainly on information internal to the institution.

Strategic planning systems provide support for actions taken by senior management that can affect an entire organization. Activities performed at this management level include setting policy, identifying potential markets, responding to regulatory agencies, and monitoring public image and community involvement. These types of systems differ in their functionality and are described using a range of terms including *executive support systems* and *executive information systems* (Rockart & DeLong, 1988). Strategic planning systems utilize information from both internal and external sources. Examples of strategic planning systems may include systems that support physician recruitment and retention, contracting activities, legal actions, and cost-containment efforts.

These three categories of information systems can be differentiated by function within the health care environment. Health care institutions can group their information systems into the broad categories of medical and business functions. Medical functions are those that support patient care. Business functions support administrative operations. The final framework, consisting of different categories for information systems and functional areas in health care institutions, can be seen in Figure 7.1. These general categories remain consistent regardless of the type of organization.

The general definitions described above provide insight into why most analysts have had difficulty in evaluating information systems. If

	Function	
Information Requirement Level	*Medical*	*Business*
Strategic planning	Physician recruitment and retention contracting	Legal actions Cost containment
Administrative	Case mix Incomplete chart reporting Care planning patient scheduling	Absence and turnover control Revenue statistics Wage and salary planning Capital spending
Operational	Admission, discharge, and transfer Census reporting	Inventory control General ledger Accounts payable

Figure 7.1. Typical Information Systems by Function and Information Requirement Level

an information system is viewed as solely the physical capital and manpower associated with its use, analysts may ignore its organizational impacts (i.e., functions) and the relevant alternatives to the proposed system and thus can ignore important costs and benefits of the system. However, Figure 7.1 describes a complex framework for information flow in an organization. Information not only flows from staff level upward through middle management to senior management but can flow also across functional areas. By not recognizing information systems as a process, analysts become confused by the objectives and production processes associated with the system.

Implications

The debate on how information systems contribute to an organization's efficiency and effectiveness continues today and has direct implications for cost-benefit and cost-effectiveness analyses. At one extreme of the management hierarchy, information systems supporting operational activities can contribute to an organization's efficiency. Belitsos (1988, p. 61) writes: "Conventional measurements of efficiency typically center on how information technology supports improved performance for a work group, department, or internal function." Most of the quantifiable elements in CBA or CEA have occurred at the *operational level*, where inputs are identifiable (for example, the labor used to perform the ADT function or the time required to perform a certain number of tests). Drazen et al. (1980, p. 4) support this by stating: "The discrete impacts of automation that are most predictable and measurable are at the level of individual task or job performance." Likewise, output can be relatively well defined (e.g., number of admissions, discharges, and transfers), measured, and realized.

CBA or CEA performed for operational systems has the greatest value. Management can expect to obtain reasonably accurate and reliable estimates of the value of these types of systems at minimal cost. The findings can be an important part of the decision-making process for this level of information system acquisition and implementation.

At the other extreme of the management hierarchy, information systems supporting *strategic planning* contribute to an organization's effectiveness. Inputs are cross-functional, that is, the executive must assemble information from multiple internal and external sources. Similarly, outputs that these systems are designed to impact include market share, profitability, physician and staff retention, and so on. The literature mentioned above supports the difficulty that analysts have had in identifying and measuring impacts at this level. The reason, in part, is because these outputs are difficult to link to any one process or input (Martin, 1990).

CBA and CEA performed on strategic planning systems by a single institution will likely be unproductive. It would be more appropriate for the government or other external organization to evaluate these types of systems. Decision making at the strategic-planning level is often unstructured (Malec, 1991), with perceptions of value and other political factors forming important components of the decision. As was observed above, technology for technology's sake may motivate the purchase. Thus spending the time and money on formal CBA and CEA does not make sense for the individual institution. Rather, formal evaluations of strategic planning systems require a social perspective and, at the least, market level data, both of which are more available and appropriate in government-sponsored research.

Between the operational and strategic systems in the management hierarchy are *administrative systems*. These systems directly influence both the efficiency and the effectiveness of institutional operations and include objective, quantifiable elements of operational systems, thus lending themselves to formal evaluation. However, these systems also have characteristics of strategic systems in that they are cross-functional within the organization. As a result, control and operational planning systems such as absence and turnover control and wage and salary planning have mixed potential for evaluation.

CBA and CEA applied to administrative systems may be the area of greatest potential value added to the institution. Melding the defined, objective elements with the somewhat unstructured needs of the system can greatly improve decision making. Institutions that concentrate the application of formal evaluations on these types of systems may be able to differentiate themselves from competitors. The future progress made in applying CBA and CEA to information system technology in the institutional setting should be with administrative systems.

Additional Reading

Introduction

Several books and articles describe the general issues surrounding health care costs and information technology and various aspects of their influence on the health care environment.

Coddington, D. C., Keen, D. J., Moore, K. D., & Clarke, R. L. (1990). *The crisis in health care: Cost, choices, and strategies.* San Francisco, CA: Jossey-Bass.

DeLuca, J. M., & Doyle, O. (1991). *Health care information systems: An executive's guide for successful management.* Chicago, IL: American Hospital Association.

Drucker, P. F. (1990). *Managing the non-profit organization: Practices and principles* (1st ed.). New York: Harper Collins.

Matta, K. F. (1988). The impact of prospective pricing on the information system in the healthcare industry. *Journal of Medical Systems, 12*(1), 57-66.

Cost-Benefit and Cost-Effectiveness Analyses

Many authors have described cost-benefit and cost-effectiveness analyses in health care but few have emerged as comprehensive treatments of the subject. Warner and Luce appear to be the accepted authority with regard to methodology.

Elixhauser, A. (Ed.). (1993). Health care cost-benefit and cost-effectiveness analysis (CBA/CEA) from 1979 to 1990: A bibliography. *Medical Care, 31* (7: Supplement), 150 pp.

Klarman, H. (1974). Application of cost-benefit analysis to the health services and the special case of technologic innovation. *International Journal of Health Services, 4,* 325-352.

Warner, K., & Luce, B. (1982). *Cost-benefit and cost-effectiveness analysis in health care: Principles, practice and potential.* Ann Arbor: Health Administration Press.

Zinn, T. K., & DiGiulio, L. W. (1988). Actualizing system benefits—Part IV. *Computers in Healthcare, 9*(8), 34-35.

Structure Impacts

The information technology explosion has had profound impacts on the structure of the health care environment and the roles of the health care manager.

Dearden, J. (1983). Will the computer change the job of top management? *Sloan Management Review, 25*(1), 57.

Johns, M. L. (1990). The CIO and IRM (information resources management) alliance: Maneuvering for competitive edge in hospital information management. *Topics in Health Records Management, 11*(1), 1-7.

Nonaka, I. (1988). Toward middle-up-down management: Accelerating information creation. *Sloan Management Review, 29*(3), 9.

Walters, R. W., & Lincoln, T. L. (1987). Using information tools to improve hospital productivity. *Healthcare Financial Management, 41*(8), 74-78.

Wyman, J. (1985). Technological myopia—the need to think strategically about technology. *Sloan Management Review, 26*(4), 59.

Applications

Although not always comprehensive applications of cost-benefit or cost-effectiveness techniques, there have been numerous applications within components of the health care delivery system. Some examples follow.

Strategic Planning

Applegate, L. M., Mason, R. D., & Thorpe, D. (1986). Design of a management support system for hospital strategic planning. *Journal of Medical Systems, 10*(1), 79-95.

Camillus, J. C., & Lederer, A. L. (1985). Corporate strategy and the design of computerized information systems. *Sloan Management Review, 26*(3), 35.

Davis, D. (1984). Computers and top management. *Sloan Management Review, 25*(3), 63.

Fredericks, P., & Venkatraman, N. (1988). The rise of strategy support systems. *Sloan Management Review, 29*(1).

Ghoshal, S., & Kim, S. K. (1986). Building effective intelligence systems for competitive advantage. *Sloan Management Review, 28*(1), 49.

Johnson, B. (1986). Developing strategic planning systems for healthcare organizations. *Healthcare Strategic Management, 4*(11), 4-8.

Kim, K. K., & Michelman, J. E. (1990). An examination of the factors for the strategic use of information systems in the healthcare industry. *MIS Quarterly, 14*(2), 201-215.

Mathis, B. W. (1985). Plan or perish: The case for long-range planning. *Computers in Healthcare, 6*(1), 40-46.

Human Resources

Calhoun, Z. F., & Lohman, P. (1987). Personnel implications for managing a hospital information system. *Topics in Healthcare Financing, 14*(2), 77-88.

Garre, P. P. (1990). A computerized recruitment program. *Journal of Nursing Administration, 20*(1), 24-27.

Clinical

Friedman, B. A. (1986). Pathologists, computers and control of the clinical laboratory database. *Pathologist, 40*(9), 40-46.

Friedman, B. A., & Mitchell, W. (1990). Horizontal and vertical integration in hospital laboratories and the laboratory information system. *Clinical Laboratory Medicine, 10*(3), 627-641.

Hindel, R., & Preger, W. (1988). Cost-effectiveness prospects of picture archiving and communication systems. *Health Policy, 9*(1), 91-101.

Szafran, A. J., & Kropf, R. (1988). Strategic uses of teleradiology. *Radiology Management, 10*(2), 23-27.

Finance

Sabin, P. (1987). Hospital cost accounting and the new imperative. *Health Progress, 68*(4), 52-57.

Tselepis, J. N. (1989). Refined cost accounting produces better information. *Healthcare Financial Management, 43*(5), 26-8, 30, 34.

Vogel, L. H. (1987). Patient accounts management: It's what's up front that counts. *Healthcare Financial Management, 41*(9), 42-44, 48, 50.

Other

Bittle, L. J., & Bloomrosen, M. (1990). QA, RM and UM functions require coordinated information management. *Journal of Quality Assurance, 12*(1), 14-19, 42.

Hanlon, P. I., & Kaskiw, E. A. (1989). Physician bonding: One hospital's experience. *Computers in Healthcare, 10*(3), 24-26, 28, 31.

Muller, J. H. (1986). Strategic Importance of MIS for home healthcare. *Computers in Healthcare, 7*(6), 31-32, 36-40.

Prussin, J. A. (1987). Automation: The competitive edge for HMO's and other alternative delivery systems. *Journal of Medical Systems, 11*(6), 431-444.

References

Altman, S., & Garfink, C. (1990). How have PPS changes affected allocation of Medicare spending for hospital care? A case study of New York State. *Inquiry, 27*(4), 19-31.

Anderson, G., & Steinberg, E. (1984). To buy or not to buy: Technology acquisition under prospective payment. *New England Journal of Medicine, 311*(July 19), 182-185.

Anser Analytic Service. (1982). *Evaluation of the Medical Information System at the NIH Clinical Center: Summary of findings and recommendations*. NTIS, PB82-190083.

Arenson, R., & London, J. (1979). Comprehensive analysis of a radiology operations management computer system. *Radiology, 133* (November), 355-362.

Austin, C. (1988). *Information systems for health services administration*. Ann Arbor, MI: Health Administration Press.

Austin, H. (1986). The economics of information systems. *Computers in Health Care, 7*(June), 43-46.

Barrett, J., Barnum, R., Gordon, B., & Pesut, R. (1975). *Evaluation of the implementation of a Medical Information System in a General Community Hospital*. Final Report to National Center for Health Services Research, Department of Health, Education and Welfare, PHS 110-73-331.

Barrett, J., Hersch, P., & Caswel, R. (1979). *Evaluation of the implementation of the Technicon Medical Information System at El Camino Hospital: Part II. Economic trend analysis.* Report to the National Center for Health Services Research (As cited in Drazen et al., 1980).

Belitsos, B. (1988). Can we measure what we do? *Computer Decisions*, August, pp. 60-63.

Carter, L. (1984). *The hospital information systems: A weapon for survival under DRGs.* Proceedings of the 13th Annual Conference of the Hospital Management Systems Society, pp. 195-205. Chicago: AHA.

Cole, R. (1985). Target information for competitive performance. *Harvard Business Review, 63*(3), 100-109.

Doubilet, P., Weinstein, M., & McNeil, B. (1986). Use and misuse of the term "cost effective" in medicine. *New England Journal of Medicine, 314*(January 23), 253-256.

Drazen, E., Feeley, R., Metzger, J., & Wolfe, H. (1980). *Methods for evaluating costs of automated hospital information systems.* Department of Health and Human Services, National Center for Health Services Research, PHS No. 233-79-3000.

Folland, S., & Stano, M. (1990). Small area variations: A critical review of propositions, methods and evidence. *Medical Care Review, 47*(4), 419-466.

Foote, A., & Erfurt, J. (1991). The benefit to cost ratio of work-site blood pressure control programs. *Journal of the American Medical Association, 265*(10), 1283-1286.

Frank, R. (1981). Cost-benefit analysis of mental health services: A review of the literature. *Administration in Mental Health, 8*(Spring), 161-176.

Fuchs, V. (1980). What is CBA/CEA and why are they doing this to us? *New England Journal of Medicine, 303*(October 16), 937-938.

Gall, J., & Norwood, D. (1977). *Demonstration and evaluation of a total hospital information system.* National Center for Health Services Research, Research Summary Series. DHEW No. (HRA) 77-3188.

Gellman, C. (1989). Automating improves OR efficiency, cost effectiveness. *OR Manager, 5*(7), 10-11.

Glandon, G., & Morrisey, M. (1986). Redefining the hospital-physician relationship under prospective payment. *Inquiry, 23*(Summer), 166-175.

Glandon, G., & Shapiro, R. (1988). Benefit-cost analysis of hospital information systems: The state of the (non) art. *Journal of Health and Human Resource Administration, 11*(Summer), 30-92.

Graig, L. (1991). *Health of nations: An international perspective.* Washington, DC: The Wyatt Company.

Hellinger, F. (1980). Cost-benefit analyses of health care: Past applications and future prospects. *Inquiry, 17* (Fall), 204-215.

Hicks, J. (1990). *Information systems in business: An introduction* (2nd ed.). St. Paul, MN: West.

Hu, J., & Sandifer, F. (1981). *Synthesis of Cost-of-Illinois Methodology.* National Center for Health Services Research, PHS Contract No. 233-79-3010.

Hubbell, M. B. (1984). *Hospital information systems (H.I.S.) impact: A post-implementation review.* Proceedings of the 13th Annual Conference of the Hospital Management Systems Society, pp. 77-86. Chicago: AHA.

Huff, W., & Bond, J. (1970). *Demonstration of a shared hospital information system.* Final report prepared for The Sisters of the Third Order of St. Francis, Peoria, Illinois.

Janssen, C., Viste, A., & Gituck, E. (1990). A simple on-line information system for quality assessment. *Medical Care, 28*(7), 567-72.

Kerr, J., & Jelinek, R. (1990). IS in the 1990s and beyond: An environmental assessment. *Journal of Health Administration Education, 8*(1), 5-10.

Kim, S., & Schmitz, H. (1975). Micro/macro cost-benefit analyses prove new data system's value to hospital, community. *Hospital Financial Management,* October, pp. 48-53.

Krobock, J. (1984). A taxonomy: Hospital information systems evaluation methodologies. *Journal of Medical Systems, 8*(5), 419-429.

Lauesen, W. D., & Kennedy, O. G. (1980). *Evaluating the benefit of hospital information systems: A management engineering approach.* Proceedings of the 8th Annual Conference of the Hospital Management Systems Society, pp. 175-186. Chicago: AHA.

Lauesen, W. D., Young. C. A., & Kennedy, O. G. (1982). *Hospital computer benefits projection/realization.* Proceedings of the 11th Annual Conference of the Hospital Management Systems Society, pp. 207-219. Chicago: AHA.

Leape, L., Park, R., Solomon, D., Chassin, M., Kosecoff, J., & Brook, R. (1990). Does inappropriate use explain small-area variations in the use of health care services? *Journal of the American Medical Association, 263* (5), 669-672.

Levit, L., Lazenby, H., Cowan, C., & Letsch, S. (1991). National health expenditures, 1990. *Health Care Financing Review, 13*(1), 29-62.

MacKenzie, G. (1989). Scientific inventory planning in materials management. *Hospital Materials Management, 14*(6), 16-19.

Malec, B. T. (1991). The benefit-cost justification of executive information systems: A model and case study. In AHA (Ed.), *Proceedings of the 1992 Annual HIMSS Conference* (pp. 133-138). Chicago, IL: American Hospital Association.

Martin, J. (1990). The environment and future of health information systems. *Journal of Health Administration Education, 8* (1), 11-24.

Mauskopf, J., Bradley, C., & French, M. (1991). Benefit-cost analysis of hepatitis B vaccine programs for occupationally exposed workers. *Journal of Occupational Medicine, 33*(6), 691-698.

Minch, D. A. (1982). *Patient care systems planning for the acquisition.* Proceedings of the 11th Annual Conference of the Hospital Management Systems Society, pp. 109-118. Chicago: AHA.

Moore, S. (1982). *Implementing a hospital information system: Can it deliver what it promises?* Proceedings of the 10th Annual Conference of the Hospital Management Systems Society, pp. 359-376. Chicago: AHA.

Napoli, J. G., & Russo, F. A. (1982). *Hospital information system cost and benefit analysis methodology: Structuring the ill-defined.* Proceedings of the 11th Annual Conference of the Hospital Management Systems Society, pp. 131-139. Chicago: AHA.

O'Brien, J. A. (1982). *Computers in business management* (3rd ed.). Homewood, IL: Richard D. Irwin.

Porter, M. E. (1985). *Competitive advantage: Creating and sustaining superior performance.* New York: Free Press.

Rockart, J. F., & DeLong, D. W. (1988). *Executive support systems: The emergence of top management computer use.* Homewood, IL: Dow Jones-Irwin.

Rogers, W., Draper, D., Kahn, K., Keeler, E., Rubenstein, L., Kosecoff, J., & Brook, R. (1990). Quality of care before and after implementation of the DRG-based prospective payment system. A summary of effects. *Journal of the American Medical Association, 264*(15), 1989-1994.

Schmitz, H. (1974). An evaluation of the immediate financial impact of the hospital information system at Deaconess Hospital. In Koza, R. (Ed.), *Health information systems evaluations.* Boulder, CO: Colorado Associated University Press.

Shapin, P. (1979). Unpublished and untitled report. (As cited in Drazen et al., 1980)

Sinclair, V. (1991). The impact of information systems on nursing performance and productivity. *Journal of Nursing Administration, 21*(2), 46-50.

Steele, L. (1989). *Managing technology: The strategic view.* New York, NY: McGraw-Hill.

Technicon. (1975). *Cost-benefit analysis of the Technicon Medical Information System (MIS) for (unnamed hospital).* (As cited in Drazen et al., 1980)

Trahey, P. (1991). A comparison of the cost-effectiveness of two types of occupational therapy services. *American Journal of Occupational Therapy, 45*(5), 397-400.

Tsevat, J., Wong, J., Pauker, S., & Steinberg, M. (1991). Neonatal screening for sickle cell disease: A cost-effectiveness analysis. *Journal of Pediatrics, 118*(4), 546-554.

Veluchamy, S., & Saver, C. (1990). Clinical technology assessment, cost-effective adoption and quality management by hospitals in the 1990s. *Quality Review Bulletin, 16*(6), 223-228.

Warner, K. (1978). The effects of hospital cost containment on the development and use of medical technology. *Milbank Memorial Fund Quarterly, 56*(Spring), 187-211.

Warner, K. E., & Luce, B. R. (1982). *Cost-benefit and cost-effectiveness analysis in health care: Principles practice and potential.* Ann Arbor, MI: Health Administration Press.

Weeks, J., Tierney, M., & Weinstein, M. (1991). Cost-effectiveness of prophylactic intravenous immune globulin in chronic lymphocytic leukemia. *New England Journal of Medicine, 325*(2), 81-86.

Weinstein, M., & Stason, W. (1977). Foundations of cost-effectiveness analysis for health and medical practices. *New England Journal of Medicine, 296*(March 31), 716-721.

Weisbrod, B. A. (1983). *Economics and medical research.* Washington, DC: American Enterprise Institute.

Weissman, C., Mossel, P., Haimet, S., & King, T. (1990). Integration of quality assurance activities into a computerized patient data management system in an intensive care unit. *Quality Review Bulletin, 16*(11), 398-403.

Westlake, G. (1983). Cost analysis and cost justification of automated data processing in the clinical laboratory. *Clinics in Laboratory Medicine, 3*(1), 63-78.

Wolfe, H. B. (1986). Cost-benefit of laboratory computer systems. *Journal of Medical Systems, 10*(January), 1-9.

Zielstorff, R. (1985). Cost-effectiveness of computerization in nursing practice and administration. *Journal of Nursing Administration, 15*(2), 22-26.

8

Clinical Information-Processing Scenarios

Selecting Clinical Information Systems

Thomas L. Lincoln
Daniel J. Essin

Introduction

A computerized clinical information system (CIS) provides an integrative focal point for all patient-related information exchange (McLinden, Carlos, & Oleson, 1990). Clinical information systems are introduced into health care facilities to augment the proper care of patients and to assist in managing the health care facility. The expense and effort associated with implementing such systems, however, can be justified only if the facility functions better with the system than without it.

There is no single proper time or method to evaluate the effectiveness of a CIS (Forsythe & Buchanan, 1991). Of necessity, however, one of the most critical evaluations must be conducted at the time of acquisition. For any health care facility, such a large purchase represents both a major investment of capital and a significant commitment of staff toward potential improvements in the delivery of patient care (Lincoln & Aller, 1991a). Thus the selection process evokes high expectations, often fueled by the vendor's sales force, tempered by concern over the ultimate utility and cost of the new system. Although subsequent system evaluations can be instructive in aiding future choices and system modifications, selection is the critical decision (Essin, 1987). The overriding concern of any selection team must be to choose a CIS that will perform well at their site in their hands when it is installed (Lincoln, 1984).

CLIPS

The use of clinical information processing scenarios (CLIPS) is a testing approach that is designed to evaluate a system's response to important nonstandard situations. The effectiveness of any CIS will depend on how well it performs certain standard functions. It is not enough, however, that a system perform well in controlled demonstration situations in which institutional uniqueness and unexpected events have been rigorously excluded. In the diverse and often unpredictable world of actual health care operations, it is essential that a CIS that supports vital health care functions operates well under the specific kinds of stress peculiar to that institution (Lincoln & Essin, 1991; Lincoln & Korpman, 1980).

The CLIPS test is based on the premise that if a vendor's product won't work for very sick patients, it is not a useful clinical system. This premise is not unfair. The scenarios that CLIPS are designed to uncover occur every day and are most frequently encountered when patients are unusually sick or when care is urgent. Although these cases generally comprise less than 20% of the patients at any time, they may represent more than 80% of the effort expended by caregivers. Although such situations are individually rare, as a group they have the capacity to seriously affect patient care (Couch, Tilney, Rayner, & Moore, 1981; Lincoln, 1990). CLIPS represents a simple and cost-effective approach that any institution can use to highlight differences in how specific CIS products handle nonstandard events. Such an evaluation will provide essential information and help clarify issues surrounding the decision to purchase a particular CIS.

The Hospital Information Environment

Hospitals are more like each other than they are like other kinds of organizations. All hospitals admit patients, locate beds, schedule appointments, order medications and treatments, and perform and review lab results. Thus, it is attractive to assume that these basic hospital activities are the same in all facilities, and, like objects or implements, are well understood and can be reduced to their smallest component parts. Were this the case, vendors could compete on packaging, price, service, and special features. Customers could consider the alternatives with the knowledge that most (if not all) of their basic needs would be satisfied by any product.

Matching customer needs with CIS products, however, is not that simple. Closer examination reveals that each hospital's information processing requirements are different. Although concrete tools for delivering patient care such as syringes, typewriters, pills, and chest X-rays may be standard, the same cannot be said for basic information-processing functions. Hospital systems for admitting, discharge, and transfer (ADT) transactions, order entry, and so on are unique—although this uniqueness is not open-ended and arbitrary but rather characterizable and classifiable. Matching the needs of an individual institution with a specific CIS is further complicated by the fact that every commercial CIS product has a preferred way of operating based on the components used in its construction and the objectives and philosophy of its designers. A review of the choices made by various hospitals demonstrates that no single vendor or configuration has been able to satisfy all institutions. Although the overall failure rate of systems is very significant, these failures do not point to any one product. Rather, what suits one hospital fails to suit another (Lincoln & Aller, 1991b).

Evaluating Systems

In evaluating system effectiveness, three questions must be answered:

1. Does each system module perform its function in a way that is acceptable and useful to the potential customer?
2. Do the modules interact in ways that fit the operational style and objectives of the institution? (Even if each individual module offers a useful function, effective performance often depends on the interaction between modules and a variety of subtle local issues.)
3. Does the system organize the data and provide general-purpose access so that the data can be used for additional applications and analysis?

The traditional approach to system selection, the request for proposals (RFP), attempts to exercise due diligence through answers to a set of checklist questions. Although preparing checklists is valuable, the process cannot ensure that the system will meet the needs of the institution. Furthermore, giving an appropriate weight in advance to the relative importance of each item on the checklist is purely guesswork (Biezer, 1988). Only experience gained from using the system under local real-world conditions can identify those issues that will be critically important. Without a priori knowledge of the critical success factors for a particular institution, checklists often fail to discriminate among competing products and may even lead to erroneous conclusions. If the first user hands-on contact takes place only after purchase and installation, the information gained from actually using the system clearly comes too late to influence procurement.

The only way to judge the fitness of a computer system is to try it before buying it under conditions that resemble those found in the specific institution. This poses some obvious problems. Clearly, a system cannot be tested in its entirety, but it is extremely important to verify that key system features work and work together as advertised. Clinical information-processing scenarios (CLIPS) provide a methodology that subjects competing vendors' systems to a "stress test" to simulate important local conditions and compare them against specific benchmarks. The following sections describe the CLIPS methodology in detail.

Clinical Information-Processing Scenarios

CLIPS represent situations that could occur within the local environment and emphasize a special need or an anticipated deviation from standard procedure. Devising CLIPS can be a natural by-product of the information-gathering process that ordinarily precedes the RFP.

Some examples appear trivial or even humorous, but they are not in reality. For example, some common family names in Korea consist of a single letter. In general, however, computer systems do not allow a single letter as a last name. Consider the dilemma of "Stephen O," reported in the *New York Times*. After 7 years in this country he has been unable to assemble a credit history. He has sometimes been identified by computers as "OO" or "Oh" or even "O'Stephen" (although he doesn't look Irish)—all for lack of a common convention to override the usual constraint on single-letter last names (Why O Why, 1991)! He would have a similar problem with most clinical information systems. This is but one of a number of problems with names. Although most names in the United States follow a predictable set of conventions, not all do. Vietnamese traditionally place their family name first, followed by their personal names. Names in Cyrillic or Chinese may be transliterated differently on different occasions. Some family names, such as Von Euler or Saint James, include a blank space, which many computer systems misinterpret. These can be challenges for every hospital, but they can be major problems in institutions that treat many minorities.

A set of CLIPS should include clinical and emergency situations that push the limits of the applications program logic. An excellent way to do this is to complicate an otherwise common set of medical events.

Members of the selection team and other interested parties can formulate their concerns by taking examples from their own experience and creating challenging scenarios from them.

One CLIPS scenario, for example, might include a woman, seven months pregnant, who has been in an automobile accident. She is injured and delivers in the ambulance but arrives in the emergency room unconscious with no identification. Mother and child are admitted separately through the emergency room. The mother goes to surgery, the baby to the neonatal intensive care unit. Can the system conform to the hospital's policies regarding "Jane Doe" admissions? How is the mother-baby linkage established in the system? What assumptions are used by the program in making such linkages? Can the linkage be made only if the mother is on an obstetrics service? Must the child's record be spawned from the previously admitted mother or can the records be linked after the fact? Marketing representatives for vendors will not be able to give satisfactory answers to such questions. The only way to find out is to simulate the event.

Design Criteria

For individuals concerned with hospital operations, CLIPS are surprisingly easy to formulate within their own area of activity. Once the concept is understood by presenting an example—such as the one given above—everyone can recall nonstandard situations that are in some sense "typical" for their domain and that could cause endless trouble if not properly addressed by the clinical computer system. Examples come from all services.

From the Laboratory: "Order a differential white cell count as an add-on test from the patient care unit two days after the original specimen was submitted. Show how the system will reject such an order as unacceptable."

From Admission: "A newborn is routinely and inadvertently discharged three days after birth, but the mother remains in the hospital with complications. It is decided that the child should remain with the mother. How is this inadvertent discharge reversed so that a well baby without a diagnosis can be returned to the hospital?"

From Billing: "An outside reimbursement agency uses the patient's birth date as a part of their patient indexing code. Bills are submitted using a birth date that turns out to be in error. This has become the permanent agency index. Show how the patient's birth date can be corrected while leaving the agency index intact."

From Registration and Demographics: "A patient's address is changed to a new one in error. Show how the old address can be recovered to reverse this process at some later date."

Doctor's Orders: "Order a peak and trough Dilantin level for a patient with the first specimen to be drawn at 3:00 p.m. and the second at 4:45 p.m. The entire procedure is delayed, and the first blood sample is actually collected by patient care unit personnel at 3:30 p.m. Change the first order to reflect this fact. Change the second order to reflect the original interval."

Archived Data: "The laboratory modifies the methodology for a glucose test, which requires a change of reference ranges. Demonstrate how the reference ranges in the historical file have not changed."

A good set of CLIPS presents a tough test. Every vendor would like to show off its system to its best advantage. Conventional demonstrations by marketing staffs are careful to take potential buyers through the vendor's scenarios, which often dramatize situations rich in information that touch on known frustrations. These are chosen to cover familiar territory and interest the user but also to avoid complications for the demonstrator. If the system has difficulties in handling other situations, these must be discovered by the prospective buyer in another way. The CLIPS approach explores territory that pushes the demonstration away from well-worn paths.

CLIPS can formalize certain test situations often used in the past. For example, it has been a common challenge to require a system to set up a series of orders in preparation for an early morning procedure, such as a barium enema, and then ask that these orders be canceled and the procedure be rescheduled. To complicate the task further, the patient may be diabetic, so that not only breakfast but also insulin orders must be changed. This scenario is a good test of the number of screens that must be traversed and the number of transactions needed to manage this frustratingly common type of occurrence.

CLIPS can address simple or complex administrative issues. For instance, one objective of a new system might be to help division administrators respond to emergency requests for management information. The corresponding scenario would test each system's ad hoc report writer with questions on patient mix, physician activity profiles, nosocomial infection rates, and the like. Such specific requests give managers a common baseline to evaluate competing products for range of operation, ease of use, readable documentation, and vendor technical support.

Some facilities have special needs. For example, teaching hospitals often group residents, interns, and staff physicians in service teams. Some functions can be performed by any member of the team, others only by specific individuals. A set of sample situations can test how well a product supports the groups of physicians as teams. This leads to further questions: Does the system adequately distinguish between unlicensed interns and senior staff members for functions such as order entry and DRG attestation? Can participating medical students and nurses in training use the system as an exercise without compromising the integrity of care?

Can the system be easily modified to respond to evolving needs? Can such modifications be made an integral part of future processing or will they forever remain, like a scar, as evidence that the modification took place? Recent examples include the introduction of the UPIN (unique physician identifying number) by HCFA and the requirement that it be used in Medicare billing and the introduction of E/M (evaluation and management) codes. One could reasonably expect a system vendor to accommodate such changes because of their nationwide scope; however, system vendors also illustrate a whole class of changes that can originate at the state, local, or institutional level. In the examples cited above, institutions were required to comply within a short mandated time period. What recourse does an individual institution have, however, if the system vendor is late or unresponsive?

Design Criteria

CLIPS should be designed around the following principles:

1. The full set of CLIPS should cover as broad a range of thematic concerns and test as many applications as possible in order to see how well the vendor's software can cope with the full range of problems that practice can present. If the system is to be truly effective in helping professionals, it should be able to deal with most nonstandard events without creating new problems. Moreover, it should not involve a computer "work-around" or an awkward alteration of hospital procedures.

2. CLIPS cannot be a prearranged set of questions. If the questions are provided to the potential vendors in advance, it is difficult to ensure that a vendor does not modify the demonstration system to provide the desired behavior without actually intending to demonstrate or

deliver any underlying flexibility. Finding appropriate new questions should be an ongoing process. However, what might seem to be a tough question to an institution with limited experience may not discriminate well enough.

3. The CLIPS should not be finalized until the written responses to the RFP are reviewed. The evaluation of the written RFP responses will highlight certain areas that should assume increased importance in the CLIPS because of ambiguity, conflict between vendor claims, or uncertainty about the vendor responses.

4. Although consultants with a wide knowledge of the performance and shortcomings of many systems in different circumstances can be particularly helpful in generating a list of questions, the overall evaluation process should be structured so that no vendor can obtain a contract based on written responses alone. It must be demonstrated that their system performs as advertised. A hands-on verification of the responses and a confirmation of system features through actual experience with the proposed products should be a deciding factor in the final decision to purchase.

Practical Considerations

There are many ways to set up a CLIPS test. The power and portability of modern hardware make it possible to explore a system at the prospective purchaser's site. Vendors can establish communications with a remote system using high-speed modems or bring a small, fully configured system with them. The less confident the vendor is, the more it will press for control. CLIPS places the flexibility in the purchaser's hands and allows as many personnel as possible to try out their own scenarios.

We recently conducted a CLIPS test at the Los Angeles County University of Southern California Medical Center that involved three different vendors of registration, ADT, and clinic scheduling systems. Separate sets of CLIPS were developed by finance, nursing, medical records, various ancillaries, a group of physicians, and the financial information system group. Each vendor was scheduled for 3 days of CLIPS testing, plus time to prepare and pack up. Although somewhat more extensive, this on-site presence involves the same kind of effort as the demonstrations and "computer fairs" that vendors often will agree to if they believe their chances for a sale are good. The test magnified the differences markedly between systems that appeared to be similar during the conventional demonstration.

Alternatively, a test can be run at the vendor's own demonstration facility or, by proper prior arrangement, in the exhibit facilities at a national meeting. Off-site tests, difficult because they require a large number of individuals to make the trip, may be effective if a small and knowledgeable group from the institution properly presents the challenges of those who could not come—and if good notes are taken.

A fairness doctrine: CLIPS can also mislead. Vendors need to be warned that a stress test is to be carried out. The knowledge of sales personnel may be limited to their own presentation, a fact that may become all too evident under a CLIPS challenge. Thus a particular test may not identify the true limitations of the system but rather show up the ignorance of the demonstrator. Experienced vendor personnel who know the applications well and are not afraid to explore their own products should be the guides in a CLIPS test.

If a system that otherwise seems desirable has received a low score during CLIPS testing, the easiest way to verify or overrule the results is to step through the problem again at a site visit to a working system. Some misunderstandings can be corrected in this way, but, in the end, it is likely that flaws and awkwardness will remain after repeat testing.

CLIPS can be a catalyst. If such challenges were to become popular, marketing departments would quickly learn more about their own products, and programming staffs would have additional motivation to improve the most egregious problems in rapid fashion.

No system is perfect. Ultimately, every hospital is compelled to make compromises and "pick its own poison" (Aller, Aller, & Weilert, 1990). The list of CLIPS failures and relative failures becomes an excellent starting place for a final, rigorous, in-depth review and comparison. Some issues might loom large in the abstract but turn out to be minor when they are considered in practice. The value of the CLIPS approach is that it allows a medical center to choose a system with the kind of shortcomings that the institution believes it can best tolerate.

Additional Reading

Acquiring a Clinical Information System

The two articles by Lincoln and Aller (1991a, 1991b) provide a general discussion of system acquisition that applies beyond the laboratory to other sorts of clinical information systems.

Computer-Based Patient Records

The Institute of Medicine report on the computer-based patient record by Dick and Steen (1991) is a discussion and evaluation, largely an advocacy document, on the present state of online records.

Ball and Collen (1992) provide what the Institute of Medicine report left out, the important details about medical record technologies.

References

Aller, R. D., Aller, D. L., and Weilert, M. (1990). Hospital patient scheduling systems. *CAP Today, 4,* 38-40.

Ball, M. J., & Collen, M. F. (Eds.). (1992). *Aspects of the computer-based patient record.* New York: Springer Verlag.

Biezer, B. (1988). *The frozen keyboard: Living with bad software.* Blue Ridge Summit, PA: Tab Professional and Reference Books.

Couch, N. P., Tilney, N. L., Rayner, A. A., & Moore, F. D. (1981). The high cost of low-frequency events: The anatomy and economics of surgical mishaps. *New England Journal of Medicine, 304,* 634-637.

Dick, R. S., & Steen, E. B. (Eds.). (1991). *The computer-based patient record: An essential technology for health care.* Institute of Medicine (U.S.), 1991 Committee on Improving the Patient Record. Washington, DC: National Academy Press.

Essin, D. J. (1987). Getting the most from data base technology in the clinical setting. *International Symposium on Computers in Critical Care and Pulmonary Medicine.* San Diego, CA: University of California.

Forsythe, D. E., & Buchanan, B. C. (1991). Broadening our approach to evaluating medical information systems. In P. D. Clayton (Ed.), *Proceedings of the 15th Annual Symposium on Computer Applications in Medical Care* (pp. 8-12). New York: McGraw-Hill.

Lincoln, T. L. (1984). Hospital information systems: What lies behind friendliness and flexibility? *Medical Informatics (London), 9,* 255-263.

Lincoln, T. L. (1990). Medical informatics: The substantive discipline behind health care computing. *International Journal of Biomedical Computing, 26,* 73-92.

Lincoln, T., & Aller, R. D. (1991a). Acquiring a laboratory computer system: Understanding the issues. *Clinics in Laboratory Medicine, 11*(1), 1-20.

Lincoln, T., & Aller, R. D. (1991b). Acquiring a laboratory computer system: Vendor selection and contracting. *Clinics in Laboratory Medicine, 11*(1), 21-40.

Lincoln, T., & Essin, D. (1991, September 9). How to tell if a clinical system is the right one for you. *Healthweek,* pp. 17-19, Information Systems Outlook.

Lincoln, T. L., & Korpman, R. A. (1980). Computers, health care, and medical information science. *Science, 210,* 257-263.

McLinden, S., Carlos, G. D'A., & Oleson, C. E. (1990). The evolution of a standard for patient record communication: A case study. In R. A. Miller (Ed.), *Proceedings of the 14th Annual Symposium on Computer Applications in Medical Care* (pp. 239-243). Los Alamitos, CA: IEEE Computer Society Press.

Why O Why, Can't That Name Compute? (1991). *New York Times,* August 28.

PART II

Evaluating Health Care Information Systems: Applications

This part includes five applications of various methodologies used to evaluate the impact of health care information systems.

Chapter 9 provides a case study of why an extension of the problem-oriented medical record system called "Knowledge Coupling" has failed to diffuse among health care organizations. This system's failure is compared to the success that other computerized decision-support systems have experienced. The author points out that success or failure hinges on the extent to which the technology can be introduced without altering traditional practice habits and engendering unwanted organizational change.

Chapter 10 reports the results of an evaluation of an expert system developed to assist physicians in the diagnosis and management of stroke. Evaluation methods included interviews and surveys with medical personnel; participant observation; and embedded software to measure the rate and type of errors, system and users' response times, and frequency of use of each module. The evaluation was designed to answer questions such as: (1) Can an expert system be implemented successfully on an emergency service? (2) How do physicians use the Stroke Consultant? (3) Is the system accepted and used by clinicians? If not, why not? (4) How do the diagnoses, test selections, and treatment recommendations of the Stroke Consultant compare to those made by attending physicians? (5) What can be done to make the system more useful to the clinician?

Chapter 11 reports the results of an evaluation of nursing use of a computerized medication order entry system in a teaching hospital. The purpose of the study was to determine characteristics and attitudes of nursing personnel that accounted for variation in the number of late and incorrect orders entered into the system on different units; to suggest measures to improve system use; and to select pilot units for future implementation of the system. The research methodology used included a survey of system users and an audit of actual system use on seven surgical units. The findings indicated that nurses who perceived the system as "confusing" and "not worth the time and effort to use it" were more likely to enter medication orders late. Errors in the accuracy of order entry, however, were mostly attributable to a small number of clerical staff.

Chapter 12 analyzes changes in communication patterns and working relationships between nursing units and the radiology and admissions departments in a hospital that resulted from the introduction of an order-entry system. The study utilized both quantitative analyses of survey data and qualitative data collected through in-depth interviews and observations of system implementation and use. The findings indicated that, although the system eliminated some areas of conflict between departments, new task arrangements as well as shortcomings of the system created new issues.

Chapter 13 reports the results of an experimental program designed to increase physician use of predesigned computer-stored personal order sets for order entry into a hospital information system. The experimental program identified and utilized educationally influential physicians to disseminate information about the program to physicians on four hospital services. Ten other services served as a control group. Utilization data were collected from system tapes and analyzed using a multivariate analysis of variance. The findings indicated that the program resulted in a significant increase in personal order sets use by physicians, physician assistants, and unit secretaries on the experimental services.

The final chapter provides a brief historical overview of the history of computer applications in health care and outlines current developments. In light of past experience, many of these new systems will result in unforeseen costs, organizational consequences, and possibly failure if developers and administrators neglect to anticipate and evaluate their social impacts. An underlying premise of this book is that the achievement of health care reform will require the development of an infrastructure based on computer technology that must be carefully evaluated. This, in turn, will require the application of the methods described in this book.

9

Evaluating the Problem Knowledge Coupler

A Case Study

Robert R. Weaver

Introduction

A broad range of computer applications now pervades modern health care. Of these, computerized decision support (CDS) systems most directly impact clinical decision making. Within the domain of CDS technologies there also exists a multitude of approaches toward helping the practitioner address a narrow or broad range of medical problems. Most CDS systems tacitly accept the existing assumptions of medical problem solving and mainly try to find some niche within the traditional structure of medical practice. Whereas most CDS systems attempt to adapt to, rather than alter, the status quo in medicine, their subsequent impact on medical organization will likely be slight (Weaver, 1991a).

In contrast, Larry Weed's *Problem Knowledge Coupler* (PKC) offers a significant departure from conventional strategies of computerized decision support. Weed questions our overreliance on the unaided mind for clinical problem solving and the memory-based system of medical education that encourages this. He developed the PKC as a computer tool designed to overcome the limitations of the human mind and to potentially transform the current system of medical education and credentialing. As such, the PKC embodies an entirely new philosophy of, and puts forth a thoroughly comprehensive approach to, medical care and education. This chapter focuses on evaluating the PKC and its early diffusion and impact.

Evaluation of Technologies

One can investigate and evaluate different aspects of technology. This chapter considers three in regard to the PKC: (1) its approach to medical problem solving; (2) its diffusion; and (3) its impact on patients, physicians, paraprofessionals, and medical organization.

Evaluating Approaches to Medical Problem Solving

CDS systems vary in terms of the range and types of problems they help solve. Is the system designed to address problems associated with a particular medical specialty, or a subset of problems within a specialty? Is it designed for finding, diagnosing, or managing particular problems? Or, does it provide a comprehensive approach to addressing these various sorts of problems in health care more generally? Also, one might wish to know about the medical knowledge contained within the CDS system's "knowledge base." Is all the knowledge relevant for solving a particular problem readily available at the time of action? Are the various relationships described in the knowledge base referenced so that the user can explore an item in greater depth? How comprehensive and accessible is that knowledge? How up-to-date is that knowledge and what human system is in place to keep it updated? Ideally, the merits of the knowledge contained in the knowledge base should be checked through feedback from its use with real patients. Does the system offer this possibility? This information would, of course, give the evaluator (and potential adopter of the system) information about the merits of the system so as to judge whether or not to adopt and use the system.

Another important focus concerns the system's program, for this reflects its underlying principles and approach to clinical problem solving. How the program operates or how the system is to be used seriously impacts the nature of the human-computer relationship. Is the approach that underlies the program one that leaves clinical discretion solely with the human, or does the program "demand" of humans certain changes in problem-solving behavior? Humans must interact with the machine and one might consider what behavioral changes would be required to make the human-machine system work correctly. Further, does the system serve to enhance or diminish the patient's role in clinical problem solving? Using CDS systems might offer adopters a certain elevated status or the potential to save time or make more money. The assumption underlying the following evaluation, however, is that CDS system's primary aim ought to be to enhance the quality of decisions and, by extension, of patient care.

Evaluating the Diffusion Process

Another aspect of evaluation involves the diffusion of technology. The concern here is with how rapidly and widely an innovation proliferates across the social system and why (Rogers, 1983). Social factors, rather than the merits of the innovation itself, intervene to impact the diffusion process. Hence worthwhile medical innovations often proliferate slowly, while others whose benefits are marginal, at best, sometimes experience rapid diffusion (Fineberg, 1979; Stern, 1927; Waitzkin, 1978). A central concern involves assessing the conditions that favor or oppose the development and proliferation of technology.

Under the present system, physicians are the primary adopters of most medical technologies. Evaluating the diffusion process, therefore, often entails examining practitioners' "perceptions" of innovations, and examining which physicians are more or less inclined to adopt (Coleman, Katz, & Menzel, 1966; Freidman, 1985; Greer, 1984; Russell, 1979). In the case of the acceptance of computer technologies, evaluation might involve examining practitioners' perceptions about, for example, the computer as a friend or foe, a system's "user-friendliness," or its usefulness in the clinical setting (Anderson & Jay, 1985; Teach & Shortliffe, 1981). Evaluating the conditions that affect the diffusion of the PKC is problematic because we are at a time of rapid change in our health care system and, hence, the social conditions themselves are changing. Although currently physicians are the primary adopters of technology, we might well be approaching a time when consumers, administrators, and the government will play a greater role in determining where and to what extent decision-support systems are used. Nonetheless this chapter offers some speculation about how existing barriers have slowed the diffusion of the PKC.

Evaluating the Impact of Technology

A third aspect of evaluation has to do with the impact of technology. In the case of the impact of computers in medicine, many have discussed potential change that might result from their widespread adoption and use (Anderson & Jay, 1987a; Brannigan, 1986; Haug, 1977; Reiser, 1978; Schwartz, 1970). For instance, one can evaluate patients' perceptions about computers in the doctor's office, or its costs and benefits to patients, physicians, hospitals, or society. One might also assess the extent to which the technology improves medical record keeping, medical quality control, the evaluation of the physician's performance, or the organizational structure of medical practice. Impact evaluation is best undertaken retrospectively. Since the PKC has only recently seen use, and not on a widespread basis (as is the case with most CDS systems), the impact assessment presented below will necessarily be tentative.

In sum, this chapter focuses on the evaluation of Weed's Problem Knowledge Coupler. Specifically, it evaluates the system's approach to problem solving and, in a preliminary fashion, the barriers to its diffusion and its impact on patient care and medical practice.

Evaluation Strategy: The Case Study Approach

Selection of the PKC for Evaluation

The investigation uses the qualitative case study method to evaluate the PKC. This CDS system was selected for two principal reasons: its *comprehensiveness* and the *new premises* that underlie the system.

First, the medical domain that the PKC covers is not limited, theoretically, to diagnosing diseases within any particular specialty. In fact the approach it offers is applicable not only to diagnosis but also to health promotion, disease prevention, and illness management, and knowledge couplers have been developed for these various purposes. In addition, the problem-solving approach can apply to any medical domain. Already knowledge couplers have been used in psychiatry, dentistry, and veterinary medicine, as well as in general medical practice. Although the software has been developed to address a substantial number of problems, still more knowledge couplers need to be developed. The rate of building knowledge couplers will likely increase in the near future, since the "editing" software has been refined to enable developers to build couplers more rapidly, and since additional resources are now being devoted to the project. Further, Weed's PKC has been under development since the early 1980s and represents an extension of his earlier innovation, the Problem-Oriented Medical Record (Weed, 1969). Thus the PKC serves an important additional function in that it enhances our ability to reliably maintain and update medical records in a standard way. The comprehensiveness of its approach to patient care distinguishes the PKC from virtually every other CDS system.

Second, the PKC's problem-solving approach and underlying philosophy departs from what is typically seen in CDS technology research. The PKC represents an alternative to and critique of traditional strategies of medical problem solving and conventional artificial intelligence approaches to decision support as well. Accordingly, deploying such a comprehensive and innovative technology becomes particularly troublesome and, hence, illustrative of institutional barriers to change. As we will see, in part because it challenges the very premises of traditional, memory-based medical practice and education, the PKC receives little attention in mainstream medical literature, a fact that, in itself, illustrates an important obstacle to innovation and social change.

Information Sources

Significant information about the design of the system derives from the numerous articles and books written by the author of the PKC. Information from open-ended interviews with the developers of the PKC and other CDS systems, along with adopters and nonadopters of CDS technology, complement materials written about the system. Because few actually use the PKC or CDS technology more generally, identifying informed candidates for interviews was difficult. Few outside the area of CDS technology research or medical computing have much more than a superficial appreciation of what the PKC does and does not offer or of its deeper philosophical underpinnings. The inability to generate a complete list of users, of potential users of the technology, or of those who know about the PKC but for whatever reason failed to adopt it, made random sampling and statistical analysis of the results both inappropriate and impossible. Respondents were identified using a "snowball" sampling approach, whereby one respondent led the researcher to others until the search was exhausted. Interviews, some numerous times, with 21 professionals provided extensive information about the processes involved in the diffusion of the PKC.

As mentioned above, the interviews were open-ended, allowing respondents to reply in various and sometimes lengthy ways to the questions that were posed. The interviews asked a range of questions concerning what is known about the PKC, the decision to adopt or reject the technology, how the technology is implemented in clinical practice, the successes and failures of its deployment, and colleagues' responses to its uses. Although the in-depth case study approach outlined here is not without limitations (discussed in the concluding section), it does offer useful information about the design and early diffusion and impact of the PKC.

Findings

The PKC's Problem-Solving Philosophy

All CDS system designs are not the same. Weed's philosophy, as incorporated in the PKC, represents a comprehensive "new paradigm" for medical education, organization, and practice. As such, it is difficult to summarize within the confines of this chapter. Moreover, whereas most other CDS systems seek mainly to improve access to medical knowledge or to help solve "difficult" or "unusual" problems, the PKC offers a new guidance system to help standardize medical care and record keeping, to empower patients, as well as to transform the present memory-based approach to medical education. Since the goals of the PKC and other CDS systems differ, direct comparisons between them are problematic. The following section, thus, first identifies the flaws inherent in "computerless" clinical problem solving before discussing how the PKC overcomes these limitations.

Flaws in Clinical Problem Solving

The patient expects the physician to gather the full range of information needed to adequately diagnose, treat, or manage his or her medical problem(s). This requires that the physician consider all the known causes of the problem as well as the various treatment or management options available to the patient. The human mind is seriously limited in its ability to memorize and reliably recall the vast body of medical knowledge required to do this. The body of medical knowledge, even within specialties, is too large and ever-changing for any individual to know and stay current with. Moreover, the mind forgets, becomes tired, or otherwise fails to perform optimally. Even if the unaided mind could always recall the knowledge that should be brought to bear on problems, it would then confront enormous complexity and the task of integrating the details of the unique patient with the relevant body of medical knowledge. The most brilliant mind can consider only a handful of variables at once and would soon be overwhelmed by such complexity and detail. Hence, the mind's memory limitations and its inability to process large numbers of variables impairs clinical problem solving.

It is not surprising, then, that the human mind relies on various rules of thumb to compensate for its memory and information-processing limitations. For instance, physicians employ the heuristic "common diseases are common" to relieve them from considering rare diseases (which they often forget or never learned about anyway) that might account for a particular problem. Patients do not choose their diseases, however, and those who contract uncommon ones can easily become shortchanged or endangered. Further, the human tendency to generate hypotheses early in the encounter with the patient biases the subsequent search for causes and solutions to the problem, a process known as *premature closure* (Voytovich, Rippey, & Suffredini, 1985). Patients' problems are often more complex than the physician initially suspects, and data collected early become weighted too heavily. Moreover, physicians are responsible for not just one but several patients, each of whom might present multiple problems. Faced with overwhelming medical knowledge and complex patients with problems, then, physicians over-rely on probabilities and can consider only a few variables thought to be most important for solving a single problem.

For most of this century we tolerated these deficiencies, since the tools required to overcome them were unavailable. More recently, however, the computer has emerged to help compensate for the inherent limits of the unaided mind. Conventional "artificial intelligence" approaches fall short of achieving this objective. In fact, in certain respects a system that incorporates the heuristics used by humans, that attempts to emulate expert decision making, or that relies on probabilistic strategies in effect embodies the very limitations it seeks to overcome. This approach to computerized decision support still depends on the physician to determine when to use the system and what information about the patient the physician will use to query the system. As suggested above, since the human mind can never consider all the causes and salient findings, the data input into the computer remain incomplete. The very first physician interviewed articulated the reality that the advice any system offers is initially limited by the deficiencies of the information on which the advice is based (in his words, "garbage in, garbage out"). Consequently, conventional strategies of computerized decision support that rely on the unaided human mind at the very outset of the doctor-patient encounter largely fail to deliver on the promises that medical computing might potentially fulfill.

In contrast, the PKC takes seriously the substantial literature that identifies the limits of the human mind and the biases that permeate the human problem-solving process but that mostly pass unnoticed. The PKC has been designed for *routine* use to identify the universe of information to be gathered about the patient, based on consideration of *all* the known causes of a problem and management options (not just the ones the physician happens to remember). Hence it offers an alternative to the more conventional approaches to decision support.

The PKC's Alternative Approach

Rather than trying to emulate human strategies or reasoning approaches, Weed's PKC system attempts to do what computers do best: reliably recall and process vast quantities of information and medical knowledge. One principle that underlies the PKC system is that *all* the known causes or available management options should be considered when addressing each problem. Whereas the clinician necessarily narrows the search to explain a problem to a few "likely" causes, the PKC identifies all the causes and asks a range of questions about findings known to be associated with each cause. For instance, the "dizziness coupler" identifies 65 causes and gathers information for almost 170 clinical findings. Although the computer accomplishes this memory feat with ease, it is well beyond the ability of human memory.

After having asked all its questions, the PKC lists, with each cause, those "findings present in the patient that support that cause, along with findings not present that might be expected for the cause" (Weed, 1991, p. 63). Again, whereas the computer can process this number of variables with ease, the human mind simply cannot do this reliably. It may now be apparent from where the name Problem Knowledge Coupler was derived: the PKC "*couple*[s] the details of *knowledge about a patient with a problem* to the *relevant knowledge from the medical literature*" (Weed, 1991, p. 34). The PKC also enables the user or the patient to find out more about the knowledge contained in its *knowledge network*. Every linkage in the knowledge coupler is accessible through the PKC's knowledge network, and every fact in the network has a reference to the medical literature. This may also be accompanied by a "comment" section that offers added details about, for instance, "the timing, frequency, and severity of findings and their relationships to causes or management options" (Weed, 1991, p. 34). This enables the user to query the literature about certain facts in the knowledge base that the practitioner or the patient might wish to explore further. What uncertainty or ambiguity remains once the information is assembled, and the related causes listed, requires discussion and negotiation between the practitioner and the patient.

To summarize the above argument: Human biases and memory and information-processing limitations interfere with clinical problem solving. CDS systems that rely on human judgment concerning when to use the system and what patient data to collect and input are, accordingly, also limited. The PKC recognizes these deficiencies and offers a guidance system to be used routinely for every patient. The system enables the practitioner to gather and process more information and to consider all the possible causes and management options in relation to any given problem. Moreover, the PKC furnishes a standard approach to medical problem solving, record keeping, and patient care. As such, it can serve as a basis for gauging the quality of care, determining the inputs to and outputs from the health care system, and, thus, providing a mechanism for improving the cost-effectiveness of health care.

Barriers to Diffusion

A deficient system design might itself prove critical in deterring the proliferation of any technology. If we agree, however, that practitioners should consider all the known causes of a particular problem or the various management options and that they cannot do so but the computer can, then the PKC appears to offer a powerful tool for improving medical problem solving and care. Yet the medical community has not embraced Weed's idea, and we have not seen the rapid deployment of the technology that one might expect. One needs to look elsewhere, then, to ascertain the factors that hinder its diffusion. Three related social factors help account for the slow diffusion of this innovation. First, the magnitude of *resources* available to develop and promote the technology will affect its deployment. Second, *awareness of and knowledge about* the technology serves to promote or hinder its proliferation. Third, the full deployment of the PKC requires considerable change in the way clinical problems are solved. Those vested in the status quo will resist this change. In short, the technology's *compatibility* with the status quo affects the speed and extent of its diffusion. The following sections discuss the impact of these three factors on the diffusion of the PKC.

Resources

The development of most modern medical technologies requires significant resources and sponsorship from at least one corporate body, be it a public or private funder, a well-endowed medical establishment, or a large medical technology corporation interested in the profit to be gained from the sale of some drug, device, or software system. The PKC has so far developed with little or no help from any such source. Working with only a few colleagues, Weed has, over several years, managed to develop a subset of the knowledge couplers required for common medical problems and worked to refine a computerized version of the Problem-Oriented Medical Record. Because a full set of knowledge couplers has not yet been developed, physicians must make certain compromises when adopting the innovation. "[Knowledge] couplers do not yet exist for many of the common problems that one sees in primary care practice," as one PKC user reported. "This requires the staff and myself to operate via two different modalities. Getting the additional couplers built, therefore, is of primary importance" (Burger, 1991, p. 281). For another practitioner, the use of the PKC takes on a moral imperative. Aware that he is unable to consider all the possible causes of a given problem, he feels obliged to use the PKC, so much so that he no longer sees patients with problems for which no coupler has been developed to help solve. Nonetheless, even those practitioners eager to embrace Weed's "new paradigm" are left with few choices: either they operate their offices in "two modalities" that combine both the traditional and the PKC approaches to problem solving while awaiting the development of new knowledge couplers, or they restrict their medical practice to handling only those problems for which software has been written. Both choices demand certain compromises even PKC enthusiasts might not be willing to make. Other potential users await the development of a more complete set of couplers.

Although developing knowledge couplers requires resources, the costs associated with maintaining a medical system that lacks standards for medical care and record keeping are significantly higher and rapidly rising. Recently, a nonprofit organization called the Center for Knowledge Coupling (CKC) has been established to address the growing concern over the quality and cost-effectiveness of our present medical system. Starting with the premises laid out by Weed, the CKC seeks to promote the further development and maintenance of knowledge couplers. With more resources being devoted to the project, the process of coupler development and proliferation will likely accelerate in the future. The emergence of this organization notwithstanding, resource limitations have curtailed the PKC's development and promotion to date. Hence the innovation is less well known than other CDS systems. As discussed in the next section, most practitioners are unfamiliar with the PKC system and this, too, hinders its diffusion.

Awareness of and Knowledge About the PKC

Medical devices today typically develop first in medical schools; only later do they become perfected and then marketed by large, private corporations. Although the development of medical innovations outside the university is not unknown in medical history, the situation does not favor the rapid dissemination of new ideas. For instance, the theory of percussion of the chest for diagnosis was slow to achieve common acceptance, in part because its main inventor, Auenbrugger, had no students "who might learn and extend his discovery among the profession" (Stern, 1927, p. 52). Researchers from prominent medical schools are better situated to advance their ideas through access to medical journals, conferences, students, and other influential colleagues. The importance of a person's position in professional networks also impacts the likelihood that one will adopt an innovation (Anderson, Jay, & Hackman, 1983; Coleman et al., 1966).

In the case of the PKC, the promoter of the innovation has written extensively and critically about the traditional, memory-based system of medical education, the credentialing system in medicine, the failure of the profession to regulate itself using conventional methods, and the customary approaches to medical problem solving (Weed, 1986, 1987a, 1987b, 1991). Foreseeing the opposition his innovation would likely face in medical schools, Weed retired early to develop the PKC outside the dominant networks of medical education and medical informatics. Weed's position outside medical education makes the communication of the PKC approach more difficult. The PKC is much less well known to mainstream medicine than was the Problem-Oriented Medical Record that Weed developed over 20 years ago while teaching at a medical school. One physician quite familiar with Weed and the PKC suggested that the innovation "should go through medical education and have as its target audience recent graduates. Most teachers are threatened by the PKC." For now, Weed has no medical students to facilitate the transfer of his invention to other professionals and throughout the medical community. Further, for the last decade Weed has had to devote almost all his time to developing the PKC to the point where only today is it truly poised for more rapid development and proliferation. Nonetheless, pursuing the larger aim of developing an integrated system for problem solving and record keeping has left Weed with little opportunity to market and promote the innovation itself.

It is no surprise that Weed's criticisms of the old ways medicine is taught and practiced probably do not endear him to the medical mainstream, and that many resist his ideas. Furthermore, physicians might well oppose the message of the PKC idea simply because of its association with its messenger. One advocate of the PKC remarked that "he [Weed] did not play the diplomatic game well, being more of a prophet than a diplomat." It is doubtful, however, that this wholly explains why his innovation has not yet been fully embraced. Few physicians are actually familiar with the PKC. Since 1983, Weed has not presented a paper at the annual Society for Computer Applications in Medical Care conference, probably the most widely attended national meeting for medical informatics. In both formal and informal interviews and discussions with various medical professionals, the researcher found few who had even heard of the PKC. Many had heard of the inventor himself, his Problem-Oriented Medical Record, and his PROMIS system. But intricate knowledge of his most recent innovation was minimal, even among those directly immersed in medical computing. Hence many in medicine remain uninformed about his knowledge coupling idea. Perhaps the least profound conclusion to be drawn from this investigation is that if few know about the system, its diffusion will remain quite confined.

Though Weed's critiques of mainstream medical practice and education likely hinder the communication and promotion of the PKC idea, even those who have heard of the invention often fail to fully understand how it is used, its goals and logic, and the new paradigm that it portends. Complex ideas are often difficult to communicate, and old ideas are often enemies of new ones. On the surface one might see the PKC as just another attempt to improve practitioners' access to medical knowledge, while its deeper and more far-reaching implications might well be missed. For instance, one physician remarked that the PKC might be useful mainly for "unusual cases," something akin to astronomer's using a telescope only when they "see something unusual up there" (Weed, 1987c, p. 244). Another physician considered the PKC to be "great for obscure problems, for education, and for complicated cases." Medical problems thought at the outset to be "routine," however, are often more complicated than first anticipated. It might seem ludicrous to consider some rare disease when explaining a set of symptoms, unless you are the patient with that disease. As mentioned above, the mind typically underestimates the complexity of problems. Further, it might appear superfluous to ask so many questions if one fails to appreciate that another, more far-reaching objective of the PKC is to build a standard clinical database that can be used as a basis of feedback for refining and modifying knowledge couplers and to make clinical knowledge cumulative. Moreover, studies that assess the "outcome" of medical practice become truly meaningful only when the input is known; the input is known only when the problem is fully examined and carefully documented in the medical record. When one fails to adequately grasp the premises that underlie the knowledge coupling approach, along with its broader implications for patient care and record keeping, the PKC's routine use might appear unnecessary or cumbersome. Hence it seems as though many physicians see certain pieces of the PKC without fully appreciating its broader goals and philosophical underpinnings. Such misunderstandings communicated about the PKC no doubt hinder the diffusion and appropriate use of the innovation.

Compatibility of the Innovation

The PKC implies a change in clinical behavior and medical organization not called for by any other CDS system. It is intended for routine use to enhance the thoroughness of data gathering and record keeping to enable the practitioner to consider all the possible causes and management options that pertain to each problem, as well as to make possible periodic audits of medical performance. In contrast, most other systems are built to adapt to the existing social context and to the needs of the "busy practitioner." In fact, the success or failure of such systems, and the extent to which they see widespread use, often hinges on the ease with which the technology can be introduced without altering traditional practice habits and without engendering organizational change. The argument here is simply that CDS systems are not useful unless doctors use them, and doctors will not use them if they are inconvenient, demanding, or require extensive changes in the way clinicians presently do business. Weed rejects this reasoning. According to him it is precisely the status quo in medicine that requires change. Hence the PKC most likely encounters resistance among the many professionals who benefit from and are interested in maintaining the status quo and the "mystique" that surrounds medical practice.

From a strictly practical standpoint, the PKC used in conjunction with the Problem-Oriented Medical Record improves medical record keeping. For instance, one physician reported that this greatly reduced the overhead and redundancy involved in medical record keeping (e.g., transcribing and filing information taken from disparate sources such as the verbal history, the physical examination, and laboratory tests). Bartholomew (1991, p. 241) writes that it "frees the medical record technician by at least 50% to accomplish other tasks in the office." This time saving, he maintains, more than compensates for the additional training time invested in the initial set-up of this integrated system. Another clinician confessed that, although "using the PKC is sometimes inconvenient when computer terminals are not available . . . the PKC software is no barrier to the PKC's implementation." Many physicians, however, do not even use computers in their offices. As one respondent indicated, "the biggest question the practitioner faces is how will the system disrupt his routine, especially those who do not have a computer." Nonetheless, although the lack of computer equipment hinders the adoption of any CDS system, this obstacle will be of lesser consequence in the future as computer technologies increasingly become integrated in office practices.

Besides making record keeping easier, the PKC provides the practitioner with an external aid to enhance problem solving. By coupling knowledge about a particular patient with a problem to the relevant knowledge from the medical literature, the PKC provides a guidance system that engenders confidence that the practitioner is bringing up-to-date medical knowledge to bear on each patient's problem(s). Hence, some physicians suggested that the PKC liberates them from their own internal constraints. Doctors' awareness of the limits of their own knowledge and their ability to keep up with expanding collective medical knowledge, however, varies, and so does the perceived need for external aids. As Dawes (1988, p. 143) writes: "The idea that a self-imposed external constraint on action can actually enhance our freedom by releasing us from predictable and undesirable internal constraints is not a popular one." For some physicians, then, the guidance system the PKC provides is a liability rather than an asset. Certain doctors indicated that the PKC would not take hold in medicine because it is "so demanding." Others failed to see the relevance of the many questions the PKC asks and considered the whole question-asking process as painstaking and "too time-consuming." In fact, the software interface is designed so that this task requires less time than one would expect, and much of the question-asking can be undertaken by paraprofessionals or patients themselves. For instance, one practitioner, after using it twice, protested that the PKC was cumbersome and time-consuming. Soon he became proficient with the system, however, and it was no longer perceived as such. Moreover, once his staff became adept at running the PKC, its use took literally none of his time. Physicians and staff must be trained in the technical aspects associated with the use of any new computer software system. In two sites where the PKC has been implemented, however, it did not take long for both physicians and staff to become comfortable handling the system (Bartholomew, 1991; Burger, 1991). Hence, although the PKC's rigor and thoroughness likely caused resistance among some practitioners, for others it became an important asset. Nonetheless, initial perceptions of the PKC as "too demanding" or "time-consuming," along with the view that an external aid may be unnecessary, rather than the benefits it promises for improved care, probably deter many physicians from adopting the innovation.

In sum, resource limitations seriously diminish the speed with which the PKC can become fully developed and the extent to which it can be promoted. Largely because of the resource constraints, few even know about the innovation and fewer fully understand its complexity and underlying philosophy. This lack of awareness of and knowledge about the PKC probably contributes the most to its rather slow diffusion.

soon, what lab work should be obtained prior to the visit, or what home treatments might be appropriate for more benign maladies. During the early development of this coupler, ambiguities in the process of problem solving became explicit and the problem further clarified. The process of building the coupler served an educational purpose, stimulating discussions between staff and physician as they attempted to rectify the ambiguities and develop and improve the coupler. As a result of this feedback, "medically untrained individuals are now making triage decisions with a high degree of sophistication backed by a coupler that incorporates my 20 years experience in medical practice and, as much as possible, information from the medical literature." Moreover, newly hired medical personnel are also trained faster and achieve a higher level of competence (Burger, 1991, p. 281).

Other Organizational Effects

Disease categories and medical specialties are human creations that nature does not respect. Individuals face problems caused by social, psychological, and biological factors; specialists in sociology, psychology, or biology cannot expect to fully grasp or reliably recall those potential causes that lie outside their area of expertise without the help of decision support tools such as the PKC. For instance, a significant minority of psychiatric patients suffer from an underlying medical disorder of which the psychiatrist is likely unaware. With the PKC, according to Yee (1991, p. 288), both psychiatric and somatic causes of mental problems are identified, breaking down the boundaries that often separate psychiatry and medicine. One practitioner suggested that the system might serve to "more precisely identify where specialists are or are not needed" by more clearly delimiting the problem. Nevertheless it is impossible now to predict whether the PKC will empower the generalist to also become a specialist or whether it will diminish referrals to specialists.

Routine use of the PKC also gives rise to certain legal questions. Whether the practitioner's liability for poor outcomes that follow decisions made with the help of computers is enhanced, diminished, or unchanged has not yet been tested. Nonetheless, the PKC used in conjunction with the Problem-Oriented Medical Record is designed to help the practitioner fully identify and document the inputs (data) used to make decisions. Better documentation might well serve to protect the practitioner in cases in which a decision yields unfavorable results for the patient but is found to be reasonable given the data available when the decision was made. Furthermore, the perception that the physician is concerned with the patient's health and is providing the best possible care (irrespective of outcomes) perhaps has as much to do with the initiation of lawsuits as do health outcomes. The greater collaboration between physicians and patients made possible with the PKC, however, may contribute to heightened patient trust, thereby diminishing the likelihood of malpractice suits in the first place. One physician stated this succinctly: "Where patients are more involved in decisions, they will be less inclined to sue." Bartholomew (1991, p. 242) suggests that furnishing patients with a medical record that they understand provides its own form of malpractice insurance: "With the amount of time spent with the patient in the use of couplers as well as the computerized medical record, the patient comes away much more satisfied that they are being cared for in the best possible manner." Although difficult to document conclusively, insofar as the PKC fosters a more egalitarian relationship between the practitioner and the patient, while encouraging and making possible greater patient responsibility for health, it probably also serves to protect the practitioner against malpractice suits.

Finally, the widespread use of the PKC has potentially far-reaching implications for the present system of medical education and credentialing physicians. Since the computer can store, recall, and process vast quantities of medical knowledge, and can do so more reliably than any human can, it becomes increasingly apparent that time, energy, and money spent requiring that future physicians memorize and regurgitate vast quantities of medical information and knowledge (only to forget most of it later) might be better spent elsewhere. Moreover, the irrationality of the current system of granting a license to practice medicine based on performance on standardized exams under conditions that are far removed from actual medical practice becomes similarly apparent, especially given the computer tools that are now available. A medical system in its present state of cost crisis might well be motivated toward significant change in the way medical practitioners are trained and licensed. Nonetheless we cannot now say for sure that the PKC will affect a broad reorganization of medical education. So far, the PKC has not penetrated the medical curriculum, and it will likely be that medical schools will most strongly resist its introduction.

Conclusion

CDS technologies do not "cure" patients. They can, however, provide a structured method of medical problem solving and record keeping that enables practitioners to more thoroughly address clinical problems and systematically record patient information. This investigation has, thereby, undertaken to evaluate the PKC's strategy toward medical problem solving and care. A central principle that underlies the PKC's approach is that all the known causes along with various management options should be considered when addressing the problems each unique patient presents. The unaided human mind cannot reliably recall all the known causes and management options, nor can it process all the information collected to thoroughly consider these causes and options; the computer, however, accomplishes this with ease. The PKC exploits the computer's special capacity to provide the necessary guidance to safeguard against the practitioner's own biases and memory and information processing limitations. Hence the PKC improves clinicians' ability to gather data and "couple" this information about the unique patient with current medical knowledge. The PKC becomes the central tool for the realization of a "new paradigm" that challenges the premises of and offers an alternative to traditional ways of clinical problem solving, memory-based medical education, and health care organization.

If we consider the PKC alternative to be an advancement over traditional strategies of clinical problem solving and computerized decision support yet find the innovation's diffusion to be slow, then we can with greater certainty argue that social factors, not the merits of the PKC itself, hinder its deployment. The above identifies, albeit in a preliminary way, several of the key social factors that impinge on the diffusion process. The inventor has developed the system with little institutional support and few resources and devoted virtually all of his time over the last decade to refining the various components of his innovation. Further, problems with communicating information about the PKC have left many medical professionals uninformed about the merits of Weed's approach. Finally, it seems that the PKC faces difficulties similar to those encountered by other inventions that promised substantial change in traditional ways of practicing medicine (Stern, 1927). Although many vested in the status quo will resist change, however, other powerful social actors who foot the bill of an overly expensive health care system might just as well organize to promote it. The diffusion of the PKC, then, exemplifies how new technologies can generate conflict between tradition and change, the results of which are still to be seen.

The lack of institutional support and the change-producing quality of the PKC distinguishes it from most other CDS systems. Hence the factors that hinder the diffusion of the PKC might not apply to more conventional decision support technologies. Furthermore, the current PKC users whose experiences are expressed in this chapter probably do not represent the medical mainstream. Like Weed, early adopters of such innovations are likely to be more adventurous and probably more innovative than the average practitioner. These clinicians perhaps also offer more favorable commentary on the innovation's benefits than others would, since they are among the PKC enthusiasts. The purpose of this case study, however, is not to generalize to a larger population of CDS systems. Just as the PKC's approach emphasizes the unique qualities of patients and their clinical problems, this investigation highlights the unique features of the PKC as an innovative approach to decision support.

Mainly in retrospect are we able to more definitively evaluate the costs and benefits of medical innovations, along with the barriers to their deployment. Stern (1927) illustrates this well in his historical analysis of the diffusion of various innovations. We encounter more significant difficulties when assessing the social conditions that impact technology diffusion while the process is still underway and while those very conditions are changing. This is surely the case for evaluating the acceptance of most computer technologies in medicine, and perhaps even more with CDS technologies that are now just beginning to be introduced into clinical settings. Only a more troublesome alternative—waiting for history to pass us—justifies our efforts. Evaluating computer technologies early in the diffusion process has much to say for it, since they will be difficult to remove once they become fully deployed and entrenched in the medical system.

The analysis above reminds us that technology diffusion is influenced by factors beyond the benefits medical innovations offer, or fail to offer, to patient care. We sometimes read about the pain that follows when harmful technologies proliferate too rapidly. Less often are we made aware of what we miss when valuable innovations proliferate too slowly. By using and improving the tools available to evaluate new medical innovations we hope to alleviate the barriers that hinder the deployment of technologies with the potential to improve health care.

Additional Reading

Introduction and Evaluation of Technologies

Weed (1991) offers the most recent and comprehensive discussion of his PKC, its philosophy, and its uses, along with the Problem-Oriented Medical Record.

Rogers (1983) provides both an in-depth and comprehensive general discussion of the various phases of the diffusion process, along with an extensive survey of studies on technology diffusion.

Buchanan and Shortliffe (1984) discuss the problems with the empirical assessment of the performance of the MYCIN program; similar problems are associated with the evaluation of other systems. R. Weaver (1991) discusses other problems associated with comparing computerized decision-support systems.

Evaluation Strategy: The Case Study Approach

Stern (1927) offers a classic illustration of using historical documents to uncover social factors that affect opposition to medical innovation.

Anderson and Jay (1987a) provide a useful collection of papers that employ both survey and case study research strategies to assess the diffusion and impact of computer technologies in medicine.

Findings

Weed's (1982) article titled "Problem-knowledge couplers: Philosophy, use and interpretation," written for the PKC Corporation, offers perhaps the most succinct discussion of the premises that underlie the PKC. Weed (1991) provides a more lengthy examination along these lines and contributors also discuss their clinical experiences with the PKC.

Weaver (1991b) compares the development, proliferation, and potential impact of the PKC and other artificial intelligence systems.

References

Anderson, J. G., & Jay, S. J. (1985). Computers and clinical judgment: The role of physician networks. *Social Science and Medicine, 20*, 969-979.

Anderson, J. G., & Jay, S. J. (1987a). Hospitals of the future. In J. G. Anderson & S. J. Jay (Eds.), *Use and impact of computers in clinical medicine* (pp. 343-350). New York: Springer Verlag.

Anderson, J. G., & Jay, S. J. (Eds.). (1987b). *Use and impact of computers in clinical medicine*. New York: Springer Verlag.

Anderson, J. G., Jay, S. J., & Hackman, E. M. (1983). The role of physician networks in the diffusion of clinical applications of the computer. *International Journal of Bio-medical Computing, 14*, 195-202.

Bartholomew, K. A. (1991). The perspective of a practitioner. In L. L. Weed (Ed.), *Knowledge coupling: New premises and new tools for medical care and education* (pp. 235-277). New York: Springer Verlag.

Brannigan, V. M. (1986). Medical informatics and the regulation of decision making: The challenge of a new technology. In R. Salamon, B. Blum, & M. Jorgenson (Eds.), *Proceedings of the 10th Annual Symposium on Computer Applications in Medical Care* (pp. 1064-1068). New York: Elsevier Science Publishers.

Buchanan, B. G., & Shortliffe, E. H. (1984). The problem of evaluation. In B. G. Buchanan & E. H. Shortliffe (Eds.), *Rule-based expert systems: The MYCIN experiments of the Stanford Heuristic Programming Project* (pp. 571-588). Reading, MA: Addison Wesley.

Burger, C. S. (1991). Implementation of Problem Knowledge Couplers in a primary care practice. In L. L. Weed (Ed.), *Knowledge coupling: New premises and new tools for medical care and education* (pp. 279-282). New York: Springer Verlag.

Coleman, J. S., Katz, E., & Menzel, H. (1966). *Medical innovation: A diffusion study.* New York: Bobbs-Merrill.

Cross, H. D. (1991). Computers in a private practice in Hampden, Maine. In L. L. Weed (Ed.), *Knowledge coupling: New premises and new tools for medical care and education* (pp. 282-286). New York: Springer Verlag.

Dawes, R. M. (1988). *Rational choice in an uncertain world.* New York: Harcourt Brace Jovanovich.

Fineberg, M. (1979). Gastric freezing—A study of diffusion of a medical innovation. In Committee on Technology and Health Care (Ed.), *Medical technology and the health care system: A study of the diffusion of equipment-embodied technology* (pp. 173-200). Washington, DC: National Academy of Sciences.

Freidman, M. (1985). The rate of adoption of new procedures among physicians: The impact of specialty and practice characteristics. *Medical Care, 23,* 939-945.

Greer, A. L. (1984). Medical technology and professional dominance theory. *Social Science & Medicine, 18,* 809-817.

Haug, M. R. (1977). Computer technology and obsolescence of the concept of profession. In M. Haug & J. Dofny (Eds.), *Work and technology* (pp. 215-228). Beverly Hills, CA: Sage.

Lesse, S. (1983). A cybernated health diagnostic system—An urgent imperative. *American Journal of Psychotherapy, 37,* 451-455.

Lesse, S. (1986). Computer advances towards the realization of a cybernated health-science system. *American Journal of Psychotherapy, 40,* 321-323.

Maxmen, J. S. (1976). *The post-physician era: Medicine in the twenty-first century.* New York: John Wiley.

Reiser, S. J. (1978). *Medicine and the reign of technology.* New York: Cambridge University Press.

Rogers, E. (1983). *Diffusion of innovations* (2nd ed.). New York: Free Press.

Russell, L. B. (1979). *Technology in hospitals: Medical advances and their diffusion.* Washington, DC: The Brookings Institution.

Schwartz, W. B. (1970). Medicine and the computer—The promise and problems of change. *New England Journal of Medicine, 283,* 1257-1264.

Stern, B. J. (1927). *Social factors in medical progress.* New York: AMS Press.

Teach, R. L., & Shortliffe, E. H. (1981). An analysis of physicians' attitudes regarding computer-based clinical consultation systems. *Computers and Biomedical Research, 14,* 542-558.

Voytovich, A. E., Rippey, R. M., & Suffredini, A. (1985). Premature conclusions in diagnostic reasoning. *Journal of Medical Education, 60,* 302-307.

Waitzken, H. (1978). How capitalism cares for its coronaries: A preliminary exercise in political economy. In E. B. Gallagher (Ed.), *The doctor-patient relationship in the changing health scene.* DHEW Publication No. (NIH) 78-183. Washington, DC: Government Printing Office.

Weaver, R. R. (1986). Some implications of the emergence and diffusion of medical expert systems. *Qualitative Sociology, 9,* 237-255.

Weaver, R. R. (1987). Editorial comments, 1974-1986: The case for and against the use of computer-assisted decision making. In W. W. Stead (Ed.), *Proceedings of the*

11th Annual Symposium on Computer Applications in Medical Care (pp. 143-149). New York: IEEE Computer Society Press.

Weaver, R. R. (1991a). The assessment and diffusion of computerized decision support systems. *International Journal of Technology Assessment in Health Care, 7*(1), 42-50.

Weaver, R. R. (1991b). *Computers and medical knowledge: The diffusion of decision support technology in medicine.* Boulder, CO: Westview Press.

Weed, C. (1982). Problem-Knowledge Couplers: Philosophy, use, and interpretation. Unpublished paper written for the Problem-Knowledge Coupler Corporation.

Weed, L. L. (1969). *Medical records, medical education, and patient care.* Cleveland, OH: The Press of Case Western Reserve University.

Weed, L. L. (1978). *Your health care and how to manage it.* Essex Junction, VT: Essex Publishing.

Weed, L. L. (1986). Knowledge coupling, medical education and patient care. *CRC Critical Reviews in Medical Informatics, 1*(1), 55-79.

Weed, L. L. (1987a). Flawed premises and educational malpractice: A view toward a more rational approach to medical practice. *The Journal of Medical Practice Management, 2,* 239-254.

Weed, L. L. (1987b). Medical education and patient care: Mistaken premises and inadequate tools. *Physicians & Computers,* February, pp. 30-35.

Weed, L. L. (1987c). The premises and tools of medical care and medical education: Perspective over 40 years. In B. I. Blum & K. Duncan (Eds.), *A history of medical informatics* (pp. 224-249). Reading, MA: Addison-Wesley.

Weed, L. L. (1991). *Knowledge coupling: New premises and new tools for medical care and education.* New York: Springer Verlag.

Yee, W. K. (1991). Problem Knowledge Couplers in psychiatry. In L. L. Weed (Ed.), *Knowledge coupling: New premises and new tools for medical care and education* (pp. 286-289). New York: Springer Verlag.

10

Reaction of Medical Personnel to a Medical Expert System for Stroke

Loretta A. Moore

Medical expert systems have been the object of considerable research. However, very few are in routine clinical use, even when their performance has been shown to be acceptable. This indicates that it is a mistake to primarily concentrate research efforts on methods of improving the computer's decision-making performance when clinical impact depends on solving other problems of acceptance as well (Shortliffe, Buchanan, & Feigenbaum, 1984). Bischoff, Shortliffe, Scott, Carlson, and Jacobs (1983) have suggested that successful medical consultation systems must not only provide advice at the expert level but also fit smoothly into the physician's daily routine. Friedman and Gustafson (1977) list several major impediments to successful implementation of clinical computer systems: poorly defined user interfaces, systems whose performance does not exceed that of the physician, inability to prove that the system has a beneficial impact on patient care, and systems with an inflexibility that inhibits transferability.

AUTHOR'S NOTE: This chapter is based on the author's doctoral dissertation (Moore, 1991) and is an expansion of concepts presented initially elsewhere (Moore et al., 1990).

The development of the Stroke Consultant was supported in part by NIH Grant No. NS25811-01 from NINCDS to Michael Reese Hospital, a grant from the Amoco Foundation, and an equipment grant from AT&T Bell Laboratories. The author was supported by AT&T's Doctoral Support Program.

I wish to thank Dr. Martha Evens, Dr. Daniel Hier, Dr. Margaret Huyck, Chris Grode, Janet Coleman, Lori Jones, and the medical personnel of the Neurology Ward of Michael Reese Hospital. I would also like to thank Dr. Stephen Seidman for his comments on earlier drafts of this chapter.

The primary goal of the research was to explore this problem of acceptance by studying reactions of medical personnel to the clinical use of an expert system for stroke. A second goal was to discover which changes in the human-computer interface could make medical expert systems more attractive and effective in the clinical context. The particular target of the research project was the evaluation of the Stroke Consultant at Michael Reese Hospital, a large teaching hospital in Chicago. The Stroke Consultant is a medical expert system developed to assist physicians in the diagnosis and management of stroke. It was developed as a joint research project of Illinois Institute of Technology and Michael Reese Hospital (Moore, 1991; Moore, Evens, & Hier, 1990).

Evaluation methods included interviews and surveys with medical personnel, participant observation, and embedded evaluation techniques. Pre-use and post-use surveys and interviews were conducted to assess user satisfaction with the system. The embedded software measured the rate of errors, types of errors, system response time, user response time, and frequency of use for all modules. The system maintained a complete record of all clinical sessions, which were later reviewed.

The data collected were intended to answer the following questions: (1) Why are medical expert systems not effectively utilized in clinical settings? (2) What can be done to encourage the use of these systems? (3) Can a medical expert system be implemented in a busy clinical service (such as an emergency room)? (4) How do physicians use the Stroke Consultant in its present form? (5) Is the system accepted by the users for whom it is intended? If not, why? (6) Do the diagnoses, test selection, and treatment recommendations of the Stroke Consultant compare favorably with those of the attending physician? (7) Is the user interface adequate? If not, how can we improve it? (8) What is needed to make the Stroke Consultant more useful? (9) What can be done to make the system friendlier and more informative? and (10) Does the system function well outside of a research setting and is it suitable for dissemination?

The future usefulness of medical expert systems ultimately depends on user acceptance. One way to ensure this acceptance is to survey users to determine their satisfaction with a system and then make necessary modifications to the system to improve its usefulness and user acceptance. I was interested in discovering why physicians and nurses would not use the system. Also, I wanted to improve the acceptability of the Stroke Consultant, if it was found to have value.

Description of the Stroke Consultant

Stroke is generally sudden in onset, and most stroke victims are taken to hospital emergency rooms where they are seen by house physicians who usually are not well trained in neurology (Weiner & Levitt, 1974). The Stroke Consultant was designed to advise emergency room physicians on the diagnosis and management of stroke patients. It was developed jointly by the Computer Science Department at Illinois Institute of Technology and the Department of Neurology at Michael Reese Hospital. The expert system is programmed in C for portability and speed, and has been installed on a variety of computers, from minicomputers to mainframes.

The system has a blackboard architecture (Hill, 1985; Hill, Curt, Kozar, Hier, & Evens, 1985). In such an architecture, system components communicate with each other by posting information on a blackboard. In this case, the blackboard stores all information collected about the patient by the component modules and also records any intermediate hypotheses and decisions. The blackboard also contains the system agenda, a collection of rules that determine what modules are executed and when. All system components run under the control of a system executive, and all communication with the user is handled by a common user interface, which presents a consistent view of the system.

The blackboard architecture has made it possible to design the system so that all components, including the system executive and user interface, can be replaced with functional equivalents, possibly using a different knowledge base or inference engine, as necessary. The use of modular components for each aspect of the system gives the whole system greater flexibility and efficiency. For example, modules have been incorporated that represent a variety of approaches to determining Mechanism of Stroke, including decision trees, Bayesian methods, nearest neighbor algorithms, and set covering algorithms (Desai et al., 1985; Neapolitan et al., 1987; Peeters, Evens, & Hier, 1987).

Physicians generally approach diagnosis and treatment of stroke in a series of steps: (1) anatomical diagnosis, (2) mechanism of stroke diagnosis, (3) test ordering, (4) treatment, and (5) prognosis. The Stroke Consultant goes through this same series of steps, each handled by a separate component of the system. Each component has its own knowledge base, inference engine, and local data store, and uses whatever type of reasoning is most appropriate for the problem for which it is responsible. The user interface is designed for the busy clinician in a stressful situation who uses the system infrequently and has little or no typing or computer experience. Using menus and question and (multiple choice) answers formats and with all data entry interactions initiated by the system, the Stroke Consultant is intended to be fast and easy to use as well as simple to learn (Curt, 1986; Hill, 1985).

Methods

Evaluation Site

The setting for this evaluation was Michael Reese Hospital, a teaching and research center that supports primary as well as specialty care programs. It is one of the Midwest's largest private medical centers with 750 available beds, a staff of more than 650 full-time and voluntary physicians, 1,000 nursing personnel, and 300 interns, residents, and fellows. The hospital is located in an urban "stroke-belt" where more than 500 stroke patients per year are admitted to the hospital from the surrounding community.

Participants

Thirty-nine people participated in the study: 20 males and 19 females. The participants ranged in age from 26 to 49 with a mean age of 35 years. The participants included 11 attending physicians, 5 residents, 3 interns, 11 nurses, 3 medical students, 4 technicians, 1 social worker, and 1 health administrator, all from the Neurology ward. The mean number of years the participants had been working in medicine was 8 years, with a range of 0 to 27. Most participants had a limited amount of computer experience with computer-based office equipment or with the computer-based patient care system at Michael Reese Hospital.

Design

This study investigated factors relating to variability in the users' responses to the Stroke Consultant. The research included a quasi-experimental design. Interaction between the participants and the Stroke Consultant was measured over a span of 4 months (January 1990 through May 1990). The study was initially designed for continuous use of the system during this time period, with a pre-test and post-test. Project participation was to begin with an introductory session in which the research was described and an initial interview was conducted. The second session was to include use of the Stroke Consultant and an exit interview. It was also expected that interested participants would use the system on an occasional basis. The study design was changed, however, to limit participants' interaction with the system to a single session lasting about an hour and a half, which contained both the pre-test and the post-test. The decision to limit the time was made because most medical personnel were not willing to participate in two sessions and also because we feared that staff rotations and departures would cause some people to drop out of the study. The investigator also spoke with participants informally, however, throughout the 4-month study period.

Procedure

The Stroke Consultant was introduced to the Department of Neurology at Michael Reese Hospital during Neurology Grand Rounds, a weekly forum where topics relating to neurology are discussed. Presentations were given by the author and Dr. Hier, who was then Head of the Neurology Department and the domain expert. Members of the teaching staff, attending physicians, residents, interns, medical students, and nurses were invited to attend this session and to participate in the research.

Interviews

Interviews were scheduled with all participants. All interviews were audiotaped, transcribed verbatim, and later coded in general categories. The beginning of the interview examined attitudes toward medical expert systems in general and participants' previous computer experience. They were then asked to fill out the first two surveys.

The participants were then given brief verbal instructions and asked to use the Stroke Consultant. Users were encouraged to make comments regarding what they found useful about the system and what they would like to see changed. They were not disturbed while they worked with the system, unless they requested assistance or it appeared that they needed help in order to continue. This was an attempt to simulate use of the system in the clinical setting.

Once the participants had finished using the system, they were given the last four surveys and an exit interview. During the sessions it was stressed that the physician is the ultimate decision maker about the patient's care, and that the Stroke Consultant is intended to be an aid to the physician. The exit interview included questions about their interaction with the system and their comments about the system as a whole.

Surveys

The surveys included: (1) *Survey of Biographical Information*; (2) *Attitude Toward Computers in General* (Kjerulff & Counte, 1984); (3) *User Evaluation of Interactive Computer Systems* (Shneiderman, 1987); (4) *Attitude Toward the Stroke Consultant* (adapted from Kjerulff & Counte, 1984); (5) *How Computers Will Affect the Practice of Medicine* (Teach & Shortliffe, 1981); and (6) *What Computers Should Be Able to Do* (Teach & Shortliffe, 1981).

The *Attitude Toward Computers in General* survey (Kjerulff & Counte, 1984) was selected to measure preexisting attitudes toward computers in general. It consists of 20 bipolar semantic differential statements rated on a 7-point scale. The format asks the participant to choose a number between two opposite positions (e.g., smart 1 2 3 4 5 6 7 stupid). The positive items were reversed so that high scores indicated a positive attitude. A total score for each participant was calculated by summing the scores for the 20 items.

The *User Evaluation of Interactive Computer Systems* survey (Shneiderman, 1987), administered immediately after participants used the Stroke Consultant, allowed users to identify problem areas in the user interface. It consisted of 23 bipolar semantic differential statements each rated on an 11-point scale. This format asks the participant to choose a number between two opposite positions (e.g., the characters in the displays were: unreadable 0 1 2 3 4 5 6 7 8 9 10 readable). The survey focused on several areas: the display layout; the sequence of displays; the terminology and instructions; and user's overall reactions.

The *Attitude Toward the Stroke Consultant* survey, also administered after participants had used the system, was adapted from Kjerulff and Counte (1984) and was designed to measure attitudes toward the Stroke Consultant. The statements focus on several areas: how the Stroke Consultant would affect them personally; how the Stroke Consultant would affect the hospital; how they would respond if the system was implemented at the hospital; and how they felt about the Stroke Consultant. Participants rated each statement on a 6-point Likert-type scale (1 = Strongly Agree, 2 = Agree, 3 = Neutral/Mixed, 4 = Disagree, 5 = Strongly Disagree, 0 = No Opinion). Ratings for positive items were reversed so that high scores indicated a positive attitude toward the Stroke Consultant. A total score for each participant was calculated by summing the scores for the 13 items.

Users' expectations about the effect of computer-based consultation systems on the practice of medicine were measured using a 17-item scale developed by Teach and Shortliffe (1981). This survey, *How*

Computers Will Affect the Practice of Medicine, was selected to measure physicians' views about the effect computer-based consultation systems are likely to have on the practice of medicine. Each statement is rated on a 5-point Likert-type scale (1 = Strongly Agree, 2 = Agree, 3 = Not Sure, 4 = Disagree, 5 = Strongly Disagree). A high score on this scale indicated that the participants thought that the statement was not likely to occur and a low score indicated that it was likely to occur. Items such as "Computer-based consultation systems will be hard for physicians to learn" and "Computer-based consultation systems will increase government control of physician's practices" were included.

Users' demands regarding the performance capabilities of computer-based consultation systems were measured by a 15-item scale developed by Teach and Shortliffe (1981). This scale, *What Computers Should Be Able to Do*, was selected to measure what performance capabilities physicians consider important for computer-based consultation systems. The scale contains statements about what computers should be able to do. Participants rated each of the items on a 5-point Likert-type scale (1 = Strongly Agree, 2 = Agree, 3 = Not Sure, 4 = Disagree, 5 = Strongly Disagree). Ratings for all items were reversed so that a high score indicated an item was evaluated to be an important capability and a low score meant that it was unimportant. They included items such as "Computer-based consultation systems should be able to explain their diagnostic and treatment decisions to physician users" and "Computer-based consultation systems should never make an incorrect diagnosis."

Participant Observation

Participant observation was chosen as a data collection technique so that the clinician's view of a medical expert system in the context of the social environment of the hospital could be understood. Participants' interactions with the Stroke Consultant were studied and notes were made of problems with the system, both those mentioned by participants and those that were observed by the investigator. Aspects of the interaction that users found particularly useful or interesting were also recorded. Notations about individual user's interaction style and the familiarity with the keyboard were also listed.

Both diary notes and session notes were taken. Diary notes were recorded both during the day and at the end of the day and contained statements that described the events that were experienced by the investigator through observation. They also contained statements made by participants about computers or computerization. Session notes were recorded both during and immediately after the session and included information about the sessions and any problems that participants encountered. Comments and suggestions made by the participants regarding the system were also recorded. Casual informal interviews were also conducted during observation. For example, several nurses mentioned that physicians were initially resistant to use the hospital's computerized patient care system. Several participants were subsequently asked about this system and its use.

Embedded Evaluation Techniques

The embedded evaluation techniques included Capture/Playback and Performance Analysis. The Capture/Playback tool allowed for the "capturing" of sessions for later review and also maintained statistics on which features of the system were being used and which were not, user errors, corrections, requests for online help, transaction aborts, and system usage. The tool also provided programs to analyze errors and system usage. Unnecessary actions on the part of users are one obvious activity to trace, such as deletions, transaction aborts, requests for online help, and so on. Excessive unnecessary actions indicate that the interface may be confusing. If one section of the dialogue is producing excessive problems it clearly needs redesign. The data were analyzed to determine the frequency with which certain options were chosen. The frequency of use versus the number of stroke patients can also be monitored. Capture/Playback not only suggests problem areas but it also points out those features that are attractive in the system.

The Performance Analysis tool measures the user response time, the system response time, and the screen display rate. This tool helps discover whether screen response and display times fall within acceptable limits and, if not, helps identify the problem areas. Examination of the user response time provides important clues as to whether or not each menu is easily comprehensible to the user.

Constructs and Measures

The research was initially motivated by the general hypothesis that a combination of users' predispositions and their experiences with the system would be a good predictor of whether a particular medical expert system is accepted. The user predisposition measure was multidimensional, including demographic variables, prior computer experience, general attitude toward computers, and initial reaction to medical expert systems. The demographic variables utilized in this study were age, sex, occupation, and number of years in medicine. The user experience measure had the following components: user exposure to the system, user error rates and types of errors, user response time and consultation time, system response times and display rates, and observer notes on user interaction styles. The user response outcome measure was also multi-dimensional. It included measures of the user's attitude toward the Stroke Consultant; the user's evaluation of the user interface; the user's demands and expectations of computer-based medical systems; the user's thoughts about the system's usefulness and ease of use; the user's response to the results, logic, and reasoning of the system; the user's complaints; the user's likelihood of using the system; and a behavioral analysis.

Hypotheses

Three distinct sets of specific hypotheses were investigated. The first set explored the relationships between user predisposition and user response to the system by asking the following question: What effect does a user's age, sex, occupation, level of previous computer experience, and general attitude toward computers have on his or her response to the Stroke Consultant? The second set of hypotheses explored the relationship between user predisposition and experiences with the system by measuring the effect of a user's prior level of computer experience on the number and types of errors made and on response time and consultation time. The third set of hypotheses explored the relationship between user experiences with the system and user response to the Stroke Consultant. It was hypothesized that if users made many errors and had consultation times that were longer than normal, the user interface was poorly designed and users would respond negatively. The relationship between age, sex, occupation, previous computer experience, and general attitude toward computers was also explored. Specific hypotheses were not generated for all aspects of the research because much of this research was exploratory in nature, dealing with the human-computer interaction styles that were observed and with the social environment of the hospital.

Results and Discussion

A user's subjective evaluation of a computer system is as important as the evaluation of the system. If a user feels that a system is not useful or not easy to use, the system will probably not be accepted by the users. This section presents an analysis of the results obtained from the user evaluations.

Interviews

Initial Interview

The initial interview examined participants' attitudes toward medical expert systems in general and their previous computer experience. Participants' initial reaction to medical expert systems ranged from skeptical or negative to very useful. Those who were skeptical or negative said that medical expert systems could possibly be useful for library research, from an educational standpoint, in a community hospital, or for an internist if a neurologist is not available. Those people who said that the systems were very useful also recognized some significant limitations (e.g., "cannot replace physician judgment"). Some advantages of medical expert systems that were mentioned in the initial interview included: improves efficiency, offers a checklist, serves educational purposes, increases knowledge base, aids in differential diagnosis, provides database capabilities, and serves as a double check. Some disadvantages of medical expert systems mentioned included: the computer is not as flexible as the human brain, a person could become too dependent on the machine and would be disinclined to think independently and to learn, the presence of the system might erode the physician-patient relationship, physicians might be computer illiterate, computers are a potential threat to employment, and medical-legal ramifications.

Exit Interview

The purpose of the exit interview was to allow the participants to comment on the Stroke Consultant after using it. There were several ways in which participants thought that the Stroke Consultant would be useful: to organize information and the decision-making process, to use as a reference source, to use as a supplemental knowledge source, to use as a learning tool, to compare decisions, and to aid in differential diagnosis. Most participants thought that the system was very easy to use, found the results of the system medically sound, and agreed with the logic and reasoning of the system. However, there were some problem areas noted. Some participants commented that the questions were too general and that the system did not ask all of the questions they would have asked in diagnosing a patient. Participants also reported that some of the diagnoses and treatments were incorrect.

There were five categories of complaints mentioned by the participants: the system was not flexible enough, there were not enough information and options available, the system made some errors, users did not understand how it worked, and physicians would be less inclined to think independently. Most participants stated that they would be somewhat likely to use the system if it were left at the hospital.

Participants were asked what improvements they would suggest. These ranged from improvements in the modules to the addition of some new features. Participants suggested that we provide a means of using the definition module to look up a word without going through a consultation. It was suggested by some participants that a database function be added, with the capability to save a current patient and later retrieve this patient file and also to retrieve information on patients identified by the system as being similar. The retrieved information could be used in further processing or as the basis for a printed report. Participants also wanted to be able to print the information that the computer provided as references and explanations. They also suggested that the information provided be kept up-to-date. They wanted to see more articles listed, particularly references from current literature. This information was automatically displayed with each result; users wanted this display to be optional. Some participants stated they would also like the system to check for inconsistent data input by the user. Participants stated that there should be more variables included in making a diagnosis. They felt that in some cases not enough questions were asked before a diagnosis was made. They also felt that the system should provide greater flexibility. Some felt that the system should allow the user to follow through on two possible diagnoses to see the recommendations in each case. Some users asserted that the system made some errors and recommended some treatments that were controversial. These users felt that the accuracy of the system could be somewhat improved and that the system should state when it recommended a controversial therapy or treatment. A few participants felt that there were no improvements that could be made that would make them more likely to use the system. One of these individuals commented, "Impossible. Not until you get those megabyte computers that can simulate human thinking and at that stage you're talking something different. Then send the computer to medical school and it will learn everything itself."

Surveys

General Attitude Toward Computers

Participants felt that computers generally were helpful, efficient, useful, and good. In contrast, participants also felt that computers in general were cold, inhumane, complicated, and rigid. The mean total score was 103, with a standard deviation of 9.57, indicating that the group was quite positive toward computers in general. Cronbach's alpha, used to assess the internal consistency of the 20-item scale, was 0.67 ($N = 39$).

User Evaluation of Interactive Computer Systems

The mean score for the items was 8.0, indicating that there were no major problems with any of the aspects measured by the survey. Cronbach's alpha for the 19-item scale was 0.90 ($N = 26$).

Attitude Toward the Stroke Consultant

The mean total score was 47.3, with a standard deviation of 8.6, indicating that this group was quite positive toward the Stroke Consultant. Participants also responded that being required to use the Stroke Consultant would not make them consider leaving the hospital. They did not think that computers should be used in purely scientific situations. In the long run, they felt that the Stroke Consultant was a good idea and that it could increase the quality of medical education at the hospital. Cronbach's alpha for the 13-item scale was 0.85 ($N = 35$).

How Computer-Based Consultation Systems Will Affect the Practice of Medicine

The average expectation rating for this scale was slightly positive with a mean of 3.30. Three of the statements were judged likely to come true: fears that use of the consultation system would result in physician reliance on cookbook medicine and diminish judgment; concerns that systems would increase government control of physicians' practices; and concerns that the systems would result in serious legal and ethical problems. Clinicians felt that the consultation systems would not result in less efficient use of the physician's time nor would they be hard for physicians to learn. They also felt that the use of consultation systems would not reduce the need for specialists or paraprofessionals. Cronbach's alpha for the 17-item scale was 0.86 ($N = 33$).

What Computer-Based Consultation Systems Should Be Able to Do

The average demand rating for the scale was slightly positive with a mean of 3.69. The ability of a system to stimulate the physician's thought process was thought to be the most important feature of a system.

Second in importance was the ability of a system to explain its diagnostic and treatment decisions. Participants also felt that it was important that the system be portable and flexible so that physicians could access it at any time and place. They felt that it should not reduce the amount of technical knowledge physicians must learn and remember nor should it become the standard for acceptable medical practice. Cronbach's alpha for the 15-item scale was 0.66 ($N = 34$).

Hypotheses

Study findings indicated no relationships between sex and general attitude toward computers and attitude toward the Stroke Consultant, nor were there relationships between age and general attitude toward computers and attitude toward the Stroke Consultant. There was also no relationship between the expert rating of computer experience and attitudes. However, there was a relationship between the participants' self-rating of computer literacy and their general attitude toward computers. It was hypothesized that there would be a positive correlation between participants' general attitude toward computers and attitude toward the Stroke Consultant, but findings shows no correlation between these attitudes. Results also indicated that there was no association between occupation and general attitude toward computers. There was an association between occupation and attitude toward the Stroke Consultant, with nurses more positive than physicians or other non-physicians.

It was hypothesized that participants with little or no computer experience would have the highest error rate. In actuality, the highest error rate was found in precisely those users with previous computer experience, because these users were using commands that had been learned on other systems. There was no relationship between computer experience and response time. There was also no relationship between errors made while using the system and attitude toward the Stroke Consultant, but there was a negative correlation between response time and attitude toward the Stroke Consultant.

Participant Observation

Several findings emerged from the data collected through participant observation, including the participant's reaction to the Stroke Consultant, the willingness of members of the department to participate in such a study, and the effects of the hospital as a social system on the attitudes and behavior of the participants.

Reaction to the Stroke Consultant

Participants' reaction to the Stroke Consultant varied. There were those who enjoyed using the system very much. They used terms such as "fun" and "interesting" to describe the system. Some of the participants thought aloud while using the system. There were other participants who did not comment during the session but acknowledged the system as being accurate. Some of the participants would nod their heads in agreement with the system as results were displayed. If there was something that they didn't agree with they would mention it so that a notation could be made. Some participants were negative toward the system. One participant stated that he was one of the more negative or pessimistic users. There were also the participants who came in with the idea that the system was accurate and tried to find ways to "trick it" with patient symptoms that were not related to the stroke.

Participants found the system very educational, taking notes as they read the information. Even the most negative and pessimistic users noted that the system did have educational value. One participant who was using the system with a current patient wrote down a reference and said he would have to go to the library and look it up. There were participants who said it could be a useful learning tool.

Observations suggested that participants would be willing to use the Stroke Consultant, but it needed to provide them with some capability not otherwise available. There were some participants who stated that they would not use the system solely for its diagnostic purposes, since they could go next door and consult a colleague. The references provided, however, were beneficial to everyone: physicians, residents, interns, and nurses. Observation also suggested that participants may be willing to use a system that is not 100% accurate, but they would not use a system with software malfunctions. Furthermore, participants would simply not use a system that is not easy to use. The Stroke Consultant was very easy for participants to use; however, there were features of the system that participants tried once, had difficulty with, and never used again. Several participants had used the Stroke Consultant's correct feature and had some problems with it; rather than use this feature again, most participants wanted to stop the case and start over from the beginning.

Finally, some participants were initially hesitant to use the system. After they had gone through a session, many said it was not as hard as they thought it would be, that they actually had fun. This initial hesitancy and later acceptance also applied to the use of computers in general. The idea was mentioned by participants in an open-ended initial interview when asked how they thought other health care professionals would react to the idea of medical expert systems. It was also mentioned throughout the period of participant observation that physicians were very hesitant about using the hospital's patient care system, but after several years more and more physicians were using it. Participants summarized this idea by saying that as people use computers more they become more positive toward computers.

Willingness to Participate

In order to gain voluntary participation, participants must be convinced of their importance to the research. One physician, who did not want to participate, stated that he had a negative bias toward computers and did not understand why anyone would recommend him as a participant. It was explained that feedback was being requested from all members of the department, not just the ones who felt positive about computers. He agreed to participate and provided very useful comments and several recommendations about how to make the system better and more acceptable to all.

There was also a difference in physicians' and nurses' willingness to cooperate. As recorded in the session notes, most nurses easily agreed to participate and were willing to set up an appointment as soon as possible. Interns and residents responded similarly. Physicians, however, usually requested that an appointment be made with their secretaries for a week or two later, and in some cases even longer.

Finally, without participant observation, the participation of all members of the Neurology Department would not have been obtained. After members of the department became familiar with the investigator, it was easier to convince members of the department to participate.

Effects of the Social System

The Neurology Department as a social system and the possible effects this system might have on attitudes were also of interest. The manner in which the personality, attitudes, motivations, and behavior of the individuals influenced and were influenced by the social group were studied. The Neurology Department as a whole was very positive about computers in general. Almost all members of the department had some prior computer experience, using computers for word processing, statistics, or for the hospital's computerized patient care system. Several members of the department stated that Dr. Hier, then Head of the Neurology Department, had gotten them interested in computers and supported the use of computers. Other departments, without such a strong acceptance of computers in general, might be less receptive to the idea of medical expert systems.

Within this social system, some members felt that using computers was for secretaries, nurses, and technicians. One participant responded that physicians may be hesitant to use a medical expert system because they would feel that they were relegated to the role of a technician. It was suggested by several participants that the physicians might want the results and information provided by the system, but they might not be willing to use the system themselves. It was believed that they would want the nurses or technicians to enter the information and give them the results.

When the research first began, some members of the department also questioned the investigator's presence and purpose. After having been there for a while and having helped members of the department with computer-related problems, the investigator was accepted as a member of the team.

Conclusion

This research examined the interaction between the Stroke Consultant and medical personnel in the Neurology Ward at Michael Reese Hospital. Data collection strategies included pre-use and post-use interviews and surveys and participant observation. User errors and other kinds of system interaction were also measured. Participant observation was essential in obtaining the cooperation of almost all of the staff on the ward. It was also extremely valuable in helping interpret user comments, identifying points of user frustration, and understanding the source of many user errors. The Capture/Playback and Performance Analysis tools proved to be very effective for objective evaluation of the human-computer interface of the Stroke Consultant.

A clear majority of the participants displayed a positive overall attitude toward computers in general and indicated a willingness and even a desire to learn more about computers and apply them in their daily work. Most participants indicated that they would be likely to use the Stroke Consultant if it were installed at the hospital. The results of the research also suggest, however, that although the Stroke Consultant is clearly valuable, its attractiveness and convenience in the clinical setting could be enhanced in many ways. Users requested a number of enhancements that had not been envisioned and showed a total lack of interest in others that had been planned. User errors and system performance measurements suggested that the system is easy to use at a micro level but that the overall structure of the consultation was not clear to the users. It is also clear that health care personnel will not use a system that just recommends a diagnosis but will demand more information, such as definitions, references, explanations, reports, and database capabilities. These findings provide valuable information on the reactions of different medical personnel to the clinical use of an expert system and the changes required to make the system more effective in the clinical context.

Additional Reading

Participant Observation

Carroll, Landauer, John, Whiteside, and Wolf (1989) discuss the role of using laboratory experiments, participant observation studies, and field studies in human-computer interaction in order to answer design questions about the user interface, to evaluate the usability of computer systems, and to improve the developer's understanding of usability.

Rubin and Babbie (1989) and Guy, Edgley, Arafat, and Allen (1987) provide a discussion of observation in field research.

Embedded Evaluation Techniques

Bannon, Cypher, Greenspan, and Monty (1983) and Gaines and Shaw (1983) discuss the logging of user activities.

Neal and Simons (1984) developed a playback program for obtaining objective measures of product usability. Their playback methodology proved to be very effective for objective evaluation and comparison of software including the user interface design and software documentation.

Measuring Attitudes

Kjerulff and Counte (1984) developed two questionnaires to measure attitudes toward computers. The first questionnaire measures general attitudes toward computers, and the second questionnaire measures attitudes toward a specific medical information system.

Startsman and Robinson (1972) developed a scale to assess attitudes toward computers in general.

Teach and Shortliffe (1981) developed a questionnaire to assess physician attitudes toward computer-based consultation systems. The questionnaire evaluated the acceptability of different medical computing applications, expectations about the effect of computer-based consultation systems on medicine, and demands regarding the performance capabilities of computer-aided consultation systems.

Evaluation

Miller (1985) describes three forms of evaluation of artificial intelligence systems in medicine and discusses how several previous evaluations fit into his framework.

Kirakowski and Corbett (1990) present a methodology for the study and evaluation of the human-computer interface.

References

Bannon, L., Cypher, A., Greenspan, S., & Monty, M. (1983). Evaluation and analysis of users' activity organization. *Proceedings of the CHI 1983 Conference on Human Factors in Computing Systems* (pp. 54-57). New York: ACM Press.

Bischoff, M. B., Shortliffe, E. H., Scott, A. C., Carlson, R. W., & Jacobs, C. D. (1983). Integration of a computer based consultant into the clinical setting. *Proceedings of the 7th Annual Symposium on Computer Applications in Medical Care* (pp. 149-152). Washington, DC: IEEE Computer Society Press.

Carroll, J. M., Landauer, T. K., John, B. E., Whiteside, J., & Wolf, C. G. (1989). The role of laboratory experiments in HCI: Help, hindrance, or ho-hum? *Proceedings of the CHI 1989 Conference on Human Factors in Computing Systems* (pp. 265-268). New York: ACM Press.

Curt, C. L. (1986). *Human factors in computerized medical systems.* Unpublished doctoral dissertation, Loyola University, Chicago.

Desai, B., Beachy, M., Biss, K., Evens, M., Hier, D., Hill, H., & McCormick, W. (1985). Comparing Bayes' rule and the nearest neighbor rule for medical diagnosis. *Proceedings of the 1985 Conference on Intelligent Systems and Machines* (pp. 22-24). Oakland, CA: Center for Robotics.

Friedman, R. B., & Gustafson, D. H. (1977). Computers in clinical medicine: A critical review. *Computers in Biomedical Research, 8,* 199-204.

Gaines, B. R., & Shaw, M. L. (1983). Dialog engineering. In M. E. Sime & M. J. Coombs (Eds.), *Designing for human-computer communication* (pp. 23-53). London: Academic Press.

Guy, R. F., Edgley, C. E., Arafat, I., & Allen, D. E. (1987). *Social research methods: Puzzles and solutions.* Newton, MA: Allyn & Bacon.

Hill, H. (1985). *An expert system to assist physicians with stroke diagnosis and treatment.* Unpublished doctoral dissertation, Illinois Institute of Technology, Chicago.

Hill, H., Curt, C. L., Kozar, B. K., Hier, D. B., & Evens, M. W. (1985). The architecture of the IIT-MRH Stroke Consultant. *Proceedings of the 9th Annual Symposium on Computer Applications in Medical Care* (pp. 314-317). Washington, DC: IEEE Computer Society Press.

Kirakowski, J., & Corbett, M. (1990). *Effective methodology for the study of HCI.* North Holland, The Netherlands: Elsevier Science Publishers B.V.

Kjerulff, K. H., & Counte, M. A. (1984). Measuring attitudes toward computers: Two approaches. *Proceedings of the 8th Annual Symposium on Computer Applications in Medical Care* (pp. 529-535). Washington, DC: IEEE Computer Society Press.

Miller, P. L. (1985). Evaluation of artificial systems in medicine. *Proceedings of the 9th Annual Symposium on Computer Applications in Medical Care* (pp. 281-286). Washington, DC: IEEE Computer Society Press.

Moore, L. A. (1991). *A methodology for the evaluation of the human-computer interface of medical expert systems.* Unpublished doctoral dissertation, Illinois Institute of Technology, Chicago.

Moore, L. A., Evens, M., & Hier, D. B. (1990). Physician use of an expert system for stroke in a clinical setting. *Proceedings of the Second IASTED International Symposium on Expert Systems and Neural Networks* (pp. 171-174). Anaheim, CA: ACTA.

Neal, A. S., & Simons, R. M. (1984). Playback: A method for evaluating the usability of software and its documentation. *IBM Systems Journal, 23,* 82-96.

Neapolitan, R., Evans, M., Jiwani, H., Kenevan, J., Moore, L., Rinaldo, F., & Hier, D. (1987). Applying reasoning under uncertainty to set covering. *Proceedings of the EDS/SMI Conference on Expert Systems* (pp. 171-183). Detroit, MI: Engineering Society of Detroit.

Peeters, M., Evens, M., & Hier, D. (1987). A comparison of the generalized set covering algorithm with a decision tree algorithm for the diagnosis of stroke. *Proceedings of the ESD/SMI Conference on Expert Systems, Dearborn* (pp. 153-169). Detroit, MI: Engineering Society of Detroit.

Rubin, A., & Babbie, E. (1989). *Research methods for social work.* Belmont, CA: Wadsworth.

Shneiderman, B. (1987). *Designing the user interface: Strategies for effective human-computer interaction.* Reading, MA: Addison-Wesley.

Shortliffe, E. H., Buchanan, B. J., & Feigenbaum, E. A. (1984). Knowledge engineering for medical decision making: A review of computer based clinical decision aids. In W. J. Clancey & E. H. Shortliffe (Eds.), *Readings in medical artificial intelligence: The first decade* (pp. 35-71). Reading, MA: Addison-Wesley.

Startsman, T. S., & Robinson, R. E. (1972). The attitudes of medical and paramedical personnel toward computers. *Computers and Biomedical Research, 5,* 218-227.

Teach, K. H., & Shortliffe, E. H. (1981). An analysis of physician attitudes regarding computer-based clinical consultation systems. *Computers and Biomedical Research, 14,* 542-558.

Weiner, H., & Levitt, L. (1974). *Neurology for the house officer.* New York: Medcom.

11

Predicting Effective Use of Hospital Computer Systems

An Evaluation

Carolyn E. Aydin
Rosemary Ischar

Introduction

Information handling for interdepartmental communications constitutes a large proportion of a nursing unit's work. Increasingly, hospitals are adopting computers to support these communications. Evaluations have shown that computer communication systems can improve the timeliness of message transmission, improve access to medical information, and reduce errors (Blum, 1986). Little attention, however, has been paid to system maintenance as computers become a routinized part of the daily work of the hospital. Most implementation studies are short-term (Tornatzky et al., 1983) and almost no research has focused on errors in computer system use (Kling & Scacchi, 1980).

The purpose of this chapter is to determine the demographic characteristics and attitudes of system users, as well as the aspects of work on each unit, that predict ongoing use or discontinuance of an established computerized medication information system in a large medical center. System users are not viewed as potential resisters but as adopters of an

AUTHORS' NOTE: An earlier version of this chapter appeared in the *Proceedings of the 12th Annual Symposium on Computer Applications in Medical Care* (pp. 862-868), 1988. Los Angeles, CA: IEEE Computer Society Press.

innovation who make ongoing decisions concerning the innovation's characteristics and continued use.

Specifically, respondents' perceptions of three characteristics of the innovation are addressed: relative advantage, compatibility, and complexity (Rogers, 1983). These respondent perceptions are used to predict system use, which is defined in terms of timely and accurate medication order entry.

Background

Setting

The study was conducted at Cedars-Sinai Medical Center, a 1,200-bed private teaching hospital located in Los Angeles, California. A computerized medication order entry system (HART MEDS) was developed in-house by the medical center's computer staff beginning in 1978 and implemented throughout the hospital by 1981 (Ischar, 1987). The system called for unit clerks to enter medications in the computer, followed by verification by both nursing and pharmacy. The RN or LVN II was also to chart the medication on the computer. The computerized charting function, however, resulted in problems on the pilot unit and online charting was discontinued. Currently, the system operates with computerized order entry by unit clerks or RNs and LVN IIs, followed by computer verification by both nursing and pharmacy (Aydin, 1989; Ischar, 1987).

Purpose

In 1986, a hospital audit of computerized medication order entry highlighted late (defined as 2 hours or more after the order is written) and inaccurate order entry by clerical staff and RNs/LVN IIs. Although these problems are detected during the double verification process and do not result in errors in administration of medications, correction of each entry is time-consuming and costly. In addition, the audit showed large differences between units in the number of late or incorrect orders. The purpose of the present study is: (1) to determine characteristics or attitudes of individual nurses or units that account for the variation in the number of late and incorrect orders for the different units, (2) to suggest measures to improve system use in all units, and (3) to make recommendations concerning selection of pilot units for future computer implementation.

Hypotheses

Personal and situational factors, attitudes of computer system users, and characteristics of the work on different hospital units are hypothesized to affect users' ongoing decisions to use the computer system (Lucas, 1975, 1981). Six specific hypotheses are listed below.

Individual Differences

Two individual differences hypothesized to influence use of the medical information system include cognitive style (Aydin, 1987; Keen & Morton, 1978; Kilmann & Mitroff, 1976; Mason & Mitroff, 1973; Myers & McCaulley, 1985) and age. Thinking types, who rely on logical structures to clarify a situation, should have less difficulty adapting to computers and a more positive attitude toward computer use (Keen & Morton, 1978). Younger workers may also have more positive attitudes toward the computer system. In addition, the effects of type and level of nursing education, number of years in nursing, tenure at this hospital, and job title are also explored.

Hypothesis 1: Thinking types exhibit more effective use of the medical information system than feeling types.

Hypothesis 2: Age is negatively associated with effective use of the medical information system.

Attitudes Toward the Innovation

According to Rogers (1983, p. 15), "the characteristics of innovations, as perceived by individuals, help to explain their different rate of adoption." We hypothesize that these characteristics of the computer system are also essential to system maintenance on an ongoing basis. Each of the hypotheses listed below predicts the relationship between a characteristic of the computer system as perceived by the user (i.e., "relative advantage," "complexity," or "compatibility") and effective use of the system.

Hypothesis 3 predicts that users' perceptions of the relative advantage of the information system will predict effective system use:

Hypothesis 3: Acceptance of the information system is positively associated with effective system use.

Hypothesis 4 states that the perceived complexity of the computer system will also predict effective system use:

Hypothesis 4: Perception of the information system as confusing to use is negatively associated with effective system use.

Hypothesis 5 concerns the compatibility of the innovation with the user's values and expectations concerning computerization. Specifically, general attitudes and expectations for computer applications in the hospital are expected to predict effective system use:

Hypothesis 5: Positive general attitudes toward hospital computer applications are associated with effective system use.

Unit Characteristics

In addition to individual determinants of effective information system use, characteristics of the nursing units themselves and the work context are hypothesized to affect use of the computer system by nurses on each unit. Aydin (1987) found that units with a larger volume of intravenous medications charted a lower percentage of those medications correctly on the computer. Unit specialty, shift, and level of clerical staffing are also explored as predictors of effective use of the information system. All of these elements provide additional measures of the compatibility of the computer system with the daily routine of the system user.

Hypothesis 6: The volume of medications on a unit is positively associated with the proportion of medication errors on the computer.

Methodology

Research methodology involved a quantitative study with comprehensive survey of computer system users throughout the hospital as well as an audit of actual system use on seven surgical units. Each of these procedures is described in detail below.

Survey

Survey questionnaires were mailed to the 463 RNs and LVNs at the medical center currently using the computerized medication order entry system. The questionnaire included questions about the order entry system, general questions concerning hospital computer applications, questions concerning their work and job satisfaction, demographic characteristics, and the short form of the Myers-Briggs Type Indicator. The questionnaire took approximately 20 minutes to complete. To ensure the confidentiality of responses, the questionnaires were mailed to the researchers at the University of Southern California rather than being returned to the hospital. Respondents did not put their names on the questionnaires but were identified by code number so the response rate could be tracked by unit and survey results could be matched with the audit of computer use.

Respondents

One hundred and ninety nurses responded for a response rate of 41%. Response rates for the 20 units surveyed range from 21% to 80% of the nurses assigned to the unit. Nurses responding to the survey were 97% female with an average age of 36 years. Nurse managers and assistant nurse managers, as well as clinical nurses and LVN IIs, responded to the survey. The average tenure at the medical center is 8 years and 56% of the respondents have bachelor's or master's degrees.

To determine how well the sample represented the nurses at the medical center, a nonrespondent study was conducted by contacting a random sample of the nonrespondents and requesting that they complete the questionnaire. An additional 15 nurses completed the survey. Statistical analyses indicated that these initial nonrespondents did not differ from the original sample. With the addition of these 15 responses, the final sample for analysis totalled 205 nurses.

Measures

Cognitive style was measured using the thinking/feeling scale on Form AV of the Myers-Briggs Type Indicator (Myers & McCaulley, 1985). Respondents were grouped into four categories: 1 = high thinking (thinking score higher with a difference between thinking and feeling categories of more than 5 points), 2 = low thinking (thinking score higher than feeling score, but with a difference of 5 points of less), 3 = low feeling (feeling score higher than thinking score, but with a difference of 5 points or less), and 4 = high feeling (feeling score higher with a difference of more than 5 points between thinking and feeling) (Aydin, 1987).

The attitude variables included on the questionnaire were all measured on 7-point Likert scales ranging from "Strongly disagree" to "Strongly agree." Thus, a higher score indicated agreement with the statement. Acceptance of the information system (relative advantage) was measured by agreement with the following statement: "The HART MEDS System is worth the time and effort required to use it" (Aydin, 1987; Schultz & Slevin, 1975). Perceived complexity of the system was measured by level of agreement with the following statement: "The HART MEDS System is confusing to use."

Attitudes toward hospital computer applications in general were measured by asking for level of agreement with these statements: "Hospital computer applications will (a) improve the technical quality of care, (b) reduce costs of medical care, and (c) allow nurses more time for patients" (Anderson, Jay, Schweer, & Anderson, 1987). Responses to the three statements were added to form a scale with a reliability coefficient (Cronbach's alpha) of .80. Job satisfaction was measured by summing responses (1 to 7 from "Strongly disagree" to "Strongly agree") on the following four questions adapted from standardized measures of job satisfaction: "I am satisfied with the nature of the work I perform," "The job offers me the opportunity to use my personal initiative or judgment in carrying out my work," "The job gives me considerable opportunity for independence and freedom in how I do the work," and "I am satisfied with my relations with others in the organization with whom I work—with my co-workers" (Hackman & Oldham, 1975; Schriesheim & Tsui, 1981). Reliability for the job satisfaction scale (Cronbach's alpha) was .84.

The dependent variable was self-reported entry of medications on the computer in response to the following question: "When medications are entered on the computer for the patients you are assigned to care for, what percentage of these are entered within 2 hours after the order is written?"

Audit

An audit of the information system was conducted by the pharmacy department to determine the number of late entries and errors in order entry for seven surgical units, more than one third of the 20 units included in the survey. The audit covered four days of medication entries. Pharmacy copies of physician medication orders were compared with computer entry of the orders. The audit report identified each error by type, unit, date, and (where possible) clerk or nurse responsible for the entry. To aid in data analysis, each unit was categorized according to the approximate volume of medications administered on that unit. Of the 20 units using the order entry system, 3 were classified as having a high volume of medications relative to other hospital units. Twelve units were classified as having a medium volume of medications and 5

TABLE 11.1 Correlation Matrix Among Variables

	1	*2*	*3*	*4*	*5*	*6*	*7*
1 Percentage meds entered within 2 hours	—						
2 Cognitive style	.003	—					
3 Age	−.02	−.11*	—				
4 Attitude toward system	.39**	−.06	−.15	—			
5 System confusing	−.17*	−.05	.12	−.31**	—		
6 Hospital computer applications	.21**	−.03	−.11	.45**	−.21*	—	
7 Job satisfaction	.05	.02	.21*	.12	.001	.09	—
Mean	72.03	2.48	36.21	5.79	2.18	14.14	22.32
Standard deviation	23.48	1.24	9.24	1.40	1.38	4.35	4.46

NOTE: $n = 205$; $^*p \leq .05$; $^{**}p \leq .01$

units were classified as having a relatively low volume of medications to administer.

Two types of analyses were performed on the audit data. The errors were analyzed by unit, combined with survey data for the same seven units, to gain a more complete picture of the problems on each unit related to computer use. In addition, the errors that could be attributed to individual unit clerks or nurses were analyzed in detail to determine the distribution of different types of errors among different individuals. The results of these analyses, as well as results of the survey analysis, are discussed below.

Results

User Characteristics and Attitudes

Table 11.1 shows the zero-order correlations between the dependent variable, self-reported computer entry of medications within 2 hours, and the survey variables hypothesized as predictors of effective computer use.

A regression analysis was performed to determine the predictive power of each variable on the dependent variable (respondent's self-report of the percentage of medications entered within 2 hours), controlling for the effects of all other variables. Predictor variables included were cognitive style, age, attitude toward the HART MEDS system,

TABLE 11.2 Regression Analysis to Predict Percentage of Medications
Entered Within 2 Hours From User Characteristics and Attitudes

Variable Entered	b (s.e.)	t	Sig. t
Cognitive style	1.34 (1.37)	.98	.33
Age	.08 (.21)	.40	.69
Attitude toward system	5.92 (1.45)	4.08	.0001[***]
System confusing	−.31 (1.26)	−.24	.81
Hospital computer applications	.71 (.46)	1.53	.13
Job satisfaction	−.06 (.41)	−.15	.88

Adjusted R^2 = .16
$F (6,146) = 5.98$
Sig. $F = .0000$[***]

NOTE: $n = 153$; [*]$p \le .05$; [**]$p \le .01$; [***]$p \le .001$

perception of the system as confusing, attitude toward hospital computer applications, and job satisfaction. (Job satisfaction was included as an exploratory variable to determine whether individuals who were dissatisfied with their jobs in general also had negative attitudes specifically toward the computer system.)

Results of the regression analysis show that the only statistically significant predictor of computer use is the respondent's attitude toward the system (see Table 11.2). Contrary to previous research (Aydin, 1987), cognitive style does not predict computer use in the current setting.

As shown in Table 11.2, respondent attitude toward the value of the computerized order entry system (acceptance) is the only predictor of computer use. It is possible, however, that other variables act as predictors of this attitude (Schultz & Slevin, 1975). Thus, an additional regression analysis was performed to investigate the other variables as determinants of respondent's attitude. Results show that age, perceptions of the system as confusing, positive attitudes toward hospital computer applications in general, and job satisfaction are statistically significant predictors of the respondents' acceptance of the computer system (Table 11.3).

TABLE 11.3 Regression Analysis to Predict Respondent Attitude Toward
HART MEDS From Other User Characteristics and Attitudes

Variable Entered	*b* *(s.e.)*	*t*	*Sig. t*
Cognitive style	−.03 (.08)	−.41	.68
Age	−.02 (.01)	−2.21	.03*
System confusing	−.14 (.07)	−1.99	.05*
Hospital computer applications	.14 (.02)	6.11	.0000***
Job satisfaction	.06 (.02)	2.51	.01**
Adjusted R^2 = .28 F (5,148) = 13.06 Sig. F = .0000***			

NOTE: n = 154; *$p \leq .05$; **$p \leq .01$; ***$p \leq .001$

Based on the survey analysis, Hypothesis 1 is rejected. Cognitive style does not predict either self-reported use of the HART MEDS system or the respondent's acceptance of the system. Age is, however, a significant negative predictor of the respondent's acceptance of the system, which, in turn, does predict self-reported system use. Thus Hypotheses 2 and 3 are accepted. Hypotheses 4 and 5 are also accepted. Both perceptions of the system as confusing and positive attitudes toward hospital computer applications in general predict acceptance of the system, although they do not directly predict use. Job satisfaction also predicts acceptance of the system, but there were no significant differences for nurses working on different shifts.

Results of the Computer System Audit

The results of the information system audit performed by the pharmacy department are also important in considering effective system use. Seven surgical units were included in the audit, which covered two time periods: August 31 to September 1, and September 16 to 17, 1987, a total of 4 days. Each nurse was assigned 3 to 4 patients. Clerical staffing did not differ between units.

A total of 136 errors was detected by the audit (all of which were corrected through pharmacy verification). Forty-seven (35%) of the errors detected were late entries. The balance were errors in duration, frequency, dose, drug, or other errors such as duplicate entries or entry for the wrong patient. The clerk or nurse responsible for order entry on 76 of these errors (56%) could not be identified from the information available.

The audit data were first examined along with data from the survey for each of the seven units. Table 11.4 summarizes this information. The first column identifies the unit by number. The next three columns contain data from the survey of system users. The data include the unit's response rate on the survey, mean self-reported percentage of medications entered within 2 hours, and mean of respondents' attitudes toward the system. The audit data (next four columns) include the total number of errors in order entry for the unit over the 4-day period, number and percentage of those errors that were late entries, and volume of medications on the unit.

Examination of Table 11.4 reveals several interesting points. First, there is an inverse relationship between the volume of medications administered and the number of order entry errors. Of the units audited, Units 12 and 13 typically have a higher volume of medications than the other five units. These units, however, are also the units with the fewest errors in the audit and the highest survey self-reports of percentage of medications entered within 2 hours (80% and 84%). Thus Hypothesis 6 was rejected. A higher volume of medications is not associated with more computer order entry errors.

The audit results also validate the relative accuracy of the self-report information collected on the questionnaires. The three units (Units 12, 13, and 16) that report the highest percentage of medications entered within 2 hours also show the fewest late entries in the computer audit. Two of these units (13 and 16) also show the most positive attitudes toward the computer system. Interestingly, the nurses on one of the units (13) are also younger and newer to the medical center than nurses in the survey as a whole, validating the regression findings for age.

The units with the highest number of total errors on the audit, however, also indicate (survey data) that they enter a lower percentage of medications within 2 hours (15 and 17). One of the two units (17) also shows a relatively negative attitude toward the computer system. Unit 11 also shows a low percentage of medications entered, although the error count on the audit was lower than that of Units 15 and 17.

In addition to the analysis by unit, the errors that could be attributed to specific unit clerks or nurses were analyzed in detail. These errors were typically not late entries but errors in duration, frequency, instruction, route, and the like. Thirty-six errors were attributed to 11 different

TABLE 11.4 Summary of Survey and Audit Data for Seven Surgical Units

Unit	Survey Data Response Rate	Survey Data % Meds Entered/ 2 Hours	Mean Respondent Attitude	Audit Data Total Errors	Audit Data Number Late	Audit Data % Late	Meds Volume
11	43%	60%	5.8	13	5	38%	low
12	21	80	5.5	2	0	0	med
13	47	84	6.7	6	2	33	med
14	25	75	5.4	14	9	64	low
15	50	71	5.7	45	14	31	low
16	80	77	6.2	17	0	0	low
17	43	70	5.2	39	17	44	low

clerks. Some clerks were held responsible for as many as 9 errors of different types over the 4 days. On many units, the bulk of the medication order entry is done by the clerks. Nursing verification of all orders is required, however, and should correct these errors.

In addition to the errors attributed to clerks, 26 errors were attributed to 19 different nurses. Approximately 133 nurses are regularly assigned to these seven units, however, indicating that problems with inaccurate entry are concentrated in less than 15% of the nurses.

These results are in contrast to the survey data regarding late medication entries. Although the more specific types of errors described above are concentrated in a few staff members, late order entry is common for a large proportion of nurses. Although the percentage of late entries varies widely between units, only 14% of nurses surveyed responded that 100% of their medications are typically entered within 2 hours. Thirty percent of survey participants responded that less than 70% of their medications were entered within 2 hours. Undoubtedly even more are entered late than respondents are willing to admit.

Discussion

The most important findings for the management of information system use in the hospital environment concern the different results for the different types of errors. The late entry of orders is a relatively widespread phenomenon among a large proportion of the nursing staff, although the audit suggests differences between units. Furthermore, respondent attitude toward the system is a strong predictor of late order entry.

The fact that nurses often do not enter medication orders in the computer according to hospital guidelines reflects a reaction to the competing pressures of the job (Fed Up, Fearful, and Frazzled, 1988). Timely computer entry of medication orders is perceived as less important than other aspects of the job. Nurses as adopters of an innovation are evaluating the relative advantage of the innovation to them in the delivery of patient care.

However, other types of order entry errors are made mainly by clerical workers and a small minority of the nursing staff. Thus, dealing with the two types of errors requires different strategies. Late order entry was traced to the relative value respondents place on the computer system. Attitude was measured by asking whether the system was "worth the time and effort required to use it." In this case, as in the case of numerous computer applications, the advantage is greater for the pharmacy department and for the institution as a whole than it is for nursing. Using the system requires extra work on the part of the individual nurse for no immediate or apparent benefit. Thus it is a matter of persuading individual workers, who bear the costs of using the system, that it is beneficial to patient care or to the hospital for which they work (Lucas, 1981).

Cognitive style did not predict computer use in this study of an established computer system, although previous research on nurses using a newly implemented system showed cognitive style as a significant predictor of use (Aydin, 1987). It may be that this variable is most important when workers are faced with computers for the first time and diminishes in importance as the computer becomes part of the daily routine.

Viewing the system as confusing was also a statistically significant predictor of attitudes. Both training and good screen design and sequencing are essential in encouraging employees to use the system, especially when work pressures are high and finding time to learn to use computer systems that seem confusing or difficult is problematic.

Identifying the minority of nurses making most of the other order entry errors is also important. Automatic system audits that record this information as corrections are made during the verification process would allow for counseling and additional training of nurses or clerical personnel who make more than a specified number of errors.

Adequate nursing verification of clerical order entry is also essential. Although the majority of the order entry errors were made by clerical staff, all of these entries were verified by an RN or LVN II without detecting the errors. This indicates the necessity for both additional training of clerical staff and changes in the flow of nursing work so adequate time is taken during the order verification process. All of these issues need to be dealt with on an ongoing basis if a computer system is to continue to benefit the institution and improve the quality of patient care.

Conclusion

The results of this study will be used to make recommendations concerning the selection of appropriate pilot units for the implementation of additional computer systems. In selecting pilot units, it is important to both (1) take advantage of the positive attitudes and support available in units currently using the HART MEDS System effectively and (2) involve the units that are currently having difficulty with HART MEDS in order to address their problems and enlist their support as well. As the results of the present study show, user perceptions of the relative advantage and compatibility of the innovation in particular are still predictive of effective use many years after implementation.

Additional Reading

Alavi and Joachimsthaler (1992) summarize information systems research findings and make suggestions for future research.

Burkes (1991) provides a review of nurses' attitudes toward computer systems.

Kraemer and Dutton (1991) provides a detailed analysis of the major findings that have emerged from surveys of information technology in organizations.

Rogers (1983) is the standard introduction to the study of diffusion of innovations.

References

Alavi, M., & Joachimsthaler, E. A. (1992). Revisiting DSS implementation research: A meta-analysis of the literature and suggestions for researchers. *MIS Quarterly, 16*, 95-116.

Anderson, J. G., Jay, S. J., Schweer, H. M., & Anderson, M. M. (1987). Physician utilization of computers in medical practice: Policy implications based on a structural model. In J. G. Anderson & S. J. Jay (Eds.), *Use and impact of computers in clinical medicine.* New York: Springer Verlag.

Aydin, C. E. (1987). The effects of social information and cognitive style on medical information system attitudes and use. In W. W. Stead (Ed.), *Proceedings of the 11th Annual Symposium on Computer Applications in Medical Care* (pp. 601-606). New York: IEEE Computer Society Press.

Aydin, C. E. (1989). Occupational adaptation to computerized medical information systems. *Journal of Health and Social Behavior, 30*, 163-179.

Blum, B. I. (1986). *Clinical information systems.* New York: Springer Verlag.

Burkes, M. (1991). Identifying and relating nurses' attitudes toward computer use. *Computers in Nursing, 9*, 190-201.

Fed Up, Fearful and Frazzled. (1988, March 14). *Time,* p. 77.

Hackman, J. R., & Oldham, G. R. (1975). Development of the Job Diagnostic Survey. *Journal of Applied Psychology, 60*, 159-170.

Ischar, R. (1987). *Diffusion of a medical information system from the organizational and individual perspective.* Unpublished manuscript. Annenberg School of Communications, University of Southern California, Los Angeles, CA.

Keen, P. G. W., & Morton, M. S. S. (1978). *Decision support systems: An organizational perspective.* Reading, MA: Addison-Wesley.

Kilmann, R. H., & Mitroff, I. I. (1976). Qualitative versus quantitative analysis for management science: Different forms for different psychological types. *Interfaces, 6*, 17-27.

Kling, R., & Scacchi, W. (1980). Computing as social action: The social dynamics of computing in complex organizations. *Advances in Computers, 19*, 249-327.

Kraemer, K. L., & Dutton, W. H. (1991). Survey research in the study of management information systems. In Kraemer, K. L. (Ed.), *The information systems research challenge: Survey research methods* (pp. 3-57). Boston, MA: Harvard Business School.

Lucas, H. C., Jr. (1975). Behavioral factors in system implementation. In R. L. Schultz & D. P. Slevin (Eds.), *Implementing operations research/management science* (pp. 203-215). New York: American Elsevier.

Lucas, H. C., Jr. (1981). *Implementation: The key to successful information systems.* New York: Columbia University Press.

Mason, R. O., & Mitroff, I. I. (1973). A program for research on management information systems. *Management Science, 19,* 475-487.

Myers, I. B., & McCaulley, M. H. (1985). *Manual: A guide to the development and use of the Myers-Briggs Type Indicator.* Palo Alto, CA: Consulting Psychologists Press.

Rogers, E. M. (1983). *Diffusion of innovations.* New York: The Free Press.

Schriesheim, C., & Tsui, A. (1981). *Development and validation of a short satisfaction measure for use in survey feedback interventions.* Paper presented to Academy of Management Western Region Meeting, April.

Schultz, R. L., & Slevin, D. P. (1975). Implementation and organizational validity: An empirical investigation. In R. L. Schultz & D. P. Slevin (Eds.), *Implementing operations research/management science* (pp. 253-270). New York: American Elsevier.

Tornatzky, L. G., Eveland, J. D., Boylan, M. G., Hetzner, W. A., Johnson, E. C., Roitman, D., & Schneider, J. (1983). *The process of technological innovation: Reviewing the literature.* Washington, DC: National Science Foundation.

12

Computerized Order Entry in a Large Medical Center

Evaluating Interactions Between Departments

Carolyn E. Aydin

Managing communication between the diverse departments in health care organizations is becoming an increasingly important issue as institutions aim to control rising health care costs. Health care organizations of all sizes are typically organized along functional lines, with departments composed of members of a single occupational group such as nurses, pharmacists, or radiologists. Although all health care providers share a common mission—the delivery of patient care—employees from different professions also pursue their own interests, making coordination between departments difficult. The struggle for limited resources resulting from pressures to control costs has also exacerbated traditional conflicts between departments.

Lack of communication across departmental boundaries can delay the diagnosis and treatment of patients and increase patient length of stay. Delays may affect not only the delivery of medical care but have important financial consequences for the organization in which reimbursement for patient costs is based on standard lengths of stay per diagnosis. Computerized order entry systems have been adopted in health care settings in recent years to improve communication and coordination between departments, as well as to store information, control costs, and regulate the provision of health care (Packer, 1985).

Social Impacts of Computing

Computerized order-entry systems are designed to link patient care areas with ancillary departments such as the laboratory, radiology, or pharmacy. These systems require departments to share and maintain a common database of information necessary for effective patient care. Recent research focusing on the social impacts of such systems has shown increases in interdepartmental communication and interdependence accompanying their implementation (Aydin, 1989; Aydin & Rice, 1992; Majchrzak, 1988; Sproull & Kiesler, 1991; Zuboff, 1988). Although remote access to information may eliminate the need for some routine interpersonal communication such as telephone calls to obtain lab results, individuals in departments that share common databases meet face-to-face at least as often as before the computer system. These meetings may be formal, regularly scheduled meetings or informal conversations to solve day-to-day problems such as clarifying terminology or discussing orders for a specific patient. In essence, the maintenance of the database becomes a "superordinate goal" shared by all of the departments involved (Aydin, 1989; Sherif & Sherif, 1969). Furthermore, the increase in communication accompanying computer implementation may also provide an opportunity to encourage better working relationships between the departments involved (Aydin, 1989; Aydin & Rice, 1992; Connelly, Werth, Dean, Hultman, & Thompson, 1993; Kraemer & Danziger, 1990; Majchrzak, 1988; Pryor, Gardner, Clayton, & Warner, 1983).

The purpose of this study is to investigate the conditions under which increases in communication and improved working relationships between departments might be expected following system implementation (Aydin & Rice, 1992; McGuire, 1983). Using both quantitative and qualitative methods, the research focuses specifically on the effects of (1) organizational size and (2) the nature of past interactions between departments on potential changes accompanying a new centralized computer system.

Organizational Size and Increased
Communication Between Departments

Health care organizations vary widely in size, from small offices and clinics to large medical centers with hundreds of beds and several thousand employees. Although all health care providers face the challenge of coordinating numerous health care professionals, individual employees in large medical centers are often insulated within their departments and communicate less frequently with members of other departments than employees in smaller hospitals or clinics. Although research has been conducted in both large and small settings, key questions remain.

Aydin (1989), for example, showed increased interaction between departments in two large medical centers as a result of the implementation of a pharmacy order-entry system. Her findings, however, were based on retrospective interviews with key individuals involved in system implementation. Although these respondents reported increased communication and cooperation between departments, the study did not include employees who were less involved in system implementation. Aydin and Rice (1992) also focused on interdepartmental interaction, studying the implementation of a centralized scheduling system in a university student health clinic over a 2-year time period. Results included detailed examples of new informal communication patterns created by employees at all levels of the organization to support their use of the new computer system. The clinic, however, had only 100 permanent employees, making generalization to larger organizations difficult. Thus, although we know that sharing a common database can lead individuals to have contact with different people and depend on one another differently, the pervasiveness of such changes in larger health care organizations is unclear.

History of Conflict or Cooperation Between Departments

Past history of conflict or cooperation may also affect the changes that can be expected in working relationships between departments. Aydin (1989) found important differences between two medical centers in the amount of change reported by informants, noting that organizational history as well as size might be important in determining computer impacts. Although interdepartmental conflict as well as cooperation is common in health care organizations, the studies cited above included only departments with a history of cooperation before computer implementation.

This chapter presents preliminary results of a longitudinal research project that includes system users at all levels, from clerical employees to managers, of a large medical center. Furthermore, the project describes the working relationships between nursing and two different departments with different histories of interdepartmental relations. Results compare findings for the department with a past history of conflict with those for another department in the same institution with a history of cooperation with nursing. The chapter then discusses the practical implications of these findings and makes recommendations for future modifications in system implementation procedures.

Research Questions

The introduction of a computerized order-entry system has the potential to affect both routine communication between departments as well as more substantive, issue-oriented communication. Routine communication includes the frequent telephone calls required between nursing areas and ancillary departments such as radiology or laboratory to order and schedule tests and to obtain test results. Literature documenting the effects of computerization on work activities of nurses has shown that nurses spend less time telephoning other departments following computer implementation (Staggers, 1988).

Research Question 1: Will the frequency of telephone calls between nursing units and ancillary departments decrease following computer implementation?

Although use of the computer system to order tests and communicate results may decrease routine telephone communication, meetings and negotiations during the computer implementation process may improve relations between nursing and other departments as individuals meet to address the computer as an issue of common concern (Aydin, 1989; Aydin & Rice, 1992). In fact, research has shown that working toward a common goal can induce cooperation between previously competitive groups (Worschel, 1986). Furthermore, such negotiations should allow nursing and other departments to better coordinate their efforts, using the computer system, to support the delivery of patient care (Aydin, 1989; Connelly et al., 1993). Use of the computer system to communicate orders between nursing and other departments may also defuse issues. By eliminating problem-laden telephone calls and standardizing the requirements for the information to be transmitted, computer use may reduce ongoing conflict between departments. In large medical centers, however, only a few individuals may be involved in these negotiations as representatives of their departments. Individual computer users may remain insulated within their departments and see little change in their relationships with members of other departments as a result of computer implementation.

Research Question 2: Will nursing employees in a large medical center perceive improvements in the overall quality of communication with other departments following computer implementation?

Methods

Setting

This chapter explores changes in communication patterns and working relationships between four different nursing units and the Radiology and Admissions departments in a large medical center. The hospital began installation of a commercially developed order-entry system in four patient care areas and three ancillary departments (Radiology, Nuclear Medicine, and Admissions) in 1990. This study focuses on the relationships between the four nursing areas and the Admissions and Radiology departments.

The computer-based system, called ORDERS, replaced the transcription of physician orders onto paper requisitions with entry of physician orders by clerks and nurses into the ORDERS system. As orders are entered, electronic requests are routed to the appropriate department. Each department receives notification of requests via computer printouts. The Radiology and Nuclear Medicine departments also use ORDERS as a charge capture system.

The unit secretaries, as traditional order transcribers, are the most frequent users of ORDERS among the nursing staff. With ORDERS implementation, the secretaries' job responsibilities have expanded to include basic computer skills and a better understanding of medical terminology. The latter responsibility results from the need to match physician requests for radiology procedures with a list of menu selections. Unit secretaries are promoted, with a salary increase, to the position of communication technician in recognition of the expanded role. All unit secretaries are eligible for promotion following successful completion of an ORDERS training class and proficiency examination. Operational changes affecting communication between nursing and Radiology and Admissions, respectively, are described in the following sections.

Radiology

Nursing staff transmit physician orders to Radiology using the ORDERS system. Radiology and nursing then schedule the time for the procedure via telephone. The Radiology staff still maintains a paper trail of printout requests until procedures are completed. Radiology is currently purchasing an additional computer system to automate their internal operations and allow an electronic ORDERS interface to be developed. In the interim, updating of ORDERS once procedures are completed is done by clerical staff in the Radiology department—thus the reason for the paper trail.

Admissions

As in many large medical centers, the efficiency of the admissions process has long been an area of concern. Since the summer of 1985, the Department of Admissions has used a computer system called the Patient Management (PM) system to automate admission, discharge, and transfer (ADT) functions for the medical center. Difficult telephone communication between nursing areas and Admissions, however, has continued to be an issue. Admissions employees maintain that nurses delay notification of discharges to put off having a new patient admitted until the next shift. Nurses, in contrast, cite poor communication and short staffing in Admissions as the root of the problem.

When ORDERS was implemented, an electronic interface was developed to upload PM patient registration information into ORDERS patient files. This interface was designed to allow nursing staff to manage patient transfers and discharges using ORDERS as a message-only function. The initial "pending" message puts the Admissions department on alert to locate a bed on a new unit in event of patient transfer, or, on patient discharge, the message signals the department that a bed may soon be vacated. The "completed" message indicates that either (1) the patient has been discharged from the hospital or (2) the transferred patient has been received in the new unit. Changes to the patient census, however, are performed by the Admissions staff on receipt of computer printouts. The patient census is maintained within the PM system but can be displayed on the nursing units using ORDERS.

Measurement

This study is based on both quantitative analyses of survey results and qualitative data collected through in-depth interviews and observations of system implementation and use.

Surveys were administered to all registered nurses, licensed vocational nurses, and unit secretaries during training sessions for the pilot units prior to implementation of the order-entry system in 1990. The pilot units included two 32-bed adjacent surgical nursing units ("East" and "West") under the supervision of a single nurse manager. In addition, a surgical intensive care unit ("ICU") and the pre- and post-operative holding ("P/P Op") area also piloted the system. A second survey was distributed by unit managers 6 months following implementation during regular unit staff meetings to all staff currently working on the unit (a smaller number of respondents than those in the initial training sessions at Time 1).

Although responses were anonymous, participants were asked to write their social security number on the surveys to make it possible for computer analyses to match responses for the two surveys. A total of 71 respondents returned the first survey (47%), and 46 respondents (62%) returned the second survey. A number of individuals omitted their social security number, resulting in a total of 22 matched pre-post responses. The majority of respondents were staff nurses, although nurse managers and unit secretaries completed the surveys as well.

Both surveys asked respondents to (1) indicate how often they usually spoke to someone from Admissions and Radiology by telephone (ranging from 1 = Never to 6 = Many times a day) and (2) rate the communication between their area and Admissions and Radiology (ranging from 1 = Poor to 7 = Excellent). Test-retest reliability for survey items ranged from .70 to .80 when administered at the beginning and end of a 3-hour training session. These reliability statistics, however, may have been influenced by users reconsidering their relationships with other departments during the training session itself. (The survey also included additional questions to be used for other aspects of a larger research project.)

Qualitative methods included observation of unit secretaries at work both before and after computer implementation; participant observation in systems development and implementation meetings that were attended by representatives of nursing, Admissions, and Radiology; semi-structured interviews with representatives of each department prior to computer implementation; and informal discussions with computer implementation staff throughout the study period.

Quantitative Results

Tables 12.1 and 12.2 depict the quantitative results for relationships between nursing and the Admissions and Radiology departments, respectively. Mean ratings are shown for the total sample at both time periods.

TABLE 12.1 Changes in Communication With Admissions Department

Unit	N	Time 1 Mean	SD	N	Time 2 Mean	SD
Frequency of Telephone Communication With Admissions Department[1]						
Total Respondents						
ICU	26	2.42	1.47	15	2.07	1.28
P/P Op	7	4.43	1.51	7	4.71	1.11
East	11	4.27	1.49	11	4.09	1.92
West	23	4.13	1.52	11	4.18	1.33
Total	67	3.52	1.71	44	3.52	1.77
Pre-Post Respondents Only[3]						
Total $N = 20$; Mean Change: Time 2 − Time 1 = −.15; $p = .72$						
Overall Rating of Communication With Admissions Department[2]						
Total Respondents						
ICU	27	3.77	1.37	15	4.00	1.00
P/P Op	7	3.86	1.07	7	4.86	1.21
East	11	2.73	1.42	11	2.81	1.60
West	23	3.52	1.73	12	3.33	1.30
Total	68	3.53	1.50	45	3.66	1.41
Pre-Post Respondents Only[3]						
Total $N = 20$; Mean Change: Time 2 − Time 1 = −.35; $p = .34$						

[1]Scale: 1 = Never, 2 = Once/Week, 3 = Few Times/Week, 4 = Once/Day, 5 = Few Times/Day, 6 = Many Times/Day
[2]Scale: 1 = Poor, 4 = Neutral, 7 = Excellent
[3]Includes only those respondents who completed both surveys *including* their social security numbers to allow matching. Significant *t*-test results indicate that the *difference* between the Time 1 and Time 2 scores was significantly different from 0.
*p ≤ .05

Findings are also presented by unit to explore the possibility that system impacts differed by unit. In addition, paired *t*-tests for respondents completing both surveys (matched by social security number) test for statistically significant changes between the first and second surveys.

Results for communication with the Admissions department (Table 12.1) showed no significant changes between time periods in telephone contact or ratings of communication between departments. Results for Radiology (Table 12.2), however, showed a significant decrease in telephone communication, as rated by respondents completing both surveys. Examination of results for individual units, however, indicated that this decrease in telephone contact was not experienced by all units, with East in particular showing an increase rather than a decrease in telephone communication. Furthermore, the pre-post respondents also showed somewhat lower ratings for the quality of communication with

TABLE 12.2   Changes in Communication With Radiology Department

Unit	N	Time 1 Mean	SD	N	Time 2 Mean	SD
Frequency of Telephone Communication With Radiology Department[1]						
Total Respondents						
ICU	27	3.77	1.45	15	3.27	1.44
P/P Op	7	5.71	.49	7	5.14	.90
East	11	4.09	1.45	9	4.56	1.42
West	22	4.32	1.25	11	3.63	1.29
Total	67	4.21	1.41	42	3.95	1.46
Pre-Post Respondents Only[3]						
Total $N = 19$; Mean Change: Time 2 − Time 1 = −.63; $p = .02$*						
Overall Rating of Communication With Radiology Department[2]						
Total Respondents						
ICU	28	4.18	1.54	16	3.75	1.65
P/P Op	7	2.14	.90	7	3.00	2.00
East	11	4.36	1.36	10	4.00	1.25
West	23	3.87	1.42	11	3.91	1.38
Total	69	3.90	1.52	44	3.73	1.55
Pre-Post Respondents Only[3]						
Total $N = 18$; Mean Change: Time 2 − Time 1 = −.56; $p = .09$						

[1]Scale: 1 = Never, 2 = Once/Week, 3 = Few Times/Week, 4 = Once/Day, 5 = Few Times/Day, 6 = Many Times/Day
[2]Scale: 1 = Poor, 4 = Neutral, 7 = Excellent
[3]Includes only those respondents who completed both surveys *including* their social security numbers to allow matching. Significant *t*-test results indicate that the *difference* between the Time 1 and Time 2 scores was significantly different from 0.
*$p \leq .05$

Radiology at Time 2, although the decrease was not statistically significant. In answer to the Research Questions posed, telephone communication decreased with Radiology only. Furthermore, there was no improvement in the ratings of overall communication with either Admissions or Radiology.

Further examination of Tables 12.1 and 12.2 reveals differences between the nursing units in their communication patterns with both Admissions and Radiology. Findings for Admissions showed significant differences between nursing units in both the frequency of telephone communication and their overall ratings of communication with Admissions, all of which are likely attributable to the different functions performed by Admissions for different types of units. ANOVA results showed that the ICU respondents had significantly less telephone communication with Admissions, both before ($F = 7.58$, $p = .0003$) and after ($F = 7.05$, $p = .0007$) computer implementation. However, the East unit rated their overall communication with Admissions significantly lower than did the other three units at Time 2 ($F = 3.42$, $p = .03$).

Radiology results showed a different pattern than those for Admissions. P/P Op had significantly more telephone communication with Radiology (Time 1: $F = 4.07$, $p = .01$; Time 2: $F = 3.77$, $p = .02$), especially when compared with the ICU. P/P Op also, however, gave Radiology somewhat lower ratings than the other units at Time 1 for overall communication ($F = 4.25$, $p = .009$). The ratings had, however, increased somewhat by Time 2. The other units showed a decrease in telephone contact but no significant change in ratings of communication with Radiology. The qualitative results described below shed further light on the study findings.

Qualitative Results

Nursing and Admissions

Results from detailed interviews with system implementers helped clarify the quantitative findings detailed above. According to these respondents, several factors may explain the lack of change in both frequency and rating of communication with the Department of Admissions. Order entry for this department is a message-only function requiring two messages to complete a single transfer or discharge of a patient. The initial message, a "pending" message, puts the Admissions department on alert to locate a bed on a new unit in event of patient transfer or, on patient discharge, this message signals the department that a bed may soon be vacated. Although computer order entry may reduce the telephone volume by half, the potential for complete elimination of telephone communication did not exist at the time of the pilot study. The Admissions department was required to telephone the nursing unit during the transfer function on location of a suitable bed for the transferring patient. (The system was later modified to allow online notification of the new bed assignment.) The lower volume of telephone communication with the ICU perhaps reflects the fact that only patient transfers, not discharges, are precipitated from this area.

The lower rating on communication quality depicted by the East unit may be driven by the larger volume of patient transfers carried out on this unit. As a monitored unit transitioning between the ICU and the general care unit, tighter bed control is mandated on the East unit. These conditions may require heavier dependence on the telephone to keep the patient flow continual. Interviews indicated that this higher volume of telephone contact concerning the tense issue of bed vacancy and patient movement may create the potential for more dysfunctional communication patterns.

Nursing and Radiology

Findings concerning communication patterns between the Radiology department and the nursing units stem from a different set of circumstances. Prior to computerization, Radiology requisitions were handwritten, initiated on the nursing units by a secretary or nurse copying the physician's exact language or terminology for tests to be ordered. The decision as to the appropriate test to be performed and charge code was in the command of the Radiology department on receipt of the order. With computer order entry, the decision making and translation of radiology test names are transferred to the computer user at the nursing unit level, either a secretary or a nurse. This individual, who has limited expertise in radiology, now enters orders into the radiology database by selecting from menu options, significantly magnifying the potential for error. Although the errors are detected and corrected by Radiology, the clarification process results in a significant increase in telephone communication between Radiology and nursing. A growing concern over this issue on the part of Radiology may actually impair relations between the departments. This shift in tasks from Radiology to nursing points to the need for additional training of nurses and secretaries in radiology terminology.

Discussion

Overall, although the results of this project indicate some decrease in the frequency of telephone communication with Radiology for some units, the ORDERS system at the time of the pilot study had not yet produced predicted improvements in the quality of communication between departments. Furthermore, interviews with system users in all departments indicate that, although ORDERS may have eliminated some previous areas of conflict between departments, the new task arrangements have also created new issues.

Prior to the implementation of ORDERS, for example, interactions between Admissions and nursing had revolved around time delays in nursing notifying Admissions that a patient had been discharged, thus freeing a bed for a new admission. With the ORDERS system, however, Admissions receives a "pending" message that a bed may soon be vacated.

Immediately following system implementation, informants in both Admissions and Nursing reported a decrease in interdepartmental tensions and judged the system to be functioning well. As nurses and secretarial staff became more proficient with the new system, however, they continued to send the "pending" message promptly but were no longer as prompt with the "discharge complete" message. This may reflect the fact that both unit secretaries (who most frequently enter orders) and nurses are engaged in many other tasks and may not stop to discuss which patients have left the unit. In some units "discharge complete" messages are delayed until the workload or change of shift permits. This practice has resulted in frequent telephone calls from Admissions to some nursing units inquiring about the status of pending discharges, creating new tensions between departments.

The issues surrounding Radiology, however, stem from the Radiology department's loss of control over its "own" data entry function. A similar loss of control on the part of a Pharmacy department was documented by Aydin (1989). In that case, the Pharmacy department attempted to regain at least partial control over data entry by acting as expert consultants, training secretaries and nurses to use the system, and continuing the consulting relationship after system implementation. In the present research, however, the Radiology department has been less active in the training of secretaries and nurses to use the system.

Organizational Size

The results detailed above seem to indicate that, at least in this large medical center, employees were less likely than respondents in a small clinic setting (Aydin & Rice, 1992) to initiate changes in their own communication patterns to interact with system users in other departments. Rather, one system implementer described her role as that of an "ambassador" between nursing and the ancillary departments, constantly trying to convince each group that the others are there to help them. Furthermore, few of the daily computer users were personally involved in interdepartmental meetings concerning the computer system.

Past History

The present results also indicate that a past history of interdepartmental conflict or cooperation may influence, but not determine, the outcome of computer implementation. In the case of nursing and the Department of Admissions, for example, interview respondents reported an improved working relationship immediately following system implementation. Nurses and secretaries in some units, however, returned to their previous interaction patterns, delaying the "discharge complete" message once they were experienced in system use.

The relationship between nursing and the Radiology department, however, was characterized as "good" before system implementation. The difficulties encountered by nursing employees with radiology terminology, however, resulted in new issues between Radiology and nursing at Time 2. Rather than focusing on the shared goal of patient care, both nursing and the ancillary departments returned to a focus on their own departmental issues.

Recommendations

Immediately following evaluation of the implementation process, system implementers took several steps to address some of the issues described above. A detailed *Radiology Service Item Manual* was developed to help secretarial and nursing staff determine the correct codes for entry of radiology orders. The number of nurses expected to be able to enter orders was also reduced. Rather than training all nursing staff to enter orders, a core group of users, including all unit secretaries and selected nursing staff, was identified for updated training. Thus the systems staff could focus on helping this smaller group improve their ability to enter orders for the various ancillary departments. The ORDERS screens were also revised for easier use and Radiology was encouraged to increase its use of online, rather than paper, reports to ensure working from the most up-to-date orders.

In addition to these efforts, a concerted plan to encourage the identified group of users to communicate with each other about the system through meetings, electronic mail, or informal interpersonal contacts might also improve interdepartmental communication and system use. According to Papa (1990), the more co-workers an employee talks to and the more frequently he or she talks about a new computer system, the more productive the employee will be on the new system. In smaller organizations, employees may establish their own contacts to talk about the system (Aydin & Rice, 1992). In large organizations, however, it may be necessary to counteract the inhibiting effects of organizational size by providing employees with the time and support necessary to develop these ties.

Finally, despite the common pressures of today's rapidly changing health care environment, departments still focus their attention inward on their own concerns rather than on the challenges facing the institution as a whole. Few departments even recognize the importance of establishing and maintaining relationships with other departments, and liaison functions are seldom defined in the job descriptions of their members. Actual improvements in communication and cooperation may need to be triggered by an institutionwide emphasis on a process such as *total quality management* (Sahney & Warden, 1991) or Ackoff's (1981) "interactive planning," through which departments work together to plan for organizational change. Specific topics for joint action might include more involvement by ancillary departments such as Radiology in expanded training for secretaries and nurses and identifying potential sources of friction between departments for intervention as soon as issues arise. Financial constraints, however, make most managers reluctant to invest time and resources in issues that extend beyond their own departmental boundaries.

Conclusion

The system described in this chapter had many shortcomings and had been in use on the pilot units for only 6 months at the time of the survey. Thus, recommended modifications may result in different communication patterns over time. The results of the study, however, also reinforce past findings on computer impacts in a wide variety of settings. Overall, the impact of computerization is usually less dramatic than anticipated. According to Danziger (1985), the effects of computing emerge in a varied, subtle, and evolutionary manner. Furthermore, the changes that occur are a product of decisions made for the system and organization as a whole, existing task arrangements and interactions, and the actions of individual employees as they incorporate the new technology into their everyday work.

Additional Reading

Aydin (1989) and Aydin and Rice (1992) conducted similar studies focusing on changes in interaction patterns between departments in different health care settings.

Majchrzak (1988) and Zuboff (1988) address increased interdependence and communication in comprehensive studies of technology implementation in settings outside of health care.

Kraemer and Danziger (1990) provide an overview of recent research findings on the impacts of computerization on worklife.

In Karasek and Theorell (1990), Chapter 9, "Job Design Strategies for Different Occupational Groups," addresses the issue of occupational boundaries and different strategies for work redesign.

Lyytinen (1987) reviews different perspectives on information systems problems, including models of negotiation and bargaining between groups involved in implementation. Greenbaum and Kyng (1991) focus on the design of computer systems and on the importance of day-to-day communication in making sense of the workplace and innovations within it.

References

Ackoff, R. L. (1981). *Creating the corporate future*. New York: John Wiley.

Aydin, C. E. (1989). Occupational adaptation to computerized medical information systems. *Journal of Health and Social Behavior, 30*, 163-179.

Aydin, C. E., & Rice, R. E. (1992). Bringing social worlds together: Computers as catalysts for new interactions in health care organizations. *Journal of Health and Social Behavior, 33*, 168-185.

Connelly, D. P., Werth, G. R., Dean, D. W., Hultman, B. K., & Thompson, T. R. (1993). Physician use of an NICU laboratory reporting system. In M. E. Frisse (Ed.), *Proceedings of the 16th Annual Symposium on Computer Applications in Medical Care* (pp. 8-12). New York: McGraw-Hill.

Danziger, J. N. (1985). Social science and the social impacts of computer technology. *Social Science Quarterly, 66*, 3-21.

Greenbaum, J., & Kyng, M. (1991). *Design at work*. Hillsdale, NJ: Lawrence Erlbaum.

Karasek, R., & Theorell, T. (1990). *Healthy work: Stress, productivity, and the reconstruction of working life*. New York: Basic Books.

Kraemer, K. L., & Danziger, J. N. (1990). The impacts of computer technology on the worklife of information workers. *Social Science Computer Review, 8*, 592-600.

Lyytinen, K. (1987). Different perspectives on information systems: Problems and solutions. *ACM Computing Surveys, 19*, 5-46.

Majchrzak, A. (1988). *The human side of factory automation*. San Francisco: Jossey-Bass.

McGuire, W. J. (1983). A contextualist theory of knowledge: Its implications for innovation and reform in psychological research. In L. Berkowitz (Ed.), *Advances in experimental social psychology* (vol. 16, pp. 1-47). New York: Academic Press.

Packer, C. L. (1985, January 16). Historical changes in hospital computer use. *Hospitals, 59*, 115-118.

Papa, M. J. (1990). Communication network patterns and employee performance with new technology. *Communication Research, 17*, 344-368.

Pryor, T. A., Gardner, R. M., Clayton, P. D., & Warner, H. R. (1983). The HELP System. *Journal of Medical Systems, 7*, 87-102.

Sahney, V. K., & Warden, G. L. (1991). The quest for quality and productivity in health services. *Frontiers of Health Services Management, 7*, 2-40.

Sherif, M., & Sherif, C. W. (1969). *Social psychology*. New York: Harper.

Sproull, L., & Kiesler, S. (1991). *Connections*. Cambridge: MIT Press.

Staggers, N. (1988). Using computers in nursing: Documented benefits and needed studies. *Computers in Nursing, 4*, 164-170.

Worschel, S. (1986). The role of cooperation in reducing intergroup conflict. In S. Worschel (Ed.), *Psychology of intergroup relations* (pp. 288-304). Chicago: Nelson-Hall.

Zuboff, S. (1988). *In the age of the smart machine: The future of work and power.* New York: Basic Books.

13

Modifying Physician Use of a Hospital Information System

A Quasi-Experimental Study

James G. Anderson
Stephen J. Jay
Jane Perry
Marilyn M. Anderson

Introduction

Diffusion of Innovations Among Professionals

A number of studies indicate serious underutilization of clinical computer applications long after they have been implemented (Freidman & Gustafson, 1977). In some instances, physicians have adopted circumventing strategies to avoid using clinical computer systems (Fischer, Stratmann, Lundsgaarde, & Steele, 1987). In other cases, hospital staff have interfered with their implementation (Dowling, 1980).

Studies suggest that, in collegial organizations or bureaucracies largely made up of professionals, adoption of innovations depends largely on individual decisions (Mintzberg, 1979). Burt (1987) provides a model for this process. He suggests that individuals who are structurally

AUTHORS' NOTE: This research was supported by Grant No. HS05398 from the National Center for Health Services Research and Health Care Technology Assessment. This chapter was published as "Diffusion of Computer Applications Among Physicians: A Quasi-Experimental Study" in *Clinical Sociology Review, 8* (1990), pp. 116-127, and is reprinted with the permission of the Sociological Practice Association.

equivalent or who share similar positions in the social structure will largely interact with the same group of individuals and will share similar beliefs, attitudes, and behaviors. Competition among individuals in an organization will motivate them to adopt an innovation soon after they perceive that structurally equivalent individuals have done so.

The findings of a number of studies support these contentions. One survey of innovations in health care organizations concluded that, in addition to a leader, it is important to identify and utilize early adopters who can influence their colleagues to adopt an innovation (USDHEW, 1973). Also, Stross and Harlan (1979) found that two thirds of the family practitioners and internists they surveyed, who were aware of an important study 18 months after publication of the results, had been informed about the study by another physician. Evidence from the Columbia University drug diffusion study (Coleman, Katz, & Menzel, 1966) found that, in general, physicians did not adopt a new drug, tetracycline, unless they had direct contact with a physician who had. A reanalysis of the data from the study by Burt (1987) suggests that the dominant factor driving the diffusion of the drug was physicians' perceptions of the actions of other doctors with comparable standing in the medical community and not just conversations with colleagues. These studies clearly point to the importance of peer influences in understanding the diffusion process. The importance of informal advice and information seeking among physicians is underscored by the results of other studies as well (Maxwell, Bashook, & Sandlow, 1984; Weinberg, Ullian, Richards, & Cooper, 1981; Wenrich, Mann, Morris, & Reily, 1971).

Hospitals are a particularly important setting for the diffusion of new technology because the medical staff constitutes a social system based on shared norms, expectations, and functional interactions (Wenrich et al., 1971). Acting on this, researchers at the University of Michigan have identified educationally influential physicians in community hospitals and used them to informally influence the practice of their colleagues (Stross & Bole, 1979, 1980; Stross, Hiss, Watts, Davis, & MacDonald, 1983). Substantial improvements in the utilization of diagnostic procedures and patient management were observed in the three community hospitals that utilized influential physicians.

The results of these studies demonstrate the importance of peer networks in communicating information about innovation and persuading physicians to try them out in practice. They also indicate that certain physicians are central to these communication networks and are educationally influential in the dissemination of information concerning medical innovations. Our previous research indicated that physician attitudes toward clinical computer applications significantly affect the extent to which they use a hospital information system (HIS) to communicate medical orders and test results to and from ancillary services (Anderson, Jay, Schweer, & Anderson, 1985). Furthermore, once physicians form their initial attitudes and practice patterns involving the use of the HIS, they are likely to persist over long periods of time (Anderson, Jay, Anderson, & Schweer, 1988). This research also found that prominent physicians who were frequently consulted by other physicians on their hospital service were the first to adopt the HIS in their clinical practice. Moreover, physicians who were structurally equivalent (i.e., had similar consultation patterns with other physicians on the hospital service) adopted the HIS at approximately the same time and evidenced similar patterns of HIS utilization (Anderson, Jay, Schweer, & Anderson, 1986, 1987; Anderson, Jay, Schweer, Anderson, & Kassing, 1987). This suggests that a strategy that utilizes educationally influential physicians may be an effective means of changing physicians' practice behavior.

Objective

The primary objective of this research was to design, implement, and evaluate a program to change the procedure that physicians use to enter orders into a hospital information system (HIS). The intervention used members of the medical staff identified as being educationally influential in the peer network to influence practice behavior.

Research Methods

Practice Setting

This study was conducted in a 1,120-bed private teaching hospital that implemented the TDS HC 4000 hospital information system in 1976. The hospital information system is a communication system that links patient units to ancillary services and various departments throughout the hospital. All patient data (e.g., admission information, medical orders, test results, progress notes) are entered into the computer at terminals throughout the hospital. Most data entry is menu driven. Hospital personnel make selections from predesigned lists using a light pen (Anderson, 1992a).

Physicians generally write medical orders in the chart. These orders in turn are entered into the HIS by unit secretaries or by physician assistants who are frequently RNs. Alternatively, physicians may directly enter orders at a terminal instead of writing them. Order entry requires

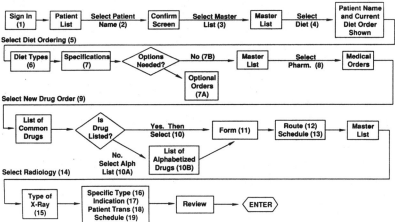

ORDER ENTRY - REGULAR HIS PATHWAYS

Figure 13.1. Standard Order Entry Into the Hospital Information System

numerous selections from generic menus as shown by the flowchart in Figure 13.1.

As an alternative, physicians can create personal order sets for order entry. These personal order sets are tailored to the specific types of procedures that the physicians frequently order for their patients (see Figure 13.2). Personal order sets are like preprinted order forms but appear on the computer monitor. The use of a light pen to make selections from these precomposed lists minimizes the use of the keyboard.

Quasi-Experimental Design

The study used a quasi-experimental design. Physicians on the following hospital services were assigned to the experimental group: cardiovascular disease, general surgery, obstetrics and gynecology, and orthopedic surgery. The four services were selected because of the large number of orders written for patients. Also, these physicians are somewhat specialized so that many of the same medical orders are used for multiple patients with minor modifications. Consequently, the development and use of personal order sets are potentially useful to physicians on these services.

We initiated an experimental program on the four services aimed at physicians identified as educationally influential among their peers. The program was designed to increase the use of personal order sets for

ORDER ENTRY - PERSONAL ORDER SETS

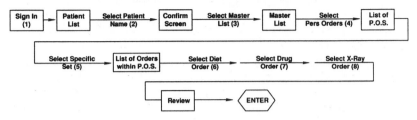

Figure 13.2. Order Entry Into the Hospital Information System Using Personal Order Sets

the entry of medical orders. Physicians on 10 other hospital services were assigned to a control group. Data on order entry were collected from 109 and 231 physicians on the experimental and control services, respectively.

Identification of Influential Physicians

Six weeks of patient data were extracted from the hospital information systems' purge tapes used to store clinical data once the patient is discharged from the hospital. These tapes indicate the attending physician and all consulting physicians for each patient. From these data, binary consultation networks were constructed for each of the experimental services. These matrices indicated the physicians on the service who were consulted by each physician during the 6-week period. STRUCTURE, a hierarchical clustering algorithm, was used to analyze the networks (Burt, 1982). Groups of physicians with similar consultation patterns were identified on the four experimental hospital services.

An influential physician was identified in each group using the following criteria: social network measures of each physician's prestige in the consultation network, and participation in the hospital's medical education program and/or on medical staff committees. Influential physicians are professionally active, technically proficient, frequently consulted by other physicians, and generally early adopters of new procedures. Each of these physicians was then contacted and asked to participate in a research project designed to increase use of personal order sets to enter orders into the hospital information system. All of the physicians who were contacted agreed to participate in the study.

Experimental Program

The objective of the experimental program was to demonstrate to the educationally influential physicians the advantages of developing and using personal order sets for medical order entry into the hospital information system. First, however, it was necessary to assess the degree to which each of these physicians used the HIS in practice as well as their knowledge and use of personal order sets. This was accomplished in two steps. First, a questionnaire was used to determine the extent to which physicians used the system to obtain patient lists, laboratory test results, and current medical orders; to print test results; and to enter new medical orders. From this information, a profile of HIS use was created for each influential physician.

Second, prior to meeting with each influential physician, a packet was delivered to the physician's office. This packet contained a short questionnaire as well as listings of any personal order sets they had created and all departmental order sets for their hospital service. The physician was asked to answer questions regarding his or her use of personal and departmental order sets. This material was then picked up and analyzed prior to the meetings with each of the influential physicians.

At the meeting, the physician was provided with data that indicated his or her overall use of the hospital information system as well as his or her use of personal and departmental order sets for order entry. Individual physician profiles were compared to usage profiles for physicians on their service and to the profile for the hospital medical staff as a whole. During the meeting, the project staff discussed with the physician the advantages of using personal order sets to enter medical orders into the HIS. The use of personal order sets for medical order entry, especially when used by physicians themselves, has the following advantages: (1) faster order entry, (2) elimination of transcription errors, (3) faster execution and results reporting, and (4) decreased clerical work. Following the meetings, the physicians continued their normal practice on their hospital services. The project staff did not ask these physicians to engage in any special activities to promote personal order sets.

Six months later, the second phase of the experimental program was implemented. A second meeting was held with the educationally influential physicians. At this meeting, the influential physicians were provided with information concerning the use of the HIS by the house staff. Second, they were provided with comparative utilization data based on both modes of order entry (i.e., regular HIS pathways and personal order sets). The time that it took to enter orders and the number and type of errors made in order entry were compared. Third, a summary of physicians' perceptions of the advantages and disadvantages of using personal order sets in practice was developed from the first set of meetings with the influential physicians. This summary was used to review the value of the educational program and to reinforce its content.

Evaluation

In order to determine whether increased use of personal order sets occurred on the experimental services as a result of informal consultations with the influential physicians, data were collected at three points in time—prior to the intervention, 2 months after the first meeting with the influential physicians, and 2 months after the second meeting with these same physicians. At each point in time, 4 weeks of patient data were extracted from the discharge data contained on the HIS tapes. For each physician who had discharged patients during this period, the following statistics were computed: the number of medical orders entered per patient by the physician using his or her own personal order sets, departmental order sets, and the generic order sets that are a standard part of the hospital information system.

These data were analyzed by means of a multivariate analysis of variance with repeated measures over time. A major advantage of this design is the control that it provides for individual differences between physicians that often are quite large relative to differences due to treatment or intervention effects that this study is attempting to evaluate.

Results

Identification of Influential Physicians

For each of the experimental services, a matrix was constructed with the rows and columns representing the physicians on the service. A 1 in a cell indicated that the row physician had consulted with the column physician at least once during the 6-week period. STRUCTURE, a hierarchical clustering program, was used to generate groups of structurally equivalent physicians with similar consultation patterns (i.e., they generally consulted the same physicians in the course of caring for patients). This resulted in the identification of five groups on cardiovascular disease and general surgery and three groups of physicians on obstetrics and gynecology and orthopedic surgery.

An influential physician was identified in each cluster of structurally equivalent physicians. Selection was based on the frequency with which the physician was consulted by others on the service as well as by whether or not the physician was an active participant in the hospital's medical education program and/or medical staff affairs.

Evaluation

The evaluation was aimed at determining whether a change in physician behavior took place on the experimental services as a result of providing educationally influential physicians with information documenting the advantages of using personal order sets for order entry into the hospital information system. In order to accomplish this, a multivariate analysis of variance with repeated measures was performed. Order entry by physicians, unit secretaries, and physician assistants were analyzed simultaneously. Figure 13.3 compares the mean number of medical orders entered into the HIS by means of personal order sets on the experimental and control services.

The results of the analysis indicate significant differences between the experimental and control groups ($F1,338 = 15.58$, $p < 0.000$) and between persons entering the orders ($F1,338 = 10.78$, $p < 0.000$). In general, a greater number of orders per patient was entered on the experimental services using personal order sets. Also, unit secretaries entered the most orders using personal order sets and physicians the least. Furthermore, the group by time interaction was significant ($F1,338 = 5.80$, $p < 0.003$). The use of personal order sets on the experimental services by physicians, unit secretaries, and physician assistants increased significantly over time.

Discussion

This study was based on the hypothesis that, within medical practice settings such as hospitals, there are physicians who significantly influence the behavior of their colleagues through interaction in the informal consultation network. These individuals have been called *educationally influential physicians* (see Stross & Bole, 1979, 1980; Stross et al., 1983). This study was undertaken to determine whether or not educationally influential physicians could be identified and used to introduce innovative procedures into groups of physicians on hospital services.

The study developed a new methodology that can be used to identify educationally influential physicians using data from hospital information systems. Moreover, these physicians were successfully recruited and participated in the study. This involved approximately two 1-hour meetings with project staff over a 12-month period. After these meetings, the physicians resumed their normal activities as members of the hospital's medical staff. The hypothesis was tested by analyzing data

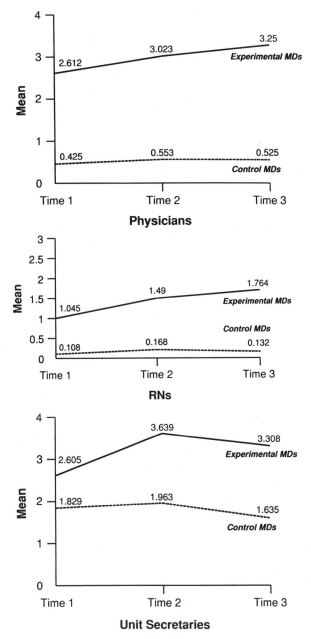

Figure 13.3. Mean Number of Medical Orders Entered Into the Hospital Information System Using Personal Order Sets

on medical order entry obtained from the hospital information system to determine if the educationally influential physicians had influenced the behavior of their colleagues as expected.

Significant changes were observed on the experimental hospital services as a result of the experimental program. The use of personal order sets for order entry into the HIS significantly increased on these units. At the same time, no significant change in patterns of order entry were observed among physicians on the control services.

It appears from the results that the influence of the educationally influential physicians extended beyond the other physicians on the service. Not only did the use of personal order sets increase among physicians on the four services, but their use increased among physician assistants and unit secretaries on these services as well.

The earlier studies that were reviewed have documented that physicians learn about medical innovations from one another. Also, Stross and his colleagues demonstrated that key individuals in informal physician networks play a critical role in the dissemination of information concerning medical innovations. The results of our study indicate that the influence of these educationally influential physicians extends to the entire network of health care providers involved in the care of patients on a hospital unit.

Based on the results of this study, we conclude that the recruitment and deliberate use of educationally influential physicians is an effective means of changing practice behavior. Such an approach to the introduction of new procedures and approaches has great potential given the large number of diverse practice settings. At the same time, many additional questions need to be answered by future research. Are educationally influential physicians equally effective in all specialties and in practice settings other than the hospital? Should the initial sessions with the influential physicians be supplemented with other forms of continuing medical education? Will changes in practice behavior diminish with the passage of time unless reinforced?

Additional Reading

Health Care Information Systems

Anderson (1992a, 1992b) and Blum (1984, 1986) provide comprehensive reviews of a number of clinical information systems used in patient care. The Anderson articles also review the literature on the evaluation of the use and impact of these systems.

Diffusion of Medical Innovations

Rogers's (1983) book contains a comprehensive review of the body of research findings related to the diffusion of innovations. The Anderson and Jay (1987) volume provides a number of empirical studies related to the adoption and diffusion of medical computer systems.

Experimental and Quasi-Experimental Research Designs

Chapter 5 in this book by Anderson and Jay reviews the use of experimental research methods to evaluate health care information systems.

Campbell and Stanley (1966) and Cook and Campbell (1979) provide excellent overviews of experimental and quasi-experimental research designs.

References

Anderson, J. G. (1992a). Medical information systems. In A. Kent & J. G. Williams (Eds.), *Encyclopedia of microcomputers*(vol. 9, pp. 39-65). New York: Marcel Dekker.

Anderson, J. G. (1992b). Computerized medical record systems in ambulatory care. *Journal of Ambulatory Care Management, 15*, 1-8.

Anderson, J. G., & Jay, S. J. (Eds.). (1987). *Use and impact of computers in clinical medicine*. New York: Springer Verlag.

Anderson, J. G., Jay, S. J., Anderson, M. M., & Schweer, H. M. (1988). Why do doctors use computers? Findings from a longitudinal study. In *Proceedings of the AAMSI Congress 1988* (pp. 109-113). Washington, DC: AAMSI.

Anderson, J. G, Jay, S. J., Schweer, H. M, & Anderson, M. M. (1985). A structural model of the impact of physicians' perceptions of computers on the use of hospital information systems. *Behaviour and Information Technology, 3*, 231-238.

Anderson, J. G., Jay, S. J., Schweer, H. M., & Anderson, M. M. (1986). Physician utilization of computers in medical practice: Policy implications. *Social Science and Medicine, 23*, 259-267.

Anderson, J. G., Jay, S. J., Schweer, H. M., & Anderson, M. M. (1987). Diffusion and impact of computers in organizational settings: Empirical findings from a hospital. In G. Salvendy et al. (Eds.), *Social, ergonomic and stress aspects of work with computers* (pp. 3-10). Amsterdam: Elsevier.

Anderson, J. G., Jay, S. J., Schweer, H. M., Anderson, M. M., & Kassing, D. (1987). Physician communication networks and the adoption and utilization of computer applications in medicine. In J. G. Anderson & S. J. Jay (Eds.), *Use and impact of computers in clinical medicine* (pp. 185-199). New York: Springer Verlag.

Blum, B. I. (1984). *Information systems for patient care*. New York: Springer Verlag.

Blum, B. I. (1986). *Clinical information systems*. New York: Springer Verlag.

Burt, R. S. (1982). *Toward a structural theory of action*. New York: Academic Press.

Burt, R. S. (1987). Social contagion and innovation: Cohesion versus structural equivalence. *American Journal of Sociology, 92*, 1287-1335.

Campbell, D. T., & Stanley, J. (1966). *Experimental and quasi-experimental designs for research*. Chicago: Rand McNally.

Coleman, J. S., Katz, E., & Menzel, H. (1966). *Medical innovation: A diffusion study.* Indianapolis, IN: Bobbs-Merrill.

Cook, T. D., & Campbell, D. T. (1979). *Quasi-experimentation: Design and analysis issues for field settings.* Boston, MA: Houghton Mifflin.

Dowling, A. F., Jr. (1980). Do hospital staff interfere with computer system implementation? *Health Care Management Review, 5,* 23-32.

Fischer, P. J., Stratmann, W. C., Lundsgaarde, H. P., & Steele, D. J. (1987). User reaction to PROMIS: Issues related to acceptability of medical innovations. In J. G. Anderson & S. J. Jay (Eds.), *Use and impact of computers in clinical medicine* (pp. 284-301). New York: Springer Verlag.

Freidman, R. B., & Gustafson, D. H. (1977). Computers in clinical medicine: A critical review. *Computers and Biomedical Research, 10,* 199-204.

Maxwell, J. A., Bashook, P. G., & Sandlow, L. J. (1984). The role of communication networks in physicians' adoption of innovations. In *Proceedings of the 23rd Annual Conference on Research in Medical Education* (pp. 231-236). Washington, DC: AAMC.

Mintzberg, H. (1979). *The structuring of organizations.* Englewood Cliffs, NJ: Prentice Hall.

Rogers, E. M. (1983). *Diffusion of innovations* (3rd ed.). New York: The Free Press.

Stross, J. K., & Bole, G. G. (1979). Continuing education in rheumatoid arthritis for the primary care physician. *Arthritis and Rheumatism, 22,* 787-791.

Stross, J. K., & Bole, G. G. (1980). Evaluation of a continuing education program in rheumatoid arthritis. *Arthritis and Rheumatism, 23,* 846-849.

Stross, J. K., & Harlan, W. R. (1979). The dissemination of new medical information. *Journal of the American Medical Association, 241,* 2822-2824.

Stross, J. K., Hiss, R. G., Watts, C. M., Davis, W. K., & MacDonald, R. (1983). Continuing education in pulmonary disease for primary-care physicians. *American Review of Respiratory Disease, 127,* 739-746.

USDHEW. (1973). *Planning for creative change in mental health services: A manual on research utilization.* Rockville, MD: NIMH.

Weinberg, A. D., Ullian, L., Richards, W. D., & Cooper, P. (1981). Informal advice and information seeking between physicians. *Journal of Medical Education, 56,* 174-180.

Wenrich, J. W., Mann, F. C., Morris, W. C., & Reily, A. J. (1971). Informal educators for practicing physicians. *Journal of Medical Education, 46,* 299-305.

14

Research and Evaluation

Future Directions

James G. Anderson
Carolyn E. Aydin
Stephen J. Jay

During the 1970s, efforts to develop and introduce computers into health care settings focused primarily on components of inpatient and outpatient systems. Inpatient systems included hospital information systems, clinical laboratory systems, and support systems for radiology and emergency medicine. There was also a parallel development of systems to support outpatient care such as ambulatory medical records, physician office systems, and telecommunications for medical consultation (Anderson, 1992a, 1992b; National Center for Health Services Research [NCHSR], 1980).

Advances in computer technology and artificial intelligence during the 1980s led to the development of expert systems and other clinical decision-support systems (Clancey & Shortliffe, 1984). In addition, the use of inpatient and outpatient systems became widespread as more health care organizations began to adopt applications such as order entry and support systems for ancillary departments (Packer, 1985). In the 1990s, the need for cost-effective delivery of health services has led to integrated databases and computer-based systems supporting outcomes research, identification of physician practice patterns, utilization review, and total quality management programs (DeTore, 1988; Jay & Anderson, 1989).

In light of past experience, however, the implementation of many of these newer systems, as well as new adoptions of more established systems, will result in unforeseen costs and organizational consequences, and even failure, because developers and administrators neglect their social impacts (Anderson & Jay, 1987; Dowling, 1980; Gardner, 1990; Lyytinen, 1988; Lyytinen & Hirschheim, 1987). These concerns are not new. In 1979, the evaluation of the Technicon Medical Information System at El Camino Hospital found that, although such a system can yield significant improvements in productivity and enhance the ability of the institution to influence the quality of care, the way in which the system is installed and developed may very much influence the degree to which these benefits can be achieved (Barrett, Hersch, & Caswell, 1979). The continued prospect of additional systems failures and unforeseen costs in the 1990s underscores the importance of developing strategies to guide implementation and evaluate the use and impacts of all types of health care computer applications.

The methods and applications included in this book provide an overview of current knowledge and emphasize the importance of a multimethod approach to system evaluation based on an understanding of the complex social and behavioral processes occurring within health care organizations. At present our understanding of how computer-based technology interacts with administrative decisions regarding the use of the system and how individual employees adapt to the system is rudimentary. Most system implementers, for example, recognize the importance of administrative support and user involvement in the implementation process for system acceptance. The physical presence of investigators or implementation team members in the clinical setting when a system is being introduced can influence practitioners' use of and reactions to a system (e.g., see Chapter 10). The importance of integrating new systems into the established practice patterns of health care practitioners is a recurring theme (see Chapters 9, 11, and 13), as is the importance of the diffusion process and the strategic use of influential early adopters of a system (see Chapters 11 and 13). Increasing attention is also being paid to the importance of negotiations between departments during system adoption and system impacts in politically charged areas such as the working relationships between departments (see Chapter 12).

What is lacking, however, are comprehensive and unifying models. Much of the research to date focuses on one or another factor such as those detailed above, in a limited context, without a systematic comparison of the relationships among them. What is needed is an integrated framework that takes into account the relative importance of the environment, both external and internal, the organization and its policies, characteristics of potential users of the system, and the attributes of the technology itself. Such a framework would enable investigators to assess the role each factor might play in explaining implementation success and failure, including the contingencies that might affect when and how different factors influence the implementation process (Kraemer, Dickhoven, Fallows, Tierney, & King, 1987).

As this book goes to press, the nation's leadership has engaged in public debate regarding health care reform aimed at reducing the cost of health care, increasing access to health services, and improving health outcomes for all Americans. The results of health care reform policy and legislative initiatives may radically alter the structure and function of the health care system in the United States. The changes that will be made in the system to accomplish short-term and long-term goals of health care reform strategies may occur as relatively smooth incremental or quantum transitions or they may occur chaotically with potentially serious and disruptive effects on the delivery of care to patients.

An underlying premise of this book is that the achievement of the goals of health care reform will depend on correction of serious deficiencies in the nation's infrastructure of health care computing technology. These deficiencies include computer system evaluative methodologies and technology transfer.

There is a critical need for those involved in health care policy and legislative reform to recognize the relationship between accomplishing cost, access, and quality goals and the need to invest resources in upgrading the nation's health care computing infrastructure. Once this relationship is recognized, public policy must be developed to support research and development in areas vital to health care reform priorities.

The purpose of this book has been to provide a practical guide for determining (1) appropriate evaluation questions based on specific underlying models of change and (2) the most effective methods available to evaluate anticipated impacts and answer the questions posed. In addition, however, we hope that this book will become a starting point for new theoretical and policy-oriented research to answer questions regarding the organizational impacts of computerized information systems and their ultimate role in the delivery of patient care.

References

Anderson, J. G. (1992a). Medical information systems. In A. Kent & J. G. William (Eds.), *Encyclopedia of microcomputers* (vol. 9, pp. 39-65). New York: Marcel Dekker.
Anderson, J. G. (1992b). Computerized medical record systems in ambulatory care. *Journal of Ambulatory Care Management, 15*, 1-8.

Anderson, J. G., & Jay, S. J. (Eds.). (1987). *Use and impact of computers in clinical medicine.* New York: Springer Verlag.

Barrett, J. P., Hersch, P. L., & Caswell, R. J. (1979). *Evaluation of the impact of the implementation of the Technicon Medical Information System at El Camino Hospital. Part II. Economic Trend Analysis.* U.S. Department of Commerce National Technical Information Service Report No. PB300869. Columbus OH: U.S. Department of Commerce (Battelle Columbus Laboratories).

Clancey, W. J., & Shortliffe, E. H. (Eds.). (1984). *Readings in medical artificial intelligence: The first decade.* Reading MA: Addison-Wesley.

DeTore, A. W. (1988). Medical informatics: An introduction to computer technology in medicine. *American Journal of Medicine, 85,* 399-403.

Dowling, A. F. (1980). Do hospital staff interfere with computer system implementation? *Health Care Management Review, 5,* 23-32.

Gardner, E. (1990, May 28). Information systems: Computers' full capabilities often go untapped. *Modern Healthcare,* pp. 38-40.

Jay, S. J., & Anderson, J. G. (1989). Computers in medicine: Dreams and realities. *Hospital Physician, 25,* 3-13.

Kraemer, K. L., Dickhoven, S., Fallows Tierney, S., & King, J. L. (1987). *Datawars: The politics of modeling in federal policy making.* New York: Columbia University Press.

Lyytinen, K. (1988). Expectation failure concept and systems analysts' view of information systems failure: Results of an exploratory study. *Information & Management, 14,* 45-56.

Lyytinen, K., & Hirschheim, R. (1987). Information systems failures—A survey and classification of the empirical literature. *Oxford Surveys in Information Technology, 4,* 257-309.

National Center for Health Services Research (NCHSR). (1980). *Computer applications in health care.* DHHS Publication No. (PHS)80-3251. Springfield, VA: National Technical Information Service.

Packer, C. L. (1985). Historical changes in hospital computer use. *Hospitals, 59*(January 16), 115-118.

Glossary

Adjacency Matrix   A matrix in which the rows and columns represent members of a network and the cells indicate direct relationships between members.

Administrative Systems   Information processing systems that support control reporting and operational planning. Control reporting systems are used to compare actual versus targeted results and operational planning systems are used to identify resources necessary to support organizational activities. These types of systems are also commonly referred to as Management Information Systems or Decision-Support Systems and tend to rely on information internal to the institution.

ADT   Admission-Discharge-Transfer—The information system module responsible for allocating patients to specific beds in the hospital and keeping track of their bed status.

Analytic Memo   Memo (for short)—Broadly defined, any reflective writing the researcher does about the research, ranging from a marginal comment on a transcript, or a theoretical idea incorporated into field notes, to a full-fledged analytic essay.

Applications Program   A computer program that is written to solve a particular problem or serve a specific need, such as word processing or data manipulation.

Artificial Intelligence (AI) Systems   A particular kind of computerized decision-support system that attempts to emulate human intelligence on the computer. In medicine, this often takes the form of an Expert System, which is a computer system that incorporates the knowledge and problem-solving strategies of experts.

Blackboard Architecture   An architecture in which system components communicate with each other by posting information on a blackboard.

Blockmodel Analysis   A mathematical procedure for grouping members of a network into subgroups that are structurally equivalent (i.e., group members have the same pattern of relations with other network members).

Case Study   An empirical inquiry that investigates a phenomenon within a specific natural setting and uses multiple sources of evidence.

Center for Knowledge Coupling (CKC) The CKC is a nonprofit organization dedicated to improving the quality and cost-effectiveness of health care and to advancing the development of knowledge couplers. The CKC is based on the new premises and tools for medical care, record keeping, and education as developed by Lawrence L. Weed, MD.

Centrality A measure of the degree of involvement of a member of a network in all the network relations.

Clinical Information System (CIS) An integrated computer system that receives information from hospital departments, processes it, maintains medical and financial records about each patient, and makes these data available throughout the health care organization.

Clinical Reminders Computer-generated reminders to clinicians about clinical events that might need corrective action.

Cluster Analysis A mathematical procedure for dividing the total set of network members into smaller and more homogenous subgroups.

Coding Segmenting the data into units and rearranging them into categories that facilitate insight, comparison, and the development of theory.

Cohort Study A study following a group of subjects over time.

Computerized Decision-Support (CDS) Systems Computer software systems designed to help the practitioner identify, diagnose (find the cause of), or manage patients' clinical problems.

Computerized Tomography (CT) Scanning A diagnostic technique in which the combined use of a computer and X-rays passed through the body at different angles produces clear cross-sectional images.

Context The cultural, social, and organizational setting in which a study is conducted, together with the history of and influences on the project and the participants in it. Context also includes the relationships between the evaluation sponsor, the researchers, and those who work in or influence the setting.

Contextual Analysis Also Narrative Analysis—Analyzing the relationships between elements in a particular text, situation, or sequence of events.

Continuous Quality Improvement (CQI) A method that uses measurements of quality indicators to initiate and drive organizational changes in a continuing cycle of improvement.

Cost-Benefit Analysis (CBA) Also Cost-Effectiveness Analysis—Analytical techniques for comparing positive or beneficial consequences with negative results of an action. Cost-benefit quantifies all of the consequences in financial or dollar terms; cost-effectiveness leaves some consequence in nonmonetary terms, such as lives saved.

Cost-Effectiveness Analysis (CEA)   See Cost-Benefit Analysis.

Cronbach's Alpha   A statistical procedure used to measure internal consistency reliability.

Cross-Sectional Study   A study in which all measurements are made at one point in time.

Decision-Support Systems   See Administrative Systems.

Dependent Variable   A variable that is affected by variation in one or more Independent Variables. In an experimental study it is the outcome measure.

Display   Any systematic visual presentation of data or theory; developed as a method of qualitative data analysis by Miles and Huberman (1984).

Educationally Influential Physicians   Professionally active, technically proficient physicians who are frequently consulted by other physicians concerning patient care, new tests and procedures, and other professional issues.

Embedded Evaluation Techniques   Software that is embedded within the computer system that measures information about the user's interaction with the system. For example, the rate of errors, the types of errors, the user and system response times, and the frequency of use of certain components of the system.

Endogenous Factors   Factors within the organization that may bring about changes.

Ethnography   A form of qualitative research that involves the researcher's relatively long-term and intensive involvement in the setting studied, which employs participant observation and/or open-ended interviewing as major strategies and attempts to understand both the cultural perspective of the participants and the influence of the physical and social context in which they operate.

Exogenous Factors   Factors external to the organization that may bring about changes within the organization.

Experimental Study   A study in which individuals are randomly assigned to groups, one (or more) of which receives a particular intervention (treatment group), while the other does not (control group).

Expert System   A computer system that emulates the decision-making process of a human expert.

External Validity   The degree to which the study conclusions made by an investigator are appropriate when applied to a larger population of individuals, settings, and times.

Field Experiment   See Quasi-Experimental Study.

Field Notes   Detailed, descriptive records of observations.

Field Research   See Fieldwork.

Fieldwork   Also Field Research—The researcher's direct engagement in the setting studied.

Formative Evaluation   Evaluation of a developing or ongoing program or activity. The evaluation is aimed at improving the program or activity while it is being developed or implemented. See also Summative Evaluation.

Grounded Theory   A theory that is inductively derived from, and tested against, qualitative data during the course of the research; also, an approach to qualitative research that emphasizes this method of theory development (Glaser & Strauss, 1967; Strauss & Corbin, 1990).

HCFA   Health Care Financing Agency of the Department of Health and Human Services.

Image Matrix   A matrix in which rows and columns represent structurally equivalent groups of network members and the cells indicate direct relationships between groups.

Incidence Matrix   A matrix in which the rows represent members of a network while the columns represent their organizational affiliation, use of different technologies, and so on.

Independent Variable   A variable that is presumed to cause variation in a Dependent Variable. In an experimental study it is the variable or variables manipulated by the investigator.

Induction   A process by which generalizations are made from many particular instances found in the data; reasoning from a part to a whole, from particulars to generals, or from the individual to the universal.

Internal Consistency Reliability   The extent to which all items on an additive scale measure the same concept.

Internal Validity   The degree to which the study conclusions made by an investigator are correct.

Iteration   Repetition of a series of steps, as in a repeating cycle of data collection, hypothesis formulation, hypothesis testing by more data collection, additional hypothesis formulation, and so on.

Knowledge Base   The information or knowledge distilled from the medical literature or from medical specialists that is encoded in a computerized decision-support system; the collection of domain knowledge.

Knowledge Network   A database of medical knowledge and a tool to be used for the development of knowledge couplers. The Knowledge Network is developed by the Lawrence L. Weed and PKC Corporation.

Management Information Systems   See Administrative Systems.

Medical Information System   See Clinical Information System.

Multidimensional Scaling   A mathematical procedure that can represent the relations among members of a network spatially in two or more dimensions.

Multiplexity   Relations between members of a network that involve more than one type of interaction (e.g., patient referrals and clinical consultations).

Narrative Analysis   See Contextual Analysis.

Network Density   The proportion of ties or connections among members of a network out of all possible ties.

Null Hypothesis   The hypothesis that there is no association between the predictor variable and the outcome variable of interest.

Open-Ended Interviewing   A form of interviewing that does not employ a fixed interview schedule but allows the researcher to follow the respondent's lead by exploring topics in greater depth and also by pursuing unanticipated topics.

Open-Ended Questions   Interview or survey questions that are to be answered in the respondent's own words rather than by selecting preformulated responses.

Operational Systems   Information processing systems that handle internal, day-to-day, real-time information processing tasks.

Paradigm   A model that guides scientific inquiry.

Participant Observation   A form of observation in which the researcher participates in the activities going on in a natural setting and interacts with people in that setting rather than simply recording their behavior as an outside observer; observation in which the researcher is involved in some recognized role as a part of the social process being investigated.

Post-Intervention Study   A cross-sectional study occurring after an intervention has taken place.

Problem Knowledge Coupler (PKC)   The PKC is an innovative strategy for the computerized decision support system developed by Lawrence L. Weed, MD. The PKC provides a guidance system to enhance the practitioner's ability to identify, diagnose, and manage patients' clinical problems. In short, the PKC is designed to "couple the details of knowledge about a particular patient with a problem to the relevant knowledge in the medical literature" (Weed, 1991, p. 34).

Problem Oriented Medical Information System   A computerized medical record keeping system based on Lawrence L. Weed's Problem-Oriented Medical Record.

Problem-Oriented Medical Record (POMR)   A system of medical record keeping, developed by Lawrence L. Weed, MD, that is organized around (1) a database (that includes facts about how an individual lives and functions), (2) a problem list (that includes the abnormalities shown in the database), (3) titled plans (including the goals, basis for the problem statement, problem's status, etc.), and (4) titled progress notes for each problem (symptomatic, subjective, and objective data, assessment, and plans) (Weed, 1991, pp. 21, 22). A computerized version of the POMR is available and can be linked to the PKC.

Prominence   Prominent members of a network are those who are highly visible to other members because of their extensive involvement in important relations.

Prospective Study   A study in which the investigator defines the sample and collects data prior to the occurrence of the intervention or outcome of interest.

Qualitative Methods   Research procedures that produce descriptive data.

Qualitative Research   A strategy for empirical research that is conducted in natural settings that uses data in the form of words rather than numbers, that inductively develops categories and hypotheses, and that seeks to understand the perspective of the participants in the setting studied, the context of that setting, and the events and process that are taking place there.

Quantitative Methods   Research procedures that depend mainly on statistical analysis of data.

Quasi-Experimental Study   A study in which full experimental control is lacking, generally because random assignment to treatment and control groups is not possible or there is no control group.

Reliability   The extent to which a data collection instrument consistently measures the concept of interest.

Research Hypothesis   A short statement indicating the expected association between the predictor variable and the outcome variable of interest.

RFP   Request for Proposal—A formal document soliciting vendor bids for a system to meet certain stated requirements, which generally include a fixed price. (An RFI, or Request for Information, would merely solicit the ability to carry out the tasks stated.)

Rich Data   Data that are detailed, comprehensive, and holistic.

Robustness   Interpretations, results, or data that can withstand a variety of validity threats because they hold up even if some of the underpinnings are removed or prove incorrect.

Snowball Sampling   A sampling technique in which each respondent is asked to name other respondents (e.g., other users of a computer technology).

Social Network Analysis   Also Structural Analysis—A methodology that attempts to explain individual attitudes and behavior in terms of the characteristics or structure of relations among the members of a social network.

Strategic Planning Systems   Information processing systems that support strategic planning activities in the organization. These systems provide senior management with information from both internal and external sources.

Structural Analysis   See Social Network Analysis.

Structural Equivalence   Groups of network members who have the same pattern of relations with other members of the network.

Study Design   The structure of a study in terms of whether experimental manipulation occurs, whether data are collected once or over time, whether random assignment to groups occurs, and when data are collected in reference to the intervention or outcome of interest.

Summative Evaluation   Evaluation that is aimed at assessing the value of a developed program for the purpose of administrative or policy decisions. This evaluation often is done by testing the impact of the program after it has been implemented. See also Formative Evaluation.

System   The hardware (input/output devices, central processing unit, storage), software, and all related components of the computer combined. May also be used to describe all the associated nodes in a local area network.

Test-Retest Reliability   The extent to which a data collection instrument yields the same scores when administered more than once to the same group of individuals.

Time-Series Study   A study in which a particular factor is measured repeatedly over time.

Tomography   See Computerized Tomography Scanning.

Total Quality Management (TQM)   See Continuous Quality Improvement.

Triangulation   The cross-checking of inferences by using multiple methods, sources, or forms of data for drawing conclusions.

Type I Error   Rejecting a null hypothesis that is true.

Type II Error   Failing to reject a null hypothesis that is false.

User-Friendly   Computer applications or software that are easy to learn and easy to use.

User Interface   The mechanism by which the user and the system communicate.

Validity   The truth or correctness of one's descriptions, interpretations, or conclusions; the extent to which a data collection instrument measures what it is supposed to measure.

Validity Threat   A way in which one's description, interpretation, or conclusion might be invalid; also known as "rival hypothesis" or "alternative explanation."

Index

About the Contributors

James G. Anderson is Professor of Sociology at Purdue University and Adjunct Professor of Medical Sociology in the Graduate Medical Education program at Methodist Hospital of Indiana. He earned his BES degree in chemical engineering, MSE degree in operations research and industrial engineering, MAT degree in chemistry and mathematics, and Ph.D. in education and sociology at the Johns Hopkins University. He is the former Director of the Division of Engineering of the Evening College of Johns Hopkins University and former Assistant Dean for Analytical Studies of the School of Humanities, Social Science, and Education at Purdue University. He has authored and edited five books and more than 130 book chapters and articles in professional journals. His research interests include the social impacts of computers in clinical medicine and health care organizations and the effects of clinical personalities on physician practice patterns.

Marilyn M. Anderson has a double major in chemistry and biology from Milliken University. She has been a Research Assistant at Wohl Clinic at Washington University Medical Center and in the Schools of Biochemistry and Pharmacy at Purdue University. Currently, she is a Senior Research Associate in the Department of Medical Research at Methodist Hospital of Indiana. Her current research interests are in physician use of computer systems. She has coauthored more than 30 journal articles and book chapters.

Carolyn E. Aydin is Assistant Administrator for Nursing Research in the Nursing Research and Development Department at Cedars-Sinai Medical Center in Los Angeles. She holds a BA from the University of California, Berkeley, and MA and Ph.D. degrees in communication theory and research from the Annenberg School for Communication at the University of Southern California. She has conducted and published research on the implementation and impacts of medical information systems at several large medical centers in Southern California, and her background includes more than 20 years of experience in evaluating the impacts of innovations in both health care and education. Her publications have appeared in the *Journal of Health and Social Behavior, Administrative Science Quarterly, Information and Management,* and the *Proceedings of the Symposium on Computer Applications in Medical Care.* Current projects include work redesign in health care, implementing patient education strategies, communication patterns in health care organizations, and changes accompanying the implementation of medical information systems.

Tracy L. Buck holds the position of Information Center Consultant in the Division of Information Services, Rush-Presbyterian-St. Luke's Medical Center. She received her EdM from the University of Illinois at Urbana-Champaign and currently teaches a graduate level course in information systems for the Department of Health Systems Management, College of Health, Rush University.

Daniel J. Essin is the Associate Chief of Clinical Information Systems, Los Angeles County and University of Southern California Medical Center, and a Clinical Assistant Professor of Pediatrics, specializing in the pulmonary physiology of children. For the past 10 years he has devoted himself almost full time to the issues of online clinical computing, and he is Director of the Women's Hospital Information Systems. He holds an AB in zoology (1969) from UCLA and an MA in zoology from UCLA (1971) with emphasis on biomathematics and minicomputer applications. He obtained his MD from the University of California, San Diego, in 1974. He is a Fellow of the American Academy of Pediatrics and the American College of Chest Physicians and a Member of the Association for Computing Machinery and an Associate Member of the Institute of Electrical and Electronic Engineers (IEEE) Computer Society.

Gerald L. Glandon received a Ph.D. in economics from the University of Washington and is currently an Associate Professor, Department of Health Systems Management, College of Health Sciences, Rush University. He also is a Research Associate in the Center for Health Management Studies and is a Senior Research Associate in the Center for Research on Health and Aging. He holds secondary academic appointments in the Departments of Psychology, Social Sciences, and Preventive Medicine, Rush Medical College. His research efforts have centered in three areas: assessment of hospital financial performance, the economics of aging, and technology evaluation in health care. He has published in a variety of journals and presented at numerous professional meetings. He teaches courses in health care economics, health care and the elderly, and applied economics: technology evaluation. Prior to coming to Rush University, he worked with InterQual, Inc., and the American Medical Association.

Rosemary Ischar is Director of Nursing and Associate Administrator for Patient Care Services at Century City Hospital in Los Angeles. She earned an MA in communication management from the Annenberg School for Communication at the University of Southern California. She formerly held the positions of Director of Special Projects and Clinical Nursing Director at Cedars-Sinai Medical Center in Los Angeles. Her research interests include the implementation of clinical information systems.

Stephen J. Jay is Senior Vice President, Academic Affairs, at Methodist Hospital of Indiana and Professor of Medicine, Indiana University School of Medicine. He has been engaged in health services research for more than 10 years. He has authored or coauthored numerous publications in scholarly journals and books regarding computer applications in health care.

Bonnie Kaplan is Associate Professor of Computer Science/Information Systems at Quinnipiac College, Hamden, Connecticut, where she directs the Medical Information Systems Program. Prior to her current position, she was on the faculty of Computer Science and Information Systems at The American University, Washington, DC. She previously was on the Information Systems faculty in the College of Business Administration and an Adjunct Professor of Clinical Pathology, University of Cincinnati. She has been a programmer/analyst and a consultant at several medical centers. Her research specialties concern social aspects of computing, evaluation of information technologies, and acceptance and implementation issues in medical computing. She has published in *Journal of Medical Systems, International Journal of Technology Assessment in Health Care, Journal of Health and Human Resources Administration, Journal of Operations Management,* and *Management Information Systems Quarterly.* She has presented her research at the annual Symposium on Computer Applications in Medical Care, at Medinfo, and at other international conferences in the United States and in Europe. She holds a Ph.D. in history from the University of Chicago.

Kristen H. Kjerulff is Associate Director of the Survey Research and Development Center and Assistant Professor in the Department of

Epidemiology and Preventive Medicine, School of Medicine, University of Maryland at Baltimore. She received a Ph.D. in psychology from the University of Illinois at Champaign—Urbana. She teaches courses in research methodology, biostatistics, health care organization, and women's health. In addition, she conducts research in women's health as well as outcomes and effectiveness of medical procedures. She is principal investigator of a study to examine outcomes and effectiveness of hysterectomy and is also conducting studies of physician practice patterns in hip fracture and hip replacement surgery, socioeconomic factors in relation to gynecological disorders, hormone replacement therapy in postmenopausal women, and breast and cervical cancer screening.

Thomas L. Lincoln is Professor of Pathology at the University of Southern California School of Medicine, a Senior Research Scientist at the RAND Corporation, and a Consultant with Anderson Consulting. He has been a Consultant to the British Health Service, the National Library of Medicine, and numerous hospitals and clinics. He now specializes in the formation and analysis of functional requirements for systems to be used in clinical settings. He was at the Jung Institute and the Institute for Applied Psychology, Zurich, Switzerland, from 1950 to 1953 and received his BS from Yale College in 1955 and his MD from Yale in 1960. He has been a Fellow in Pathology at Johns Hopkins Medical School, a member of the Operations Research Group in the School of Public Health, and Research Assistant Professor at the Institute of Applied Mathematics at the University of Maryland.

Joseph A. Maxwell is Assistant Professor at the Harvard Graduate School of Education. Prior to this, he was a Research Associate at Michael Reese Hospital and Medical Center in Chicago, where he conducted research on medical education. His areas of specialization include qualitative methodology, evaluation research, medical education, the adoption of innovations, and sociocultural theory. He has a Ph.D. in anthropology from the University of Chicago.

Loretta A. Moore is Assistant Professor in the Department of Computer Science and Engineering at Auburn University. She received the BS degree in computer science from Jackson State University in 1985. On graduation from Jackson State University, she joined AT&T Bell Laboratories as a member of the technical staff. AT&T sponsored her graduate studies in computer science at Illinois Institute of Technology, where she received the MS degree in 1986. She then returned to work in a data communications laboratory. In 1988, she was selected to participate in AT&T's doctoral support program; she returned to the Illinois Institute of Technology, where she was awarded the Ph.D. degree in computer science in 1991. Her current research interests are concentrated in human-computer interface issues involved in the design of intelligent systems.

Jane Perry formerly worked as a Systems Analyst with the hospital's computer services department and is currently the MIS Physician Coordinator and Instructor at Methodist Hospital of Indiana. She is responsible for instructing physicians and the medical staff in the use of the hospital medical information system. She has served as a Consultant for the TDS Healthcare Systems Corporation.

Ronald E. Rice received his master's degree and doctorate in communication research from Stanford University. He is currently Associate Professor at the School of Communication, Information, and Library Studies, Rutgers University, New Brunswick, New Jersey. He is coauthor or coeditor of *Public Communication Campaigns* (Sage, 1981, 1989), *The New Media* (Sage, 1984), *Managing Organizational Innovation*, and *Research Methods and the New Media*. His areas of research interest include public communication campaigns, diffusion of innovations, communication network analysis, computer-mediated communication and information settings in organizations, citation analysis, and network-based theories of social influence.

Robert R. Weaver is an Assistant Professor of Sociology at Youngstown State University in Youngstown, Ohio. He received his Ph.D. from the University of Connecticut, Storrs. Before moving to Youngstown, he worked as a Research Associate on various applied research projects at a research institute in Hartford, Connecticut. He has published numerous articles that pertain to computers in medicine and a book titled *Computers and Medical Knowledge: The Diffusion of Decision Support Technology*.